A Special Issue of
Neuropsychological Rehabilitation

Technology in Cognitive Rehabilitation

Edited by

Peter Gregor
*Department of Applied Computing,
University of Dundee, UK*

and

Alan Newell
*Department of Applied Computing,
University of Dundee, UK*

Psychology Press
Taylor & Francis Group
HOVE AND NEW YORK

Published in 2004 by Psychology Press Ltd
27 Church Road, Hove, East Sussex, BN3 2FA

Simultaneously published in the USA and Canada
by Taylor & Francis Inc
711 Third Avenue, New York, NY 10017

First issued in paperback 2015

Psychology Press is an imprint of the Taylor & Francis Group, an informa business

British Library Cataloguing in Publication Data
A catalogue record for this book is available from the British Library

ISBN 13: 978-1-138-87797-9 (pbk)
ISBN 13: 978-1-8416-9960-8 (hbk)

ISSN 0960-2011

Cover design by Hybert Design
Typeset in the UK by Quorum Technical Services, Cheltenham, Gloucestershire

Contents*

---

*This book is also a special issue of the journal *Neuropsychological Rehabilitation*, and forms issues 1 & 2 of Volume 14 (2004). The page numbers are taken from the Journal and begin with p. 1.

NEUROPSYCHOLOGICAL REHABILITATION, 2004, *14* (1/2), 1–3

Introduction

Peter Gregor and Alan Newell
University of Dundee, Scotland

Communication and information technology (CIT) has been used in a variety of ways to support older and disabled people for over 30 years and there have been many successes in this field. Until recently, however, research, development and commercial exploitation have largely concentrated on people with physical or sensory dysfunction. Computer technology has been increasingly used to support cognitive activities in able-bodied people but its use to support people with disabilities has not had much widespread recognition. Well-designed CIT systems have great and largely unrealised potential to enhance the quality of life and independence of people with cognitive dysfunction, by:

- enabling them to retain a higher level of independence and control over their lives,
- providing appropriate levels of monitoring and supervision of "at risk" people, without violating privacy,
- keeping people intellectually and physically active, and
- providing communications methods to reduce social isolation.

For example, computers are patient, consistent and tireless, and do not become emotionally involved in a shared task; multimedia and multimodal systems can provide a very rich interaction. Such systems have great potential in addressing the problems of memory loss and the more severe problems presented by dementia such as confusion, disorientation and profound personality changes. Communication systems using synthetic speech, predictive programmes which can facilitate writing, and a range of

Correspondence should be addressed to Peter Gregor, Department of Applied Computing, University of Dundee, Dundee DD1 4HN, Scotland. Tel: 01382 344153, Fax: 01382 345509 (Email: pgregor@computing.dundee.ac.uk).

http://www.tandf.co.uk/journals/pp/09602011.html DOI:10.1080/09602010343000093

non-linguistic methods of communication, can be used by those with speech and language dysfunction due to hearing loss, speech dysfunction, dementia or strokes.

This special edition of the journal recognises the potential of information technology to provide support for people with cognitive dysfunction. The overview article by Ed LoPresti et al. shows the enormous range of ways in which this technology can support such people. This includes, but is by no means limited to, the use of computers to provide traditional prostheses, albeit within the cognitive domain. The selection of papers in this issue shows that the help and support available can be far more than the "artificial replacement of part of the body" (the literal definition of prosthesis) and can include techniques to provide lifestyle support for people who would not be thought of as requiring "prosthetic support". Also, if solutions can be found which provide cognitive support where it is obviously needed, then these same solutions may be of considerable value where the need for such support is not so obvious (for example, how many "normal" people would confess to being occasionally absent minded?). This provides a significant mainstream motivation for pursuing research in this important area, in addition to the more conventional motivations of care, support and treatment.

Kapur et al. provide an excellent overview of the issues surrounding external memory aids for neurological patients, reviewing their efficacy in a clinical setting. Gartland's paper offers the wide-ranging and vital perspective of an occupational therapist in incorporating IT in the rehabilitation of brain injured patients, covering theoretical, practical and learning issues. Inglis et al. describe the development of a particular innovative interactive memory aid and its evaluation in use in a clinical setting. Manly et al. report on an experimental approach to investigating the effectiveness of auditory cueing and suggest the role of such cueing in improving executive behaviour.

Alm et al. and Mihailidis et al. describe approaches to computer-based support for people with dementia—Mihailidis et al. describe a creative approach to the development of techniques for improving executive function in a common everyday situation, while Alm et al. concentrate on supports for social communication through reminiscence, showing how a multidisciplinary approach has enabled a very challenging user group to interact beneficially with computers.

Crerar underlines the advantages of computer-based data collection and analysis, and on this basis re-examines the most appropriate ways of evaluating the effectiveness of aphasia rehabilitation, with particular reference to the neglect of processing speed. Crerar's paper is complemented by Rizzo et al., who highlight the exciting possibilities of using virtual reality systems within assessment and rehabilitation. Cognitive dysfunction can also affect processing of acoustic data, particularly speech, and Carmichael's paper addresses the issues of the perceptual effects of various techniques for automatically reducing background noise in television programmes in an attempt to improve intelligibility.

This selection of papers shows that effective research and development in this field requires a truly interdisciplinary approach, drawing on and synthesising expertise from cognitive psychology, computing, design and various medical-related disciplines. Without close collaboration and real communication between these disciplines, mistakes are likely to be made and opportunities lost. Without detailed technical and domain knowledge, the real potential of the technology will not be fully exploited. On the other hand a mainly technological focus will lead to systems which are of little or no use within any real environment or with people who display the complex symptoms, needs and wants which are so often found in those with cognitive dysfunction. Even where all the knowledge and technological expertise is in place, a creative design input is also likely to be needed to ensure an effective and enjoyable experience of the system by the user. Without these interdisciplinary components in place, there is a risk that otherwise ingenious and appropriate technical or therapeutic solutions will be abandoned for inappropriate reasons.

The use of information technology to support people with cognitive dysfunction provides a wide range of fascinating and rewarding research challenges and we are just setting out now on that journey. We hope that this special issue will provide a useful overview for those already working in this field, and that it will also encourage other researchers to consider the possibilities of applying their expertise to these challenges, and provide them with an appropriate background for the initial stages of their research.

NEUROPSYCHOLOGICAL REHABILITATION, 2004, *14* (1/2), 5–39

Assistive technology for cognitive rehabilitation: State of the art

Edmund Frank LoPresti

AT Sciences, Pittsburgh, PA, USA

Alex Mihailidis

Simon Fraser University, Vancouver, Canada

Ned Kirsch

University of Michigan Health Systems, Ann Arbor, MI, USA

For close to 20 years, clinicians and researchers have been developing and assessing technological interventions for individuals with either acquired impairments or developmental disorders. This paper offers a comprehensive review of literature in that field, which we refer to collectively as assistive technology for cognition (ATC). ATC interventions address a range of functional activities requiring cognitive skills as diverse as complex attention, executive reasoning, prospective memory, self-monitoring for either the enhancement or inhibition of specific behaviours and sequential processing. ATC interventions have also been developed to address the needs of individuals with information processing impairments that may affect visual, auditory and language ability, or the understanding of social cues. The literature reviewed indicates that ATC interventions can increase the efficiency of traditional rehabilitation practices by enhancing a person's ability to engage in therapeutic tasks independently and by broadening the range of contexts in which those tasks can be exercised. More importantly, for many types of impairments, ATC interventions represent entirely new methods of treatment that can reinforce a person's residual intrinsic abilities, provide alternative means by which activities can be completed or provide extrinsic supports so that functional activities can be performed that might otherwise not be possible.

Correspondence should be addressed to E. F. LoPresti, AT Sciences, 160 N. Craig St., Suite 117, Pittsburgh, PA 15213, USA (Email: edlopresti@acm.org).

http://www.tandf.co.uk/journals/pp/09602011.html DOI:10.1080/09602010343000101

Although the major focus of research in this field will continue to be the development of new ATC interventions, over the coming years it will also be critical for researchers, clinicians, and developers to examine the multi-system factors that affect usability over time, generalisability across home and community settings, and the impact of sustained, patterned technological interventions on recovery of function.

As clinicians and researchers seek new ways to serve people with cognitive and neuropsychological disabilities, many have incorporated computers and other advanced technologies into clinical interventions (Bergman, 1998). These technological interventions, often referred to as "cognitive orthoses" or "cognitive prostheses" (and to which we will refer collectively in this paper as assistive technology for cognition or ATC), range from alarms to remind people of their medication schedules to interactive robotic caregivers. Some draw on technology designed for the mainstream population, while others are designed for the unique needs of people with disabilities, but all are typically designed to provide extrinsic supports for individuals with compromised cognitive ability.

ATC interventions can aid people with a variety of disabilities, including traumatic brain injury (NIH, 1998; Wilson, Evans, Emslie, & Malinek, 1997), cerebrovascular accident (Evans, Emslie, & Wilson, 1998; Wright et al., 2001), learning disabilities (Higgins & Raskind, 1995; Raskind & Higgins 1995; MacArthur, Ferretti, Okolo, & Cavalier 2001), and multiple sclerosis (Allen, Goldstein, Heyman, & Rondinelli, 1998); and have shown some potential to aid people with dementia (Zanetti et al., 2000), autism spectrum disorders (Strickland, Marcus, Mesibov, & Hogan, 1996; Imamura, Wiess, & Parham, 1990; Werry, Dautenhahn, Ogden, & Harwin, 2001), and mental retardation (LoPresti, Friedman, & Hages, 1997).

Depending on the specific needs of the person, these technologies may be used in a number of ways. One approach capitalises on those of a person's skills that have *not* been compromised so that tasks can be accomplished using alternative strategies or information characteristics. For example, an ATC intervention may include a computer that allows speech recognition rather than typing for a person with poor visual letter recognition but strong verbal language skills. Similarly, a personal digital assistant (PDA) may be used for daily planning by a person with memory impairments but relatively intact executive skills or a software interface may be designed that accommodates visual–perceptual or information processing impairments.

For more severely impaired individuals, an alternative approach has been to develop extrinsic interventions that assume greater responsibility for initiation, cueing, activity guidance, and maintenance of daily information. For example, an ATC intervention may be designed that, in addition to providing simple alarms about when medications are to be taken, also provides step-by-step guidance about how to recognise the medication, how to recognise how much of the medication to take, how much water to drink, and how to refill a dispensing container to prepare for the next dose. For all of these interventions, the goal is to achieve a way of performing tasks that compensate for existing impairments by using a device that either partially takes the place of a person's impaired ability, or translates a problem into one that matches the client's strengths.

More specifically, "cognitive orthoses" or "cognitive prosthetics", collectively referred to as ATC, have been defined as compensatory strategies that alter the patient's environment and are directed to an individual's functional skills (Kirsch, Levine, Fallon-Kreuger, & Jaros, 1987). Cole expanded this definition in his 1999 review of the field to include the following attributes of a cognitive prosthetic:

- Uses computer technology;
- Is designed specifically for rehabilitation purposes;
- Directly assists the individual in performing some of their everyday activities;
- Is highly customizable to the needs of the individual (Cole, 1999).

Lynch defines a "cognitive prosthetic" as "any computer-based system that has been designed for a specific individual to accomplish one or more designated tasks related to activities of daily living (ADL), including work (Lynch, 2002)".

In keeping with these definitions, this paper will focus on interventions that provide compensatory methods and strategies for task performance. However, not all of the cognitive assistive technologies described in this article will qualify as cognitive orthoses according to all aspects of these definitions. While most attention will be given to computer-based devices, low-tech solutions will also briefly be discussed. Devices designed for both mainstream and rehabilitation applications will be reviewed, with some discussion of the advantages and disadvantages of using mainstream technology for people with cognitive impairment. Not all ATC interventions described below are designed for a specific individual, but all cognitive orthoses must indeed be customised to the individual user's needs, to varying degrees.

Scope of this article

This article reviews the state of research in cognitive orthoses through the following topics:

1. Cognitive disabilities and the human-technology interface.
2. Technology for memory and executive function impairments.
    - Compensation technologies for memory.

   - Compensation technologies for planning and problem solving.
   - Context-aware cognitive orthoses.
3. Technology for information processing impairments.
   - Compensation technologies for sensory processing.
   - Technologies for social and behavioral issues.
4. Conclusion

Since the purpose of this article is to introduce the reader to the breadth of research that has been conducted in this area, we will not review all areas of "cognitive rehabilitation" that utilise technology. For example, technology for communication deficits will not be addressed. Augmentative and alternative communication is an active field with an extensive literature of its own, addressing the technological needs of people with communication impairments, including neurologically based aphasias (Beukelman & Mirenda, 1998). This review will also not address educational software, although there are a number of software products that are directed to teaching reading, maths, and other skills to people with cognitive disabilities (Gillette, 2001). Finally, this paper will not review the use of technology for "restorative" interventions. This is a large field, with a robust history, that has been reviewed extensively. (Lynch, 1982, 2002; NIH, 1998). Most importantly, in our judgement, the literature in the area of "restorative" technological interventions is essentially indistinguishable from the more general literature addressing cognitive rehabilitation (Cicerone et al., 2000), and is subject to the same issues of efficacy that are faced by non-technological interventions, including domain specificity and limited ecological validity (Lynch, 2002). Having said this, however, we will return to the issue of restorative intervention in the concluding section, where new developments in neurorehabilitation and their implications for ATC will be addressed briefly.

COGNITIVE DISABILITIES AND THE HUMAN–TECHNOLOGY INTERFACE

Any assistive technology for people with cognitive disabilities must accommodate the individual user's skills and deficits. This is complicated by the fact that each person will have a unique combination of strengths and weaknesses. A prospective memory aid that requires a great deal of self-initiation and problem solving skills will be useful for some clients, but will only exacerbate difficulties for others. Similarly, while mainstream computer software has great potential to assist people with cognitive disabilities (for example, software for time and money management), existing software is often either too complex or not age appropriate for adults (Lynch, 2002; Wehmeyer, 1998). Therefore, accommodations for people with mental retardation and other cognitive disabilities to use computers typically need to include visual displays with reduced clutter, provision of information in non-text formats (e.g., graphics, video, audio), minimisation of the number and complexity of decision making points, presentation of information sequentially, and reduced reliance on memory (Wehmeyer, 1998).

People with cognitive disabilities will often have physical and sensory limitations, as well. In designing and prescribing cognitive aids, it is important to consider how well the technology matches the individual's physical and sensory abilities, including:

- Vision.
- Hearing.
- Tactile sense (e.g., ability to feel and touch buttons).
- Fine motor control (e.g., ability to operate small controls, ability to write).
- Ability to speak.
- Co-ordination (e.g., ability to accurately select small buttons).

All aspects of a person's cognitive, physical, and sensory capabilities must be taken into account in prescribing technology (LoPresti & Willkomm, 1997). Features that make a device more "user-friendly" for one group of users may make it less so for another group (Cole, Dehdashti, Petti, & Angert, 1994). Technology design and prescription also require consideration of all the people who will be affected by the technology, including clinicians and caregivers as well as people with the disabilities (Cole et al., 2000; Magnusson & Larsson, 1994).

Designers can better understand users' needs by referring to models of typical user needs (user modelling) or by involving the user in the design process (user-centred or participatory design). Since existing user models largely rely on data collected for individuals without disabilities, some researchers are now beginning to develop models which incorporate data for people with disabilities (Keates, Clarkson, & Robinson, 2000) or which encourage "thought" experiments in which the designer tries to put him- or herself in the position of a person with a disability (Svensk, 1997). In user-centred design, technology development is guided by frequent interactions with representatives of the user populations to discuss general needs and possible features, and to review prototypes (Cole, Dehdashti, Petti, & Angert, 1993). In participatory design, members of the user population are continually involved as members of the design team, suggesting features and pointing out possible difficulties with the design (Cole et al., 1994). Newell et al. (2000) have suggested the concept of "user sensitive inclusive design" which extends the concept of user-centred design, specifically to include users with disabilities.

High customisation is often needed for a cognitive device to be effective. Each device may need to be customised for a specific individual, and revised on a regular basis as the user's capabilities change. This customisation needs to reflect a number of factors including user priorities, functional deficits, and the environment where the activity is performed, such as home, community, school, and work (Cole, 1999; Cole & Dehdashti, 1998). Different devices approach this need for customisation in different ways.

TECHNOLOGY FOR MEMORY AND EXECUTIVE FUNCTION IMPAIRMENTS

Compensation technologies for memory

Individuals with cognitive disabilities are often unable to generalise from graded memory drills and exercises to independent completion of activities of daily living (Chute & Bliss, 1988; Middleton, Lambert, & Seggar, 1991). Therefore, interest has grown in using computers as compensatory tools in actual life situations—i.e., improving a person's performance by using the computer to support areas of cognitive weaknesses (Chute, Conn, DiPasquale, & Hoag, 1988; Rothi & Horner, 1983). Early attempts to use the computer for this purpose were limited, but growing evidence indicates that the computer has promise (Bergman, 1998).

Technological interventions can provide compensatory support for a number of executive function impairments and those complex memory deficits often associated with the integrity of executive functions. *Executive functions* are typically associated with effective adaptation and accommodation to changing environmental demands through the appropriate and efficient integration of more basic cognitive skills (Levine, Horstmann, & Kirsch, 1992; Luria 1973). This requires a range of cognitive skills, including:

- Planning.
- Task sequencing and prioritisation.
- Task switching.
- Self-monitoring.
- Problem solving.
- Self-initiation and adaptability (Cole & Dehdashti, 1998; Rubenstein, Meyer, & Evans, 2000).

Related memory skills include "prospective memory", that is, remembering tasks that need to be performed and carrying out these tasks at the appropriate time (Ellis, 1996).

Early work on prospective memory aids investigated the application of commonplace technologies, such as clocks and calendars (Harris, 1978) or timers and digital watches (Jones & Adams, 1979, Klein & Fowler, 1981, Wilson, 1984). These technologies are inexpensive, easy to use, and have no social stigma that might otherwise be attached to "rehabilitation" devices.

However, these devices have limitations in regard to the amount of information that can be stored, and how information can be presented to the user. More importantly, written lists and calendars provide no cues to the user as to when he or she needs to perform a task. For individuals with deficits in self-initiation, a device which can call itself to the person's attention will be better able to facilitate activity performance (Hersh & Treadgold, 1994, Kim, Burke, Dowds, & George, 1999, Kime, Lamb, & Wilson, 1995). However, while a standard alarm wristwatch or timer will provide an audible cue, it will not provide information about the task to be performed. An alarm wristwatch can be combined with a written list, so that whenever the watch alarm sounds the person refers to the list for information. However, this latter intervention requires that the client both associate the watch alarm with the need to refer to the list and remember to use (and carry) both the watch and the list. This can be inconvenient for people with mild memory impairments, and difficult or impossible for people with more severe memory or executive function deficits. Therefore, it is sometimes useful to have a single, easily portable device that provides both an external cue and relevant information.

Prospective memory aids are most effective when they can be customized for a specific user and his or her desired activities of daily living (ADLs) (Chute & Bliss, 1988). Chute and Bliss (1988) addressed this problem through the use of object-oriented programming, a programming approach which simplifies modification and adaptation of the properties of software "objects" or functions. Their ProsthesisWare software was designed for training and neuropsychological monitoring with four issues in mind: (1) the elderly need to be in control of their environments and ADLs; (2) the success of ProsthesisWare implementation depends on its ability to be customised to suit individual needs and abilities; (3) interconnectivity is required to provide a seamless environment among applications on the computer and other devices such as fax machines; and (4) the graphical user interface must be designed taking into account the cognitive and ergonomic capacities of its user (Chute & Bliss, 1994). ProthesisWare monitored the user, provided cues and reminders (via pictures of the user completing the required task), and supplied schedules and sequences of tasks. ProsthesisWare programs were evaluated and modified through an iterative customisation process that occurred on a case-by-case basis, and their effectiveness was measured by utility for each individual user. Outcome evaluation has been limited to qualitative analyses but the results were disappointing, in part because the subject was selected shortly after injury (Chute & Bliss, 1994).

The Institute for Cognitive Prosthetics (Bala Cynwyd, PA) has developed many ATC interventions customised to the specific needs of individual clients (Cole & Dehdashti, 1988; Cole et al., 2000). Their approach has been to meet with the individual client, identify specific functional needs, and develop a customised computer-based system designed to increase the

TABLE 1
Commercially available prospective memory aids

Device	*Manufacturer*	*Description*
IQ Voice Organizer™	Voice Powered Technology International Inc., Burlington, NJ, USA	Pocket-sized device that allows verbal messages to be recorded and played back audibly at a specified time
NeverMiss DigiPad™	ICP Inc., Montreal, Quebec, Canada	Pocket-sized device that allows verbal messages to be recorded and played back, but without an associated time function
Data Link watch	Timex™, Middlebury, CT, USA	System that includes a wristwatch and software program for a personal computer that stores the user's schedule and alerts him or her with an audible alarm when an item from the schedule is due
CellMinder	Institute for Cognitive Prosthetics, Bala Cynwyd, PA	System which utilises a cell phone as a reminder system. Software on the user's computer keeps track of a schedule and calls the user on his or her cell phone at appointed times
ISAAC	Cogent Systems, Inc., Orlando, FL	Handheld cognitive device specifically designed for individuals with a wide range of cognitive disabilities
Planning and Executive Assistant and Trainer (PEAT)	Attention Control Systems, Inc., Mountain View, CA	Handheld reminding device with intelligent support for revising schedules

client's self-sufficiency for tasks of interest to the client (Cole 1999; Cole & Dehdashti, 1990).

In one case study, a system was developed for a 54-year-old woman who was 4 years post-traumatic brain injury. A computer-based system, including a text editor and home finance software, was customised in an iterative process to match the client's strengths and weaknesses. The client was able to use the final system reliably when unattended, and able to learn the software applications in three 30-min training sessions (Cole & Dehdashti, 1990). A system was developed for a 33-year-old woman who experienced neurological dysfunction of unknown etiology followed by a series of cerebrovascular accidents. A cognitive prosthetic system was customised to her needs. The client showed increased stamina for writing, the ability to produce a two-dimensional design using drawing software and showed improvements in visual scanning and in neuromotor skills related to activities of daily living (Cole, Petti, Matthews, & Dehdashti, 1994).

Three clients with traumatic brain injury, no expectation of spontaneous recovery, and lack of remediation from alternative compensatory strategies achieved a significant increase in function using a cognitive prosthetic system (Cole et al., 1994), which included following a daily schedule, initiation of a designated activity following a cue, and maintaining a prioritised to-do list. Subjects showed additional benefits including increased relaxation and self-confidence and improved planning, problem solving, and self-initiation (Cole et al., 1994). Similar results have been observed for numerous other cases (Cole, 1999; Cole & Dehdashti, 1998; Cole et al., 1993).

The Institute for Cognitive Prosthetics has provided distance rehabilitation services (Cole, 1999; Cole et al., 2000) and remote computer connections. An integrated treatment planning system co-ordinates activities of the therapist, client, and computer programmers responsible for software customisation (Cole et al., 1994, 2000). The work in the Institute for Cognitive Prosthetics indicates a growing acceptance of the efficacy of cognitive orthotic technology by service providers.

Mastery Rehabilitation Systems (Bala Cynwyd, PA) developed the Essential Steps software to support users in a variety of daily tasks through cues presented on-screen or using a computer-generated voice (Bergman, 1996, 2002). Fifty-four people with cognitive impairments demonstrated rapid skill acquisition in individual trials with the software. It was demonstrated that this tool could be integrated into ADL tasks at home, school, and vocational settings for as much as 10 years (Bergman, 1997).

Much of the work in this area has focused on clients with prospective memory deficits resulting from traumatic brain injury or cerebrovascular accident. Zanetti and colleagues (2000) studied the ability of individuals with mild to moderate Alzheimer's disease to appropriately use an electronic agenda. Seven memory tasks, such as finding a hidden personal object or putting a newspaper in the trash, had to be completed by each of five subjects at fixed hours. Performance with the device was compared on different days with control conditions. The results showed statistically significant improvements in completion of the required tasks, with two of the five subjects achieving perfect scores when allowed to use the electronic aid (Zanetti et al., 2000).

As an alternative to specially designed cognitive orthoses, Flannery and Rice (1997) studied the efficacy of calendar software designed for the mainstream population. A laptop Macintosh computer was equipped with Easy Alarms™ software (Nisus Software, Inc, Solana Beach, CA). The software was programmed with 15 tasks that were repeated on a daily basis. The system was evaluated for a 17-year-old male with short-term memory loss. The rate of needed reminders from a caregiver dropped from 75% to 8% when the computer system was used (Flannery & Rice, 1997).

Some work on reminder systems has focused on the specific task of medication compliance. Medication compliance devices range from plastic boxes divided into sections labelled by times and day, to electronic systems that provide auditory cues (Fernie & Fernie, 1996). Devices without external cues are not effective unless the user can first remember to take his medication at an appropriate time, locate the medication dispenser and figure out which day/time compartment to open. Until recently more complex electronic devices have tended not to be portable, and the person may not respond to the audible alarms (Fernie & Fernie, 1996).

A number of electronic memory aids and recording devices are commercially available. Examples of such devices are shown in Table 1 (Hersh & Treadgold, 1994; Levinson, 1997; LoPresti & Willkomm, 1997). These are only a few examples of available products, representing a range of products of this type.

The IQ Voice Organizer™ and Data Link Watch are two examples of prospective memory aids designed for and marketed to the mainstream population, rather than specifically for people with cognitive disabilities. Scheduling and reminder software are also available for standard palmtop computers, such as those running the Palm (Palm Inc, Mipitas, CA) and Windows CE (Microsoft, Redmond, WA) operating systems. These devices may be more readily available than devices designed for people with disabilities. Also they may be more acceptable to clients, since they are "normal" devices.

Other devices, such as ISAAC (Cogent Systems, Inc.), CellMinder (Institute for Cognitive Prosthetics, Bala Cynwyd, PA), and the Planning and Execution Assistant and Training System (PEAT, Attention Control Systems Inc, Mountain View, CA), have been designed specifically for individuals with cognitive disabilities. They provide more support for people who would have difficulty independently entering their schedules into more complex devices and are designed with physical and sensory limitations in mind.

A number of investigators have studied the efficacy of electronic prospective memory aids (Herrmann et al., 1999; Tackett, Rice, Rice, & Butterbaugh, 2001). Studies have shown that older adults with memory impairments can perform as well as younger adults in prospective memory tasks if they are able to use external memory aids (Maylor, 1996). Kime et al. (1995) demonstrated improved performance of complex functional tasks by using an alarm system with a personal organiser. Subjects with attention deficit disorder have been observed to improve in punctuality for prospective memory tasks when using a Voice Organizer™ personal organiser (Willkomm & LoPresti, 1997). Hersch and Treadgold (1994) have shown that NeuroPage, a specialised paging system, can be used to facilitate prospective performance of functional tasks. Similarly, Hart, Hawkey, and Whyte (2002) have demonstrated that a portable voice organiser (Parrot Voice Mate III) can promote the retention and performance of behavioural goals (e.g., utilising relaxation techniques when episodes of anxiety occur) as well as simple prospective tasks (e.g., remembering to get the mail).

The most central work in this area has been reported by Wilson and colleagues (Evans et al., 1998; Wilson, Emslie, Quirk, & Evans 2001; Wilson et al., 1997; Wright et al., 2001) who have demonstrated that an alphanumeric paging system can facilitate the performance of functional activities for adults with a variety of neurological impairments including cerebrovascular accident and traumatic brain injury, thereby supporting independence in the home and community. In one study, Wilson and colleagues performed an ABA single case experimental design with 15 subjects who had experienced traumatic brain injuries using an alphanumeric pager to provide reminder messages at predetermined times. This intervention was associated with a significant reduction in incidents of memory failures ($p < .05$; Wilson et al., 1997).

In another study, Evans and colleagues conducted a single-subject ABAB design with a 50-year-old woman who had experienced a cerebrovascular accident resulting in impairments of planning, attention, and prospective memory. An alphanumeric paging system was compared to a paper-and-pencil checklist for efficacy as prospective memory aids. The alphanumeric paging system was able to prompt the subject to perform intended activities, to perform activities in a timely manner, and to initiate planning of future activities. For example, the subject took medication with a mean delay of 1.9 min with the pager, compared to a mean delay of 33.44 min with the checklist (Evans et al., 1998). A randomised control trial was conducted with 143 people having memory, planning, attention, or organisation problems, usually following a traumatic head injury or a stroke. More than 80% of those who completed the 16 week trial were significantly more successful in carrying out everyday activities (such as self-care, self-medication, and keeping appointments) when using the pager in comparison with the baseline period; for most of these, significant improvement was maintained when they were monitored 7 weeks after returning the pager (Wilson et al., 2001). The MemoJog project at Dundee (Inglis et al., 2002) is extending this research to develop an interactive memory aid using PDA's with data transmission via the mobile phone network. This system extends the Neuropage functionality to enable communication with the carers' computer system so that, for example, an alarm can be raised if certain critical messages are not acknowledged by a button press on the PDA.

Research has been conducted on the use of technology to support interaction with a human assistant. Videoconferencing is being explored to provide job coach services remotely to workers with cognitive disabilities in a vocational setting (Rosen et al., 2000). Telerehabilitation features were included in the Isaac and TASC projects (Fagerberg, 1999; Jonsson & Svensk, 1995). Isaac included cognitive orthotic software together with a cellular phone, a digital camera and GPS satellite navigation receiver to provide support centre staff with information about the client's needs (Jonsson & Svensk, 1995).

The Jogger system includes a portable memory aid and a home docking station, to assist caregivers and clinicians in preparing a person's schedule and monitoring performance (Jinks & Robson-Brandi, 1997). The docking station enables communication with a clinician's computer for reviewing the user's compliance with previous cues and editing his or her schedule. Researchers at the Coleman Institute are developing a Memory Aiding Prompting System (MAPS) which incorporates a PDA with a docking system, wireless communication, and data logging (Carmien, 2002). The docking system will allow a caregiver to programme the user's schedule on a stationary computer, which will download the schedule to the user's PDA. The wireless communication will allow the user or the system to contact a caregiver when problems arise that the system cannot automatically handle. Data logging facilitates evaluation of the effectiveness and appropriateness of the system.

Compensation technologies for planning and problem solving

Some ATC interventions seek to provide support with planning and problem solving as well as prospective memory. The Planning and Execution Assistant and Training System (PEAT, Attention Control Systems Inc, Mountain View, CA) uses artificial intelligence to automatically generate daily plans and re-plans in response to unexpected events (Levinson, 1997). Using manually entered appointments in conjunction with a library of ADL scripts, PEAT generates the best plan to complete all of the required steps, and assists with plan execution by using visual and audible cues. The user provides input to the device when a step has been completed, or if more time is required to complete the step (Levinson, 1997).

Most existing memory aids are designed to present scheduled, one-step tasks (e.g., "At 5:00, cook dinner"), but people may want to remember tasks that are not precisely scheduled. For example, a person might want to bake a pie sometime before 5:00, but not at any particular time. Further, many tasks are not limited to one step, e.g., cooking dinner involves a number of subtasks related to preparing kitchen utensils and following a recipe. People can be assisted in multi-step tasks by low-tech aids such as a series of cards with pictures which illustrate the steps of the task. Some research has shown that a system which combines automatic presentation of such pictorial instructions with auditory or tactile cues can improve performance (Lancioni et al., 1999, 2000).

Levine and Kirsch (1985), developed a specialised computer language called COGORTH (COGnitive ORTHotic) to support guidance through multi-step tasks. This language provided a highly structured environment for programming sequential messages, such as steps in a task. These messages could be presented as text on a video display, an audio signal, or a visual cue (Levine & Kirsch, 1985). COGORTH program could display directions at any level of specificity. COGORTH provided programming capabilities for instructional modules (IM) which could check a user's performance for errors, branch to error correcting or help procedures, manage interruptions of a task when a higher priority task must be completed, and manage a user's environment through control of electric appliances, telephone, and audio signals (Levine & Kirsch, 1985). Keyboard input from the user was required to obtain feedback regarding his or her performance. An inappropriate response, or lack of response within a certain amount of time, would cause COGORTH to conclude that assistance was required (Levine & Kirsch, 1985).

A computerised task guidance system utilising COGORTH was used in a series of efficacy studies with a wide range of patient types and cognitive disabilities. In one study, a subject with difficulty in planning and problem-solving following an anoxic episode experienced improved performance in a cooking task when using a computerised task guidance system instead of only written instructions (Kirsch et al., 1988). Four head-injured individuals used a COGORTH-based ATC intervention to perform janitorial tasks. Two subjects showed substantial improvements in accuracy when using the intervention. A third subject experienced only mild difficulty in performing the janitorial tasks with written directions and did not benefit from the introduction of the orthotic. The final subject appeared to benefit from the orthotic, but her level of motivation changed dramatically during the course of the study (Kirsch, Levine, Lajiness-O'Neill, & Schneider, 1992). More recently, the underlying concepts of COGORTH are being modified to take advantage of wireless, web-based technology (Kirsch et al., 2002) and current artificial intelligence methods (Simpson, Schreckenghost, & Kirsch, 2002).

Steele, Weinrich, and Carlson (1989) developed an ATC intervention which used a series of dynamic icons and illustrations to communicate the steps to a simple recipe. Fourteen trials were conducted for one subject with severe aphasia using six different recipes. The subject was able to accurately prepare the food during 11 of 14 trials when the device was used (Steele et al., 1989). Performance without the device was not reported.

Napper and Narayan (1994) developed a computerised ATC system to help therapists and caregivers create customised task guidance systems for people with cognitive impairments. The device guided a person through each required step of a task. The device was evaluated by assisting a subject with a head injury while shaving. With the device, the number of cues and interactions required with the caregiver was reduced compared to baseline data, and the number of errors made by the subject was reduced to zero (Napper & Narayan, 1994).

Context-aware cognitive orthoses

Many of the ATC interventions described thus far require input from the user to provide feedback to the device (e.g., pushing a button after the cued tasks has been completed). However, a person with a cognitive disability may not remember what step they had just been asked to perform and/or the need to indicate that the step had been completed (Vanderheiden, 1998). Even for those people capable of providing this input, the additional requirement increases the cognitive load on a person, and can result in the user becoming further frustrated and agitated. In addition, users who lack initiation and planning skills may not be able to actively retrieve the messages or information stored in these devices (Friedman, Kostraba, Henry, & Coltellaro, 1991). Manual re-programming is also required to customise these devices for an individual user, which can be time-consuming and difficult (especially if a caregiver or family member is expected to perform this function).

This could be remedied if a device was able to recognise the user's context; that is, his or her physical and social environment. If the device was aware of the user's location, for example, it could give reminders relevant to that location. Information about the user's environment might also provide cues to the device on what reminders might be important (handwashing if the person is in the washroom) or unnecessary (a reminder to go to the cafeteria if the person is already there). Social cues might allow the device to know when a reminder would be inappropriate; such as when the user is talking with another person and might not want to be interrupted.

Context-sensitive reminding requires a person's environment and activities to be monitored. Several researchers have used sensors and switches attached to various objects in the user's environment to detect which task the person is completing. If these devices detect an unexplainable change in the person's normal routine, then external assistance is called. Trials with several subjects indicate that this method of tracking a person's actions is a good way of monitoring the state of a person's health and independence (Bai, Zhang, Cui, & Zhang, 2000; Nambu, Nakajima, Kawarada, & Tamura, 2000; Ogawa et al., 2000).

Friedman (1993) developed an ATC device with sensing capabilities. A wearable microcomputer used a combination of radio and ultrasound to communicate with stationary ultrasound transmitters throughout the user's environment, allowing the computer to determine the person's location. Additional sensors provided task-related information. The computer provided voice prompts only as needed to help the user maintain his or her schedule. Continued evidence of difficulty adhering to the schedule would cause the computer to automatically call for human assistance (Friedman, 1993). By only providing prompts as needed, the system could "fade" cues and therefore decrease the user's dependence on them.

Cavalier and Ferretti (1993) evaluated the efficacy of this system to assist two high school students with severe learning disabilities in wiring a switch box. The task consisted of 47 component steps. If a step was completed correctly, the device waited 3 s then, if the student was not continuing to make progress, it prompted the user to start the next step using a verbal cue. If a step was incorrectly performed, the computer corrected the actions of the user using a verbal cue. If the user ignored the cues provided by the device, the teacher provided assistance. With the cognitive orthotic the subject was able to self-initiate 11% of the steps, and verbal prompts from the cognitive device were required 89% of the time (Cavalier & Ferretti, 1993). Interactions with the teacher during this phase were not required. Results from the second student were similar.

LoPresti, Friedman, and Hages (1997) instrumented a workspace with sensors to detect progress through a vocational task. A palm-top computer offered programmed advice, reminders, and praise audibly through a set of headphones. Using the device, two subjects with mental retardation were able to maintain levels of productivity comparable to those obtained when a job coach closely guided each subject (LoPresti et al., 1997).

Mihailidis, Fernie, and Cleghorn (2000) conducted a pilot study, and observed that a person with severe dementia would complete an activity of daily living in response to a computerised device that used a recorded voice for cueing. The computerised device monitored and prompted a subject through handwashing. The hardware consisted of several switches and motion sensors installed inside a fibreglass overlay, on top of a sink. The subject was independently able to complete (i.e., without a caregiver) approximately 22% more steps in the handwashing activity when the device was used. These results showed that a computerised cueing device can be effective. The current prototype however was too rigid in the way that it provided assistance to the users, and it only allowed the users to complete the ADL in one set sequence. This inflexibility in the device's algorithms resulted in several errors to occur, and for the subjects to sometimes become frustrated because the device was trying to force them to complete handwashing in a way that was different from their familiar sequence (Mihailidis et al., 2000).

Mihailidis et al. (2001) therefore used artificial intelligence to develop a new cognitive orthotic. The COACH (Cognitive Orthosis for Assisting aCtivities in the Home) was a prototype of an adaptable device to help people with dementia complete handwashing with less dependence on a caregiver. The device used artificial neural networks, plan recognition, and a single video camera connected to a computer to automatically monitor progress and provide pre-recorded verbal prompts. It was able to automatically adapt its cueing strategies according to a user's preferences and past performance of the ADL, and play multiple levels of cue detail (Mihailidis, Fernie, & Barbenel, 2001). Results from clinical trials conducted using this new device can be found in the paper by Mihailidis, Barbenel, and Fernie in this issue.

Mynatt, Essa, and Rogers (2000) are developing an instrumented environment in which an entire house will function as a cognitive orthotic. The system will have information about the user's activities through a daily schedule (e.g., a medicine regimen) and sensors (e.g., detecting that the stove is on to infer that the person is cooking). Sensors will be used to detect disruptions in a task. Auditory and visual cues will be used to both remind the person to perform a task and cue the person about the next step in a multi-step task. These sensors will be used not only to determine when the resident might need reminders or cues from a cognitive orthotic, but also when the person may need emergency assistance from a caregiver or medical professional (Mynatt et al., 2000).

Bonasso (1996) has investigated a system which would receive information from sensors in an elderly user's home and also monitor the user's vital signs. It would then incorporate this sensed information with knowledge of the user's goals and of tasks which are needed to achieve those goals. These tasks would be considered in a step-by-step fashion, with the system either prompting the user to perform tasks or assisting the user in needed tasks (Bonasso, 1996). Other researchers are developing a mobile robot assistant to monitor the needs of elderly users. The robot possesses information about the user's daily activities, monitors performance, and provides reminders when needed (Ramakrishnan & Pollack, 2000).

Sensor-based cognitive orthoses are also being developed for the mainstream population. Beigl (2000) has developed the MemoClip, a device that communicates with LocationBeacons at places of interest in the environment in order to determine the user's location. MemoClip provides an audible cue and a text message on a 4 × 5 cm display (Beigl, 2000). DeVaul (2000) has developed Memory Glasses that detect objects, locations, or people by sensing transmitters or "tags" in the environment. The Memory Glasses associate each tag with an image and/or a text description, and display this information on the glasses in a small part of the visual field. The developers plan to investigate the efficacy of this system as a memory aid for both people with normal cognitive function and people with memory impairments (DeVaul, 2000).

In addition to supporting prospective memory aids, a device which can determine a person's location, such as those developed by Friedman (1993) and Beigl (2000), could provide navigation support, providing directions to guide someone through a building. Location sensors can also help in providing care for people who are prone to wandering. Sensors can detect when someone is leaving a building or other defined area, and alert caregivers, and can assist in tracking someone who has wandered and may have become lost.

TECHNOLOGY FOR INFORMATION PROCESSING IMPAIRMENTS

Compensation technologies for sensory processing

Cognitive disabilities often result in an inability of the brain to properly process and integrate sensory information (Kielhofner, 1997). This can lead to deficits in a number of skill areas, including:

- Visual–spatial processing.
- Auditory processing.
- Sensory–motor processing.
- Language processing.
- Understanding of social cues.

Populations affected include people with learning disabilities, traumatic brain injuries, and autism spectrum disorders. By allowing information to be presented in different ways, computers can provide people with the flexibility to utilise their strengths and accommodate information-processing deficits. For example, computers can translate information between printed text and audible speech, or between audible alerts and tactile (e.g., vibrating) alarms. Adjustments to the interface between human and computer, made with attention to a particular client's needs and strengths, can greatly improve a client's performance on desired tasks (Gregor & Newell, 2000).

One area that has received considerable attention is the understanding and production of written text by people with dyslexia. Dyslexia has been defined by the World Federation of Neurology as "a disorder manifested by difficulty in learning to read despite conventional instruction, adequate intelligence, and sociocultural opportunity". It is marked by a number of possible characteristics:

1. Difficulties with visual recognition of letters, numbers, punctuation, and entire words; especially, confusion of characters or words with similar shapes (Willows & Terepocki, 1993).
2. Letter reversal (for example, interpreting a "b" as a "d"; Willows & Terepocki, 1993).
3. Poor visual memory, leading to problems with letter and word recollection (Arkell, 1997).

4. Spelling problems, often reflecting a phonic strategy with words like "of" and "all" being spelled "ov" and "olh" (Willows & Terepocki, 1993).
5. Fixation problems (Meares-Irlen Syndrome) resulting in an inability to scan text without losing one's place (Wilkins & Lewis, 1999).
6. Tendency to add duplicate or extra words, omit words, or reverse word order (Willows & Terepocki, 1993).
7. Difficulty viewing patterns of stripes, such as those produced by black text on a white background; such patterns can cause headaches or perceptions that the lines are moving or bending (Wilkins, 1995).

These problems lead to poor comprehension, since the text which is perceived may be significantly different from the actual text. They also lead to difficulties in producing original text or copying text (Gregor & Newell, 2000; Willows, Kruk, & Corcos, 1993). These difficulties are further exacerbated by motor control difficulties for some people with dyslexia, who may have hand–eye co-ordination difficulties which impede handwriting, and ocular motor control difficulties which impede smooth eye movements between lines of text (Everatt, Bradshaw, & Hibbard, 1999).

In compensating for dyslexia and related disorders, computers offer many advantages over traditional media. The computer allows variation of the appearance of text. Once text is committed to paper and ink, its appearance is permanent. Computers offer options such as changing text size and contrast (Keates, 2000). Computers also allow a user to change the colour of the text and/or the background, similar to the practice of placing coloured screens over text to increase readability (Wilkins & Lewis, 1999).

In addition to changing the appearance of printed text, computers can augment visible text using speech, so that a person with good verbal skills and aural information processing can acquire the information without the need to process printed text (Higgins & Raskind, 1997; Raskind & Higgins, 1995). Speech synthesis software can provide speech output to match text on the computer screen in a word processor or on the computer desktop. Text from books or worksheets can be scanned into the computer and read using optical character recognition software and many books are now available directly in electronic formats. In addition to using speech output as an alternative to text, it is possible to use auditory feedback while viewing the printed text. This software can therefore act as a reading assistant; the person reads most of the text, but has the computer speak unrecognisable words.

Espin and Sindelar (1988) studied the value of auditory feedback for people with learning disabilities. Ninety students took part in the study, including one group with learning disabilities, a control group matched for reading level, and a second control group matched for age. Within each group, half the subjects simply read a text passage and half the subjects listened to a recording of the passage while also having access to the printed text. Subjects were asked to identify and correct errors of grammar and syntax. For all subject groups, subjects listening to the text identified more errors than those who simply read the text (Espin & Sinclair, 1988).

More recent studies have investigated the effects of auditory feedback using speech synthesis while reading on the computer (Borgh & Dickson, 1992; Swanson & Trahan, 1992; Leong, 1995; Lundberg, 1995). In one study, subjects without learning disabilities did more editing when writing original stories on a word processor with speech synthesis compared to the word processor without speech synthesis, and preferred writing using the speech synthesis (Borgh & Dickson, 1992). In another series of studies, subjects with learning disabilities exhibited better reading and spelling performance following training with computer-generated speech feedback (Lundberg, 1995). Other studies have shown more mixed results for subjects with and without learning disabilities, with individual differences between subjects exceeding any clear effect of auditory feedback (Leong, 1995; Swanson & Trahan, 1992). These studies indicated that the value of speech synthesis depends on characteristics of the subject and of the learning goals (Leong, 1995).

MacArthur (1998) studied the use of speech synthesis and word prediction for students with learning disabilities. Five students with learning disabilities wrote in dialogue journals using a standard word processor during baseline phases and a word processor with speech synthesis and word prediction features during treatment phases. For four of five students, percentage of legible words increased from 55% to 85% during the baseline phase to 90–100% during the treatment phase, and the percentage of correctly spelled words increased from 42% to 75% to 90 to 100% (MacArthur, 1998).

Raskind, Higgins, and colleagues have conducted a number of studies on the efficacy of assistive technologies for people with learning disabilities (Higgins & Raskind, 1995, 1997; Raskind & Higgins, 1995). In one study, 33 post-secondary students with learning disabilities proofread self-generated written language samples under three conditions: (1) using a speech synthesis program that simultaneously highlighted words on a monitor and audibly "spoke" them; (2) having text read aloud by another person; and (3) receiving no assistance. Subjects detected a significantly higher percentage of errors when using speech synthesis compared to either of the other conditions. In particular, subjects detected a significantly higher percentage of capitalisation, spelling, usage, and typographical errors with speech synthesis. Subjects may have detected more errors with computer assistance than with human assistance because a person reading the text aloud may subconsciously correct errors when reading aloud; the novelty of the computer may have increased motivation in that condition; and the visual highlighting may have provided an additional benefit unavailable with the human assistant (Raskind & Higgins, 1995).

Thirty-seven post-secondary students with learning disabilities were given reading comprehension exams under three conditions: (1) using an optical character recognition/speech synthesis system; (2) having text read aloud by a human reader; and (3) reading silently without assistance. There was a significant inverse correlation between comprehension scores in silent reading and speech synthesis conditions. Subjects who had the lowest scores without assistance achieved a greater improvement with speech synthesis, but those with high scores without assistance received lower scores when using speech synthesis (Higgins & Raskind, 1997).

Computers also offer alternatives for text production. Some people have difficulty with handwriting due to motor co-ordination difficulties, or have more difficulty comprehending handwritten text compared to printed text. A keyboard can provide assistance for these individuals, since typing may be easier than handwriting. Typing is also helpful because all letters are visible on the keyboard, compensating for letter recollection difficulties. The position of the characters on the keyboard can also be used to aid recognition; if the person can remember the position of the letter he or she wants on the keyboard, he or she does not need to recall the letter's shape (Gregor & Newell, 2000).

For individuals who have difficulty typing as well as writing, speech recognition is an option for text entry in the computer. People who have good verbal skills can compose material directly through speech, and the computer will take on the task of translating the words into printed text. In one study of voice recognition, 29 post-secondary students with learning disabilities wrote essays under three conditions: (1) using speech recognition software; (2) using a human transcriber; and (3) receiving no assistance. Essays were scored according to a standardised scoring guide. Subjects received higher scores when using speech recognition than when receiving no assistance ($p < .05$). Essays written using speech recognition were longer and had a higher proportion of words with seven or more letters (Higgins & Raskind, 1995).

Whether a person is entering text through typing or speech, computer word processors have other features such as spell checkers and grammar checkers which can help compensate for spelling difficulties or a tendency to reverse word order. Word prediction software is also available, which will predict the word which a person is typing based on the letters typed thus far, or on the basis of preceding words. These features have been shown to be beneficial for people with dyslexia (Newell & Booth, 1991; Newell, Booth, Arnott, & Beattie, 1992). However, they have drawbacks. First, the unique spelling and grammar errors which are often produced by people with disabilities can confound automated spelling and grammar checkers, so that they are unable to offer appropriate assistance. Also, spelling and grammar checkers and word prediction software generally function by providing the user with a list of word to choose from (e.g., a list of possible "correct spellings" or a list of predicted words). If the user has difficulty with letter or word recognition, he or she may be unable to select the appropriate word from a list (Gregor & Newell, 2000). To alleviate this problem, students need strategies to use spell checkers effectively (Gillette, 2001), or additional tools such as talking spell checkers.

To expand upon available technologies, Gregor and Newell (2000) developed a highly configurable word processing environment, SeeWord, to assist people with dyslexia in reading and composing text. SeeWord was developed within the context of the University of Dundee's overall research programme on human–computer interaction for extraordinary users and users in extraordinary situations (Gregor, Alm, Arnott, & Newell, 1999). This software provides a variety of options related to the visual appearance of the text and of the software interface, and the means for each user to customize these settings to his or her particular preferences. Users could adjust the text font and size; spacing between characters, words, and paragraphs; and the foreground and background colours. Twelve computer-literate individuals with dyslexia evaluated the software, provided feedback during the development process, and were observed using the software after being asked to think aloud about their decisions and impressions. Subjects' preferred selections were highly individualised. They tended to prefer larger font and increased spacing between characters, words, and lines compared to typical word processor settings (Gregor & Newell, 2000). Although subjects varied in regard to their favourite colour combination, most subjects liked low contrast colour combination, such as brown text on a dark green background (Gregor & Newell, 2000), a colour combination which would be highly unusual in software for the mainstream population. These findings highlight the importance of attempting a variety of solutions and eliciting client input.

These features were implemented in a modified word processor which allows a person to set the appearance of text on the screen separately from the appearance of text produced on the printer, so that the person can compose text with his or her preferred visibility settings but print text in a standard format to share with others (Gregor & Newell, 2000). This version of the software included three additional features:

1. Users could specify a pair of characters which they have difficulty distinguishing, and have the computer increase the distinctiveness of the two characters by presenting one in a different colour, font, or size.
2. Users could reduce the width of a page to assist with fixation.
3. Users could request that selected text be read aloud.

This software was evaluated by seven people with dyslexia. Each of the users found the system easy and intuitive to use, and reported that each of the options had an effect on her or his ability to read. The option to distinguish pairs of characters (option 1 above) was reported to have a negative effect on readability by one evaluator and a positive effect by the remaining six evaluators. The reported reason for this improvement was not assistance in distinguishing characters, as intended. Rather, the occasional appearance of a character with different font, size, or colour helped in fixation by reducing the monotonous appearance of the text (Gregor & Newell, 2000).

This SeeWord software was further evaluated in a study with six students with dyslexia (Dickinson, Gregor, & Newell, 2002). Each subject was given the opportunity to select word processor settings within SeeWord. Two days later the subject was presented with a series of texts displayed with either the subject's selected settings or default word processor settings. Five out of six subjects made fewer errors when reading with their preferred settings and the mean number of errors across texts was significantly lower for the condition in which subject-selected settings were used (Dickinson et al., 2002). Following this pilot study, SeeWord was modified to allow the user to alter line spacing and more easily modify settings, and to improve users' ability to focus on a desired section of text (Dickinson et al., 2002).

In addition to difficulties with visual processing and motor co-ordination, individuals with learning disabilities often have difficulty organising their thoughts for written compositions (Newcomer & Barenbaum, 1991). Computer software can aid in this organizational process by helping the user create concept maps. Concept mapping is the process of categorizing information into a graphic form, known as a "concept map" or "semantic network". This visual representation of information can then be used to organise concepts and provide a basis for the structure of written text. Concept mapping has been shown to support more organised and detailed written texts (Ruddell & Boyle, 1989; Zipprich, 1995). Software such as Inspiration (Inspiration Software Inc, Portland, OR) provides a means to easily create and edit concept maps.

In a study of 12 eighth-grade students with learning disabilities, subjects were observed to write compositions with greater length (number of words) and quality (holistic writing scores) when using either hand-drawn or computer-supported concept maps compared to writing without maps (Sturm & Rankin-Erikson, 2002). Carry-over effects were also observed which indicate that training in concept mapping strategies improved subjects' writing performance in the no-mapping condition. Results showed that subjects' attitude toward writing was significantly more positive in the computer-supported mapping condition compared to hand-drawn mapping and no mapping (Sturm & Rankin-Erikson, 2002).

Technologies for social and behavioural issues

Sensory processing impairments can also lead to social and behavioural difficulties. If an individual is easily overwhelmed by environmental stimuli, he or she may have difficulties with concentration and social engagement (Strickland et al., 1996). Difficulties in processing visual information about faces, or auditory information about a person's tone of voice can also impair a person's ability to recognise social cues. For example, pilot data indicate that adults with autism spend much less time looking at a person's eyes compared to adults without autism (Trepagnier, 1996; Trepagnier, Gupta, Sebrechts, & Rosen, 2000). Some technological interventions have been developed to address these behavioural and social problems.

One application of such ATC is to modify speech so that individuals can more easily comprehend speech and its auditory cues. Some language learning-impaired individuals need longer neural processing times in order to process speech, making it difficult to distinguish speech sounds that have durations in the range of 10–50 ms. People may, for example, have difficulty distinguishing the speech syllables /ba/ and /da/ due to rapid frequency transitions in the initial syllables (Nagarajan et al., 1998; Tallal, Miller, & Fitch, 1993). Nagarajan and colleagues have developed software which alters the characteristics of a speech sample in a two-step process. First, the speech is prolonged, allowing more time for auditory processing. Second, sounds that are marked by high frequency or rapid transitions are made louder, so that they will be easier to comprehend (Nagarajan et al., 1998). This process has been incorporated into training software which aims to foster a reorganisation of the neural structures responsible for processing rapid speech sounds (Habib, Espresser, Rey, Giraud, Braus, & Gres, 1999; Merzenich et al., 1996; Tallal et al., 1996; Turner & Pearson, 1999;). A real-time version of this software could compensate for auditory processing difficulties and help an individual better understand a conversational partner's speech.

Technology is also being applied to allow people with dementia to communicate by augmenting their short-term memory capabilities. A multidisciplinary team of designers, software engineers, and psychologists has developed an approach to helping older people with dementia to communicate, by using an easily accessible multimedia reminiscence aid. With the age profile of most societies shifting towards a larger and larger proportion of older people, the challenges presented by dementia will increase. A significant problem with this condition is the exclusion from everyday interaction it can cause due to the person's inability to communicate effectively because of the loss of short-term memory. To address this problem a conversation support system is being developed based on touch screen access to multimedia material. The system is designed in such a way as to help users to be able to use it easily, and to be able again to enjoy holding conversations with relatives, friends, and carers. The conversations are based on reminiscence about the past, since long-term memories can remain relatively intact with dementia, even where short-term memory is ineffective (Astell et al., 2002).

A first prototype has been tested in the field with people with dementia and their carers. Both care staff and people with dementia responded positively to the system and report enjoyment in using it. People with dementia were able to use the touch screen and the multimedia presentation successfully acted as a prompt for satisfying conversation. Staff reported finding out more new information and getting to know the people with dementia better. Given the disempowerment which communication impairment can cause, an important early finding is that using this system, as compared to traditional methods of supporting reminiscence sessions, gave the people with dementia more control over the interaction (Alm et al., 2004 this issue).

Human and animal studies indicate that deep pressure is calming and reduces arousal in the nervous system (Ayers, 1979; King, 1989; Kumazawa, 1963). This research has inspired the development of tactile interventions to compensate for difficulty independently managing sensory input. Grandin developed a "squeeze machine" that provides deep pressure automatically (Grandin, 1992, 1995). Unlike other forms of deep pressure stimulation, such as rolling in mats, the squeeze machine can apply greater amounts of pressure over larger areas of the body. Also, the user has complete control over the amount of pressure applied and can enter and leave the machine at will (Grandin, 1995). Some research has shown that deep pressure administered by the squeeze machine has a relaxing effect on normal adults and may have an effect on auditory threshold (Grandin, 1992).

Beneficial effects of the squeeze machine have been described anecdotally for children with autistic disorder, attention-deficit hyperactivity disorder, learning disabilities, pervasive developmental disorder (PDD) and Tourette's syndrome. However, there is a lack of formal research data pertaining to the clinical treatment of children (Grandin, 1992). One study (Imamura et al., 1990) examined behavioural effects of the squeeze machine on nine children, aged 3–7 years, with autistic disorder or PDD. Hyperactivity was found to be reduced in four subjects, and the machine had no effect on five children. There appeared to be a relationship between longer duration of squeeze machine usage and beneficial effects (Imamura et al., 1990).

Vibration also appears to have a calming effect on individuals with sensory processing impairments, and non-contingent vibration has been found to reduce stereotypical behaviour (Grandin, 1992). One case study explored the use of automatic vibration in a seating system for an individual with developmental disability. Initially, the subject showed a reduction in stereotypical behaviours, including self-injuring behaviours. However, these behaviours increased over time, indicating that the subject acclimated to the vibration (Kelm & Pawley, 1998).

CONCLUSION

Over the past 20 years, technology has played an increasing role in the rehabilitation of persons with cognitive impairments. The literature reviewed in this paper represents a body of research which demonstrates that technological interventions can effectively facilitate participation in many activities that would otherwise not be possible. Technological interventions have been developed to assist with tasks requiring cognitive skills as diverse as complex attention, prospective memory, self-monitoring for the performance of specific desirable behaviours, inhibition of undesirable behaviours, sequential processing, and understanding of social cues. These assistive technologies can facilitate improved functioning in a number of ways. One approach has been to provide cues, reminders and sequential guidance when task completion would otherwise not be possible—in effect, serving as a "supervisory attendant" or "aide" for the person. A related approach has been to develop interventions that restructure task demands so that residual abilities can be used in place of those that are most impaired. More recently, researchers have been exploring the applications of artificial intelligence, virtual reality, and other advanced technologies to ATC systems, so that a broader range of complex tasks can be addressed and the likelihood of generalisation enhanced.

Although it can be argued that ATC interventions are still not commonplace in clinical practice, their efficacy and broad applicability clearly confirms their general importance in cognitive rehabilitation. In fact, for some types of clinical conditions, such as traumatic brain injury, technological aides such as personal digital assistants (PDA) are now viewed, at very least, as necessary therapeutic considerations, supplementing and sometimes supplanting the use of non-technological interventions such as "memory books."

Our perspective is that interventions based on ATC will continue to grow in importance as technological developments increase their ease of use, portability, and intelligence. However, this field has now grown beyond its infancy and the research approaches adopted over the past 20 years must be broadened. In the paragraphs that follow, we will briefly discuss areas that we believe constitute an ambitious, but necessary, research agenda.

First, very little is known about the relationship between, on one hand, the clinical characteristics of persons with cognitive impairments and, on the other, the specific characteristics of ATC interventions that are most suitable for those individuals. This area, sometimes referred to as "matching persons and technology" (Scherer, 2002), has received most attention for physical disabilities. The complexities of "matching persons and technology" for those with cognitive impairments is only beginning to be recognised.

Clinical experience suggests that there are many factors that influence the appropriate choice of technological cognitive interventions (and their ultimate acceptance by the user), in addition to technological considerations themselves. These factors include (but are not limited to):

1. A person's specific pattern of cognitive strengths and weaknesses (which may determine the intensity of intervention required, the person's ability to learn, or the specific cognitive skills that are to be "capitalised on" in order to promote compensation).
2. Unique issues associated with the natural history of the disorder responsible for the person's acquired cognitive profile (which may determine, for example, whether or not modifications to the intervention will be required over time or whether other considerations, such as sensory-motor adaptations will be required).
3. Specific emotional and behavioural changes associated with the disorder (which may influence motivation or the ability to sustain effort over time, despite persisting motivation).
4. The person's pre-morbid and current personality characteristics and "attitudes", (which may affect the degree to which unobtrusive or "transparent" interventions are required that do not appear to the user to be technological in nature).
5. The person's attitudes in regard to interventions that appear to exert "external control" (which will determine the degree to which participatory consultation with the user will be advantageous).
6. The person's pre-morbid and current system of psychosocial support (which will determine whether caretakers can be relied upon to rehearse and reinforce the use of the ATC intervention in the home and community).

A person's status in any one of the above areas can result in a prescribed device being used ineffectively or even abandoned, even if the intervention itself can be shown to be highly effective in a controlled setting. In order to avoid this type of disappointing outcome, our recommendation is that ATC interventions be developed and prescribed within the context of a conceptual framework that accounts for all of these "systems". Our perspective is that these types of questions must be addressed by multi-disciplinary research teams that include a broad range of rehabilitation disciplines and that represent an understanding of the technological, cognitive, emotional, behavioural, family and social factors that can influence the use of prescribed devices.

It is also crucial that clients themselves be participants in this process. Over the past several years, the National Institute of Disability and Rehabilitation Research has emphasised the importance of participatory action research (PAR) as a critical strategy for assuring that consumer input and review will be incorporated into the design and testing of new interventions. Our recommendation is that the intended consumers for new ATC interventions be incorporated into every phase of research. As an example of this approach, Cole (1999) has described a strong commitment to consumer participation during the design, feedback and implementation stages of device development. Wilson (2000) has suggested that strong consumer involvement enhances acceptance of the device and, hopefully, promotes continuing use over time. White (2002) has suggested that implementation of PAR models may actually be an ethical issue requiring consideration by all researchers.

However, it must also be noted that ATC interventions are often developed for individuals whose cognitive impairments may limit the degree to which they can contribute to any stage of device design or testing. Research teams must therefore assess the cognitive abilities of the intended consumers so that an *appropriate level of participation can be devised*, including the involvement of caretakers who may be responsible for assuring that use of the ATC intervention is maintained over time.

Second, as ATC interventions begin to incorporate changes in technological infrastructure, such as wireless wide area networks, it is inevitable that ATC interventions will be increasingly used in the community. In this regard, the issue of "context generalisability" or, to borrow a phrase loosely, the "ecological validity" of ATC interventions will have to be established, since it is still unclear whether being able to perform a task in a controlled environment will generalise to performing the identical task in a community environment. To use a very simple example, checking a personal digital assistant (PDA) to determine one's next therapy appointment may be a far different task than checking the same PDA to assure that one leaves the mall in order to return to home on time to eat supper. Our recommendation is that the generalisability of ATC devices across functional contexts cannot be assumed. As the portability of ATC devices increases, it will become increasingly important for research programmes to identify the factors that promote or hinder the effective use of ATC systems across the range of community settings in which they will be used and, most critically, to develop research programmes that actually test new interventions within those community settings.

Third, recent developments in physical neurorehabilitation suggest the very tentative hypothesis that ATC may offer a fruitful approach for attempting the "restoration" of neurocognitive functioning. For physical impairment, recent evidence suggests that sensory and motor functioning may be enhanced by "forcing" an affected limb to engage in functional activities using constraint induced therapy (CIT) or patterned neural activation (PNA) (McDonald et al., 2002; Morris & Taub, 2001). One of the critical features of this type of intervention appears to be that the affected limb is repeatedly engaged in functional activities during the course of everyday life. In regard to cognition, it is as yet unclear if there are interventions that will also qualify as PNA. However, the most likely candidates for analogous interventions would appear to be those that promote repeated, systematic and controlled performance of functional activities that require the intensive use of the cognitive skill being targeted. Potential therapeutic activities must be chosen to assure that they actually do promote activation of partially damaged neurological areas, or that they promote the activation of other neurological areas that are presumed to communicate with the damaged areas. Similarly, any functional activity chosen for this type of intervention will require that a clinically appropriate balance be achieved between demanding of the person too much of the impaired skill (making performance of the task simply impossible) or too little (making performance of the task, in effect, another compensatory intervention).

Clearly, there are many ways in which repeated, systematic and controlled performance of functional activities can be achieved. However, technological interventions seem particularly promising in this regard, because they can be used to guide a person through the stages of a functional task, in a manner analogous to the use of functional electrical stimulation for co-ordinating groups of muscles (McDonald et al., 2002). ATC interventions can be used for repeated and controlled rehearsal of activities, otherwise requiring skills that are impaired, with systematic variation of task parameters so that the level of challenge is carefully controlled. To our knowledge, this type of intervention has not yet been reported, but the implications are exciting and suggest a promising new line of research for ATC.

In conclusion, the literature reviewed in this paper establishes a 20-year history of increasingly successful technological interventions for cognition. Our perspective is that this literature serves as a strong foundation for continuing development of more sophisticated interventions that will, over time, parallel and incorporate broader technological and infrastructure changes. The "coming of age" of clinical intervention and research in this area requires that a broader perspective be adopted in regard to the development and assessment of ATC interventions. There are also many new opportunities in this area that suggest a central role for ATC in clinical and research programmes.

REFERENCES

Allen, D. N., Goldstein, G., Heyman, R. A., & Rondinelli, T. (1998). Teaching memory strategies to persons with multiple sclerosis. *Journal of Rehabilitation Research and Development*, *35*(4), 405–410.

Alm, N., Ellis, M., Astell, A., Dye, R., Gowans, G., & Campbell, J. (2004). A cognitive prosthesis and communication support for people with dementia. *Neuropsychological Rehabilitation*, *14*(1/2), 117–134.

Arkell, H. (1997). *An introduction to dyslexia: A dyslexic's eye view*. Surrey, UK: Helen Arkell Dyslexia Centre.

Astell, A. J., Ellis, M., Alm, N., Dye, R, Gowans, G., & Campbell, J. (2002). Developing computer technology to assist communication for people with dementia: The CIRCA project. *Neurobiology of Aging, 23* (1S), S543.

Ayers, J. A. (1979). *Sensory integration and the child.* Los Angeles: Western Psychology Service.

Bai, J., Zhang, Y., Cui, Z., & Zhang, J. (2000). Home telemonitoring framework based on integrated functional modules. *World Congress on Medical Physics and Biomedical Engineering.* Chicago, Illinois.

Beigl, M. (2000). Memoclip: A location based remembrance appliance. *Personal Technologies, 4*(4), 230–234.

Bergman, M. (1996). Computer orthoses: Fostering self-sufficiency in people with cognitive challenges. *Disability Today, Fall,* 54–55.

Bergman, M. M. (1997). People with cognitive challenges can enjoy rapid success in acquiring skills and managing their lives: The exciting breakthrough of Cognitive Orthoses. *California State University, Northridge, Technology and Persons with Disabilities Conference (CSUN).* Los Angeles, CA.

Bergman, M. M. (1998). A proposed resolution of the remediation-compensation controversy in brain injury rehabilitation. *Cognitive Technology, 3*(1), 45–51.

Bergman, M. M. (2002). The benefits of a cognitive orthotic in brain injury rehabilitation. *Journal of Head Trauma Rehabilitation, 17*(5), 432–445.

Beukelman, D., & Mirenda, P. (1998). *Augmentative and alternative communication: management of severe communication disorders in children and adults.* Baltimore, MD: Paul H. Brookes Publishing Co.

Bonasso, R. P. (1996). Using adjustable autonomy to extend the independence of the elderly. *Developing Assistive Technology for People with Disabilities, AAAI, Fall Symposium.*

Borgh, K., & Dickson, W. P. (1992). The effects on children's writing of adding speech synthesis to a word processor. *Journal of Research on Computing in Education, 24*(4), 533–544.

Carmien, S. (2002). MAPS: PDA scaffolding for independence for persons with cognitive impairments. *2002 Human Computer Interaction Consortium.*

Cavalier, A. R., & Ferretti, R. P. (1993). The use of an intelligent cognitive aid to facilitate the self-management of vocational skills by high school students with severe learning disabilities. *Proceedings of the Rehabilitation Engineering Society of North America (RESNA)* (pp. 216–218). Arlington, VA: RESNA Press.

Chute, D. L., & Bliss, M. E. (1988). Prosthesis ware: Personal computer support for independent living (Vol. 2000). Retrieved December 16, 2002, from http://www.homemods.org/library/life-span/prosthesis.html

Chute, D. L., & Bliss, M. E. (1994). ProthesisWare. *Experimental Aging Research, 20,* 229–238.

Chute, D., Conn, G., DiPasquale, M., & Hoag, M. (1988). Prosthesis ware: A new class of software supporting the activities of daily living. *Neuropsychology, 2*(1), 41–57.

Cicerone, K. D., Dahlberg, C., Kalmar, K., Langenbahn, D. M., Malec, J.F., Bergquist, T. F., Felicetti, T. Giacino, J. T., Harley, J. P., Harrington, D. E., Herzog, J., Kneipp, S., Laatsch, L., & Morse, P. A. (2000). Evidence-based cognitive rehabilitation: Recommendations for clinical practice. *Archives of Physical Medicine & Rehabilitation, 81*(12), 1596–1615.

Cole, E. (1999). Cognitive prosthetics: An overview to a method of treatment. *NeuroRehabilitation, 12,* 39–51.

Cole, E., & Dehdashti, P. (1988). Increasing personal productivity of adults with brain injury through interface design [Abstract]. *SIGCHI Bulletin,* October.

Cole, E., & Dehdashti, P. (1990). Interface design as a prosthesis for an individual with a brain injury. *SIGCHI Bulletin, 22*(1), 28–32.

Cole, E., & Dehdashti, P. (1998). Computer-based cognitive prosthetics: Assistive technology for treatment of cognitive disabilities. *Proceedings of the Third International ACM Conference on Assistive Technologies*. Los Angeles: ACM Press.

Cole, E., Dehdashti, P., Petti, L., & Angert, M. (1993). Design parameters and outcomes for cognitive prosthetic software with brain injury patients. *Proceedings of the Rehabilitation Engineering Society of North America (RESNA)* (pp. 426–428). Arlington, VA: RESNA Press.

Cole, E., Dehdashti, P., Petti, L., & Angert, M. (1994). Design and outcomes of computer-based cognitive prosthetics for brain injury: A field study of three subjects. *NeuroRehabilitation, 4*(3), 174–186.

Cole, E., Petti, L., Matthews, M., & Dehdashti, P. (1994). Rapid functional improvement and generalization in a young stroke patient following computer-based cognitive prosthetic intervention. *NIH Neural Prosthesis Workshop.*

Cole, E., Ziegmann, M., Wu, Y., Yonker, V., Gustafson, C., & Cirwithen, S. (2000). Use of "therapist-friendly" tools in cognitive assistive technology and telerehabilitation. *Proceedings of the Rehabilitation Engineering Society of North America (RESNA)* (pp. 31–33). Arlington, VA: RESNA Press.

DeVaul, R.W. (2000). The Memory Glasses Project. http://www.media.mit.edu/wearables/mithril/memory-glasses.html. *MIT Media Lab*. Viewed December 16, 2002; last updated March 2, 2002.

Dickinson, A., Gregor, P., & Newell, A.F. (2002). Ongoing investigation of the ways in which some of the problems encountered by some dyslexics may be alleviated using computer techniques. *Proceedings of Assets 2002: The Fifth International ACM Conference on Assistive Technologies, Edinburgh, Scotland* (pp. 97–103). New York: ACM Press.

Ellis, J. (1996). Prospective memory or the realization of delayed intentions: A conceptual framework for research. In M. Brandimonte, G. O. Einstein, & M. A. McDaniel (Eds.), *Prospective memory: Theory and applications* (pp. 1–22). Mahway, NJ: Lawrence Erlbaum Associates, Inc.

Espin, C.A., & Sindelar, P.T. (1988). Auditory feedback and writing: Learning disabled and nondisabled students. *Exceptional Children, 55*(1), 45–51.

Evans, J. J., Emslie, H., & Wilson, B. A. (1998). External cueing systems in the rehabilitation of executive impairments of action. *Journal of the International Neuropsychological Society. 4*(4), 399–408.

Everatt, J., Bradshaw, M. F., & Hibbard, P. (1999). Visual processing and dyslexia. *Perception, 28*(2), 243–254.

Fagerberg, G. (1999). TASC: Telematics applications supporting cognition. In European Commission Directorate-General, *Telematics for the integration of the disabled and elderly* (pp. 102–103). Luxembourg: Office for Official Publications of the European Communities.

Fernie, G., & Fernie, B. (1996). The potential role of technology to provide help at home for persons with Alzheimer's disease. *The 18th Annual Conference of the Alzheimer's Society of Canada*, Ottawa, ON.

Flannery, M., & Rice, D. (1997). Using available technology for reminding. *Proceedings of the Rehabilitation Engineering Society of North America (RESNA)* (pp. 517–519). Arlington, VA: RESNA Press.

Friedman, M. (1993). A wearable computer that gives context-sensitive verbal guidance to people with memory or attention impairments. *Proceedings of the Rehabilitation Society of North America (RESNA)* (pp. 199–201). Arlington, VA: RESNA Press.

Friedman, M., Kostraba, J., Henry, K., & Coltellaro, J. (1991). Hardware description of a portable electronic device. *Proceedings of the Rehabilitation Engineering Society of North America (RESNA)* (pp. 333–334). Arlington, VA: RESNA Press.

Gillette, Y. (2001). Pictures to print: A software scaffold to written literacy. *Journal of Head Trauma Rehabilitation, 16*(5), 484–497.

Grandin, T. (1992). Calming effects of deep touch pressure in patients with autistic disorder, college students and animals. *Journal of Child and Adolescent Psychopharmacology, 2*(1), 63–70.

Grandin, T. (1995). *Thinking in pictures*. New York: Doubleday.

Gregor, P., Alm, N., Arnott, J., & Newell, A. F. (1999). The application of computing technology to interpersonal communication at the University of Dundee's department of applied computing. *Technology and Disability, 10*, 107–113.

Gregor, P., & Newell, A. F. (2000). An empirical investigation of ways in which some of the problems encountered by some dyslexics may be alleviated using computer techniques. *Proceedings of Assets 2000: The Fourth International ACM Conference on Assistive Technologies, Washington, DC* (pp. 85–91). New York: ACM Press.

Habib, M., Espresser, R., Rey, V., Giraud, K., Braus, P., & Gres, C. (1999). Training dyslexics with acoustically modified speech: Evidence of improved phonological performance. *Brain and Cognition, 40*(1), 143–146.

Harris, J. (1978). External memory aids. In M. Gruneberg, P. Morris, & R. Sykes (Eds.), *Practical aspects of memory*. London: Academic Press.

Hart, T., Hawkey, K, & Whyte, J. (2002). Use of a portable voice organizer to remember therapy goals in traumatic brain injury rehabilitation: A within-subjects trial. *Journal of Head Trauma Rehabilitation, 17*(6), 556–570.

Herrmann, D., Brubaker, B., Yoder, C., Sheets, V., & Tio, A. (1999). Devices that remind. In F. T. Durso, R. S. Nickerson, R. W. Schvaneveldt, S. T. Dumais, D. S. Lindsay, & M. T. H. Chi (Eds.), *Handbook of applied cognition* (pp. 377–408). Chichester, UK: John Wiley and Sons.

Hersch, N. A., & Treadgold, L. G. (1994). NeuroPage: The rehabilitation of memory dysfunction by prosthetic memory and cueing. *NeuroRehabilitation, 4*(3), 187–197.

Higgins, E. L., & Raskind, M. H. (1995). Compensatory effectiveness of speech recognition on the written composition performance of postsecondary students with learning disabilities. *Learning Disability Quarterly, 18*(Spring), 159–174.

Higgins, E. L., & Raskind, M. H. (1997). The compensatory effectiveness of optical character recognition/speech synthesis on reading comprehension of postsecondary students with learning disabilities. *Learning Disabilities, 8*(2), 75–87.

Imamura, K. N., Wiess, T., & Parham, D. (1990). The effects of hug machine usage on behavioral organization of children with autism and autistic-like characteristics. *Sensory Integration Quarterly, 27*, 1–5.

Inglis, E., Szymkowiak, A., Gregor, P., Newell, A. F., Hine, N., Wilson, N. A., & Evans, J. (2002). Issues surrounding the user-centred development of a new interactive memory aid, In S. Keates, P. Langdon, P. J. Clarkson, & P. Robinson (Eds.), *Universal access and assistive technology* (pp.171–178). Proceedings of the Cambridge Workshop on UA and AT '02 2002.

Jinks, A., & Robson-Brandi, C. (1997). Designing an interactive prosthetic memory system. *Proceedings or the Rehabilitation Engineering Society of North America (RESNA)* (pp. 526–528). Arlington, VA: RESNA Press.

Jones, M., & Adams, J. (1979). Toward a prosthetic memory. *Bulletin of the British Psychological Society, 32*, 165–167.

Jonsson, B., & Svensk, A. (1995). ISAAC—A personal digital assistant for the differently abled. *Proceedings of the 2nd TIDE Congress* (pp. 356–361). Paris, France.

Keates, A. (2000). *Dyslexia and information and communications technology: A guide for teachers and parents*. London: David Fulton Publishers.

Keates, S., Clarkson, J., & Robinson, P. (2000). Investigating the applicability of user models for motion-impaired users. *Proceedings of Assets 2000: The Fourth International ACM*

Conference on Assistive Technologies, Washington, DC (pp. 129–136). New York: ACM Press.

Kelm, K. & Pawley, R. (1998). Good vibrations. *TeamRehab Report*, *9*(9), 37–40.

Kielhofner, G. (1997). The sensory integration model. In G. Kielhofner (Ed.), *Conceptual foundations of occupational therapy* (pp. 251–269). Philadelphia, PA: F.A. Davis Company.

Kim, H., Burke, D., Dowds, M., & George, J. (1999). Utility of a microcomputer as an external memory aid for a memory-impaired head injury patient during inpatient rehabilitation. *Brain Injury*, *13*, 147–150.

Kime, S., Lamb, D., & Wilson, B. (1995). Use of a comprehensive program of external cueing to enhance procedural memory in a patient with dense amnesia. *Brain Injury*, *10*, 17–25.

King, L. (1989). Facilitating neurodevelopment. *Autism Society of America Conference Proceedings* (pp. 117–120). Seattle, WA.

Kirsch, N. L., Levine, S. P., Fallon-Kreuger, M., & Jaros, L. (1987). The microcomputer as an 'orthotic' device for patients with cognitive deficits. *Journal of Head Trauma Rehabilitation*, *2*(4), 77–86.

Kirsch, N. L., Levine, S. P., Lajiness, R., Mossaro, M., Schneider, M., & Donders, J. (1988). Improving functional performance with computerized task guidance systems. *ICAART '88 Annual Conference*, Arlington, VA: RESNA Press.

Kirsch, N. L., Levine, S. P., Lajiness-O'Neill, R., & Schneider, M. (1992). Computer-assisted interactive task guidance: Facilitating the performance of a simulated vocational task. *Journal of Head Trauma Rehabilitation*, *7*(3), 13–25.

Kirsch, N. L., Shenton, M., Spirl, E., Simpson, R., & Schreckenghost, D. (2002). Interactive wireless cueing facilitates performance of moderately complex functional tasks for persons having severe TBI. Poster presented at *Clinical Trials in Medical Rehabilitation: Enhancing Rigor and Relevance*, Kessler Medical Rehabilitation Research and Education Corporation, West Orange, NJ.

Klein, R., & Fowler, R. (1981). Pressure relief training device: The microcalculator. *Archives of Physical Medicine and Rehabilitation*, *62*, 500–501.

Kumazawa, T. (1963). "Deactivation" of the rabbit's brain by pressure application to the skin. *Electroencephalography and Clinical Neurophysiology*, *15*, 660–671.

Lancioni, G., O'Reilly, M., Seedhouse, P., Furniss, F., & Cunha, B. (2000). Promoting independent task performance by persons with severe developmental disabilities through a new computer-aided system. *Behavior Modification*, *24*(5), 700–718.

Lancioni, G., Van den Hof, E., Furniss, F., O'Reilly, M., & Cunha, B. (1999). Evaluation of a computer-aided system providing pictorial task instructions and prompts to people with severe intellectual disability. *Journal of Intellectual Disability Research*, *43*(1), 61–66.

Leong, C.K. (1995). Effects of on-line reading and simultaneous DECtalk auding in helping poor readers comprehend and summarize text. *Learning Disability Quarterly*, *18*, 101–116.

Levine, S. P., Horstmann, H. M., & Kirsch, N. L. (1992). Performance considerations for people with cognitive impairments in accessing assistive technologies. *Journal of Head Trauma Rehabilitation*, *7*(3), 46–58.

Levine, S. P., & Kirsch, N. L. (1985). COGORTH: A programming language for customized cognitive orthoses. *Proceedings of the Rehabilitation Engineering Society of North America (RESNA)* (pp. 359–360). Arlington, VA: RESNA Press.

Levinson, R. (1997). PEAT: The planning and execution assistant and training system. *Journal of Head Trauma Rehabilitation*, *12*(2), 769–775.

LoPresti, E. F., Friedman, M. B., & Hages, D. (1997). Electronic vocational aid for people with cognitive disabilities. *Proceedings of the Rehabilitation Engineering Society of North America (RESNA)* (pp. 514–526). Arlington, VA: RESNA Press.

LoPresti, E. F., & Willkomm, T. (1997). Comparison of commercially available electronic prospective memory aids. *Proceedings of the Rehabilitation Engineering Society of North America (RESNA)* (pp. 523–525). Arlington, VA: RESNA Press.

Lundberg, I. (1995). The computer as a tool of remediation in the education of students with learning disabilities: A theory-based approach. *Learning Disability Quarterly, 18*, 89–99.

Luria, A. (1973). *The working brain: An introduction to neuropsychology*. New York: Basic Books.

Lynch, W. (1982). The use of videogames in cognitive rehabilitation. In: L. Trexler (Ed.), *Cognitive rehabilitation: Conceptualization and intervention*. New York: Plenum Press.

Lynch, W. (2002). Historical review of computer-assisted cognitive retraining. *Journal of Head Trauma Rehabilitation, 17*(5), 446–457.

MacArthur, C. A. (1998). Word processing with speech synthesis and word prediction: Effects on the dialogue journal writing of students with learning disabilities. *Learning Disability Quarterly, 21*(2), 151–166.

MacArthur, C. A., Ferretti, R. P., Okolo, C. M., & Cavalier, A. R. (2001). Technology applications for students with literacy problems: A critical review. *Elementary School Journal, 101*(3), 273–301.

Magnusson, C., & Larsson, J. E. (1994). Svarne, an expert system to be used in the care of the mentally retarded. *SAIA '94 Workshop.*

Maylor, E. A. (1996). Does prospective memory decline with age? In M. Brandimonte, G. O. Einstein, & M. A. McDaniel (Eds.), *Prospective memory: Theory and applications* (pp. 173–197). Mahwah, NJ: Lawrence Erlbaum Associates, Inc.

McDonald, J. W., Becker, D., Sadowsky, C. L., Jane, J. A., Conturo, T. E., & Schultz, L. M. (2002). Late recovery following spinal cord injury: Case report and review of the literature. *Journal of Neurosurgery (Spine 2), 97*, 252–265.

Merzenich, M., Jenkins, W., Johnston, P., Schreiner, C., Miller, S., & Tallal, P. (1996). Temporal processing deficits of language-learning impaired children ameliorated by training. *Science*, 271, 77–81.

Middleton, D., Lambert, M., & Seggar, L. (1991). Neuropsychological rehabilitation: Microcomputer-assisted treatment of brain-injured adults. *Perceptual Motor Skills, 72*, 527–530.

Mihailidis, A., Fernie, G., & Barbenel, J. C. (2001). The use of artificial intelligence in the design of an intelligent cognitive orthotic for people with dementia. *Assistive Technology, 13*, 23–39.

Mihailidis, A., Fernie, G. R., & Cleghorn, W. L. (2000). The development of a computerized cueing device to help people with dementia to be more independent. *Technology & Disability, 13*(1), 23–40.

Morris, D. M., & Taub, E. (2001). Constraint-induced therapy approach to restoring function after neurological injury. *Topics in Stroke Rehabilitation, 8*(3), 16–30.

Mynatt, E. D., Essa, I., & Rogers, W. (2000). Increasing opportunities for aging in place. *ACM Conference on Universal Usability, Washington, DC* (pp. 65–71). New York: ACM Press.

Nagarajan, S. S., Wang, X., Merzenich, M. M., Schreiner, C. E., Johnston, P., Jenkins, P., Miller, S., & Tallal, P. (1998). Speech modifications algorithms used for training language learning-impaired children. *IEEE Trans on Rehabilitation Engineering, 6*(3), 257–268.

Nambu, M., Nakajima, K., Kawarada, A., & Tamura, T. (2000). A system to monitor elderly people remotely, using the power line network. *World Congress on Medical Physics and Biomedical Engineering,* Chicago, Illinois.

Napper, S. A., & Narayan, S. (1994). Cognitive orthotic shell. *Proceedings of the Rehabilitation Engineering Society of North America (RESNA)* (pp. 423–425). Arlington, VA: RESNA Press.

Newcomer, P., & Barenbaum, E. (1991). The written composing problems of children with LD: A review. *Journal of Learning Disabilities, 22*, 262–264.

Newell, A. F., & Booth, L. (1991). The use of lexical and spelling aids with dyslexics. In C. H. Singleton (Ed.), *Computers and Literacy* (pp. 35–44). Hull, UK: University of Hull.

Newell, A. F., Booth, J., Arnott, J. L., & Beattie, W (1992). Increasing literacy levels through the use of linguistic prediction. *Child Language Teaching and Therapy, 8* (2), 138–187.

Newell, A. F., & Gregor, P. (2000). User sensitive inclusive design in search of a new paradigm. In J. Scholtz & J. Thomas (Eds.), *CUU 2000 First ACM Conference on Universal Usability* (pp. 39–44). New York: ACM Press.

NIH (United States National Institutes of Health) (1998). Rehabilitation of persons with traumatic brain injury. *NIH Consensus Statement, 16*(1), 1–41.

Ogawa, M., Ochiai, S., Shoji, K., Nishihara, M., & Togawa, T. (2000). An attempt of monitoring daily activities at home. *World Congress on Medical Physics and Biomedical Engineering.* Chicago, Illinois.

Ramakrishnan, S., & Pollack, M. E. (2000). Intelligent monitoring in a robotic assistant for the elderly. *Proceedings of the 16th National Conference on Artificial Intelligence.* Orlando, FL: AAAI.

Raskind, M. H., & Higgins, E. L. (1995). Effects of speech synthesis on the proofreading efficiency of postsecondary students with learning disabilities. *Learning Disability Quarterly, 18*(Spring), 141–158.

Rosen, M., Brennan, D., Trepagnier, C., Tran, B., Lauderdale, D., & Lathan, C. (2000). Dimensions of diversity in design of telerehabilitation systems for universal usability. *ACM Conference on Universal Usability* (pp. 61–62). Washington, DC.

Rothi, L., & Horner, I. (1983). Restitution and substitution: Two theories of recovery with application to neurobehavioral treatment. *Journal of Clinical Neuropsychology, 5,* 73–81.

Rubinstein, J. S., Meyer, D. E., & Evans, J. E. (2000). Executive control of cognitive processes in task switching. *Journal of Experimental Psychology: Human Perception & Performance, 27*(4), 763–797.

Ruddell, R. B., & Boyle, O. F. (1989). A study of cognitive mapping as a means to improve comprehension of expository text. *Reading Research and Instruction, 29*(1), 12–22.

Scherer, M. J. (Ed.) (2002). *Assistive technology: Matching device and consumer for successful rehabilitation.* Washington, DC: American Psychological Association.

Simpson, R., Schreckenghost, D., & Kirsch, N. L. (2002). A task planning, scheduling and sequencing orthotic for the cognitively impaired. *Proceedings of the AAAI Workshop on Automation as Caregiver: The Role of Intelligent Technology in Elder Care,* Edmonton, Canada, July 2002.

Steele, R. D., Weinrich, M., & Carlson, G. S. (1989). Recipe preparation by a severely impaired aphasic using the VIC 2.0 interface. *Proceedings of the Rehabilitation Engineering Society of North America (RESNA)* (pp. 218–219). Arlington, VA: RESNA Press.

Strickland, D., Marcus, L., Mesibov, G.B., & Hogan, K. (1996). Brief report: Two case studies using virtual reality as a learning tool for autistic children. *Journal of Autism and Developmental Disorders, 26*(6), 651–660.

Sturm, J., & Rankin-Erikson, J. L. (2002). Effects of hand-drawn and computer-generated concept mapping on the expository writing of middle school students with learning disabilities. *Learning Disabilities Research and Practice, 17*(2), 124–139.

Svensk, A. (1997). Empathic modeling (The Sober Version). *Proceedings 4th European Conference for the Advancement of Assistive Technology, (AAATE), Thessaloniki, Greece.* (pp. 432–435). Amsterdam: IOS Press.

Swanson, H. L., & Trahan, M. F. (1992). Learning disabled readers' comprehension of computer-mediated text: The influence of working memory, metacognition, and attribution. *Learning Disabilities Research and Practice, 7,* 74–86.

Tackett, S. L., Rice, D. A., Rice, J. C., & Butterbaugh, G. J. (2001). Using a palmtop PDA for reminding in prospective memory deficit. *Proceedings of the Rehabilitation Engineering Society of North America (RESNA)* (pp. 23–25). Arlington, VA: RESNA Press.

Tallal, P., Miller, S. L., Bedi, G., Byma, G., Wang, X., Nagarajan, S. S., Schreiner, C., Jenkins, W. M., & Merzenich, M. (1996). Language comprehension in language-learning impaired children improved with acoustically modified speech. *Science, 271*, 81–83.

Tallal, P., Miller, S. L., & Fitch, R. (1993). Neurological basis of speech: A case for the preeminence of temporal processing. *Annual New York Academy of Science, 682*, 27–47.

Trepagnier, C. (1996). A possible origin for the social and communicative deficits of autism. *Focus on autism and other developmental disabilities, 11*(3), 170–182.

Trepagnier, C., Gupta, V., Sebrechts, M. M., & Rosen, M. J. (2000). How does he look: Tracking autistic gaze. *Proceedings of the Rehabilitation Engineering Society of North America (RESNA)* (pp. 28–30). Arlington, VA: RESNA Press.

Turner, S., & Pearson, D. W. (1999). Fast ForWord language intervention program: Four case studies. *Tejas—Texas Journal of Audiology and Speech Pathology*, 13.

Vanderheiden, G. (1998). *Assistive techniques & devices for persons with cognitive and language impairments.* Madison WI: Trace Research and Development Centre: Accessible Design, University of Wisconsin.

Wehmeyer, M. L. (1998). National survey of the use of assistive technology by adults with mental retardation. *Mental Retardation, 36*(1), 44–51.

Werry, I., Dautenhahn, K., Ogden, B., & Harwin, W. (2001) Can social interaction skills be taught by a social agent? The role of a robotic mediator in autism therapy. *Proceedings CT2001, The Fourth International Conference on Cognitive Technology: Instruments of mind*, Warwick, UK.

White, G. W. (2002). Consumer participation in disability research: The golden rule as a guide for ethical practice. *Rehabilitation Psychology, 47*(4), 438–446:

Wilkins, A. (1995). *Visual stress.* Oxford: Oxford University Press.

Wilkins, A., & Lewis, E. (1999). Coloured overlays, text, and texture. *Perception, 28*, 365–370.

Willkomm, T., & LoPresti, E. (1997). Evaluation of an electronic aid for prospective memory tasks. *Proceedings of the Rehabilitation Engineering Society of North America (RESNA)* (pp. 52–522). Arlington, VA: RESNA Press.

Willows, D. M., Kruk, R. S., & Corcos, E. (1993). *Visual processes in reading and reading disabilities.* Mahwah, NJ: Lawrence Erlbaum Associates, Inc.

Willows, D. M., & Terepocki, M. (1993). The relation of reversal errors to reading disabilities. In D. M. Willows, R. S. Kruk, & E. Corcos (Eds.), *Visual processes in reading and reading disabilities* (pp. 31–56). Mahway, NJ: Lawrence Erlbaum Associates, Inc.

Wilson, B. A. (1984). Memory training in practice. In B. Wilson & M. Moffat (Eds.), *Clinical management of memory problems.* Rockville, MD: Aspen Systems Corporation.

Wilson, B. A., Emslie, H. C, Quirk, K., & Evans, J. J. (2001). Reducing everyday memory and planning problems by means of a paging system: A randomised control crossover study. *Journal of Neurology, Neurosurgery, and Psychiatry, 70*(4), 477–482.

Wilson, B. A., Evans, J. J., Emslie, H., & Malinek, V. (1997). Evaluation of NeuroPage: A new memory aid. *Journal of Neurology, Neurosurgery, and Psychiatry, 63*, 113–115.

Wright, P., Rogers, N., Hall, C., Wilson, B., Evans, J., Emslie, H., & Bartram, C. (2001). Comparison of pocket-computer memory aids for people with brain injury. *Brain Injury, 15*(9), 787–800.

Zanetti, O., Zanieri, G., Vreese, L. P. D., Frisoni, G., & Binetti, G. (2000). Utilizing an electronic memory aid with Alzheimer's disease patients. A study of feasibility. *Sixth International Stockholm/Springfield Symposium on Advances in Alzheimer Therapy*, Stockholm, Sweden.

Zipprich, M. A. (1995). Teaching web making as a guided planning tool to improve student narrative writing. *Remedial and Special Education, 16*(1), 3–15.

NEUROPSYCHOLOGICAL REHABILITATION, 2004, *14* (1/2), 41–60

Technological memory aids for people with memory deficits

Narinder Kapur
Addenbrooke's Hospital, Cambridge, UK

Elizabeth L. Glisky
University of Arizona, Tuscon, USA

Barbara A. Wilson
MRC Cognition and Brain Sciences Unit, Cambridge, UK

This paper reviews the application of external memory aids and computer-based procedures for the enhancement of memory functioning in neurological patients particularly adults with non-progressive brain injury and those with mild/moderate memory deficits. Memory aids may function as event memory aids to improve prospective memory functioning (Herrmann et al., 1999), or as knowledge memory aids to facilitate the acquisition and utilisation of factual information. We review the range of available external memory aids and evidence on their efficacy in clinical settings. Several studies have shown that external memory aids act as effective reminders and improve prospective memory functioning. Computer-based resources and procedures for improving memory functioning include those that serve similar functions to external memory aids, those which present memory tasks as memory retraining exercises, those which instruct the individual in the use of memory strategies,

Correspondence should be addressed to Professor N. Kapur, Neurosciences Unit, Box 83, Addenbrooke's Hospital, Hills Road, Cambridge, CB2 2QQ. Tel: 01223 216040, Fax: 01223 217909. Email: n.kapur@soton.ac.uk

A version of this paper appeared in Kapur, N., Glisky, E. L., & Wilson, B. A. (2002). External memory aids and computers in memory rehabilitation. In A. D. Baddeley, M. Kopelman, & B. A. Wilson (Eds.), *Handbook of memory disorders* (2nd ed.). Chichester, UK: John Wiley. Reproduced with permission.

http://www.tandf.co.uk/journals/pp/09602011.html DOI:10.1080/09602010343000138

those which directly assist in domain-specific knowledge acquisition, and those which form the basis of "virtual reality" memory rehabilitation procedures. While there may be potential for computer-based procedures, there is at present only limited evidence on their efficacy and cost-effectiveness. We outline practical issues relating to the implementation of memory aids in clinical settings. We consider future developments that may impact on the application of external memory aids and computers in the treatment of human memory disorder.

INTRODUCTION

At present, compared to conceptual frameworks that exist for considering errors in attention and memory (Reason, 1990; Schacter, 2001), or for viewing compensation strategies by memory impaired individuals (Wilson & Watson, 1996), there is no widely accepted conceptual framework for considering the functional application of memory aids in neurological rehabilitation, although some preliminary attempts have been made in specific settings, such as the use of memory aids in office environments (Reason, 2002).

In this paper, we consider mechanical (for example, pill boxes and kitchen timers), and electronic aids, together with computer-based resources. Although environmental and stationery aids are helpful and widely used in memory rehabilitation, these are not considered in detail here as we are focusing on technological memory aids in the rehabilitation of memory impaired people, particularly adults with non-progressive brain injury such as traumatic brain injury, encephalitis and hypoxia. We are not dealing with people with very severe amnesia or with dementia. The interested reader is referred to Kapur, Glisky, and Wilson, (2002). Some of the beneficial effects of memory aids can be considered in terms of the long-established distinction between experiential and knowledge memory (Nielsen, 1958), the subsequent distinctions between episodic and semantic memory (Tulving, 1972), and between memory for events and memory for facts (Warrington, 1986). Thus, aids may be used mainly to enhance event memory, or they may be more useful in knowledge acquisition and utilisation. Often, a specific memory aid can serve both purposes, and one function may merge into another.

We review both novel memory aids and also the more obvious ways in which external memory aids may be useful in clinical settings, to allow an overview of devices that can enhance memory functioning in neurological patients, and to enable us to bring the wide range of memory aids within some form of coherent conceptual framework.

ELECTRONIC ORGANISERS AND RELATED ELECTRONIC REMINDERS TO ENHANCE EVENT OR PROSPECTIVE MEMORY

The most common commercially available electronic memory aids are electronic organisers. In recent years, these have become more compact, sophisticated and diverse in their functions, and also less expensive. In general, such devices can be useful as memory aids in five main ways:

1. An electronic diary to keep a record of appointments.
2. An alarm which provides auditory cues, with or without a visual ones such as text or pictorial information, at pre-set, regular or irregular times.
3. A temporary store for items such as shopping lists, messages, etc.
4. A more permanent store for information such as addresses, telephone-numbers, etc.
5. In more expensive models, a communication device that can receive and send information such as reminders and factual knowledge.

Electronic organisers range in size from pocket-sized to the size of a wallet/filofax—palmtop devices. Alarms can be set to sound at the same time as a stored message is displayed, and for some models multiple daily, weekly or monthly alarms can be set. Many electronic organisers can be interfaced to enable them to transfer data to computers, and for certain models add-on cards can be bought to store information and allow for specialised applications. Most models have back-up devices to safeguard against loss of stored information. Electronic organisers vary greatly in features which may or may not be applicable to the needs of neurological patients with memory impairment. The following features, drawing upon the basis of our clinical experience and our appreciation of the literature, may help when selecting an electronic organiser for use with memory-impaired people.

General features

The organiser should be compact enough to fit into a shirt pocket or other handy place. Some of the more expensive electronic organisers may be too bulky to be carried around all the time, although they could still be kept in a coat pocket or a briefcase.

Databank watches are available which have many of the functions of electronic organisers. While more compact and easier to carry around, they are more limited because of the fine motor control and visual acuity needed to operate them, they have limited storage capacity, and so forth.

Although batteries may need to be changed only once every few years for watches (more frequently for personal organisers), one needs to consider the motor dexterity involved in changing the battery, and the simplicity of the instructions, in addition to the usual life of the battery and whether there is a back-up battery. Back-up batteries are useful especially where there is a large amount of stored data to be retained in the device's memory. Around 32K memory will usually suffice for most uses. More sophisticated organisers come with removable memory cards.

Patients should not have to consult the manual, but it helps if it is clear and not too intimidating in its length. Summarised forms of information such as "help cards" are useful in that they provide a quick reference to turn to without having to refer to the manual. Those using the organiser as a data gathering device in settings remote from their workplace will find it useful to be able to link up to a personal computer.

The clarity of screen display is important—some of the less expensive organisers have poor displays despite being useful in other ways. Clarity is a critical item for many neurological patients, especially older people who may have reduced visual acuity.

Since electronic organisers are designed for professionals or executives rather than for people with a disability, there are usually keys which are superfluous when the device is used as a memory aid. These may serve as a distraction, especially if the patient has visual search problems, in which case redundant keys can be masked. The keys themselves should be clearly labelled and well laid out, and, if possible, operations should be executed by a single key press rather than by a sequence of keys. Keyboards which provide tone feedback when a key is pressed are desirable.

Voice organisers are available for those who find keyboard entry difficult because of tremor or other movement disorder. These have the same text storage and alarm features as most conventional electronic organisers, but rely on voice input. The device is "trained" to recognise the voice of the user, but even then occasional errors may occur. While current devices are compact, the input keys require a degree of motor control that may be outside the capacity of many neurological patients. (See Gartland, this issue, for further discussion of these factors.)

Storing and retrieving information

There are three basic operations which memory-impaired people need to learn—*entering* information, *reviewing* stored information, and *deleting* information from storage. Check whether these basic operations are simple or complicated for patients. Consider whether word-processing features are useful—for example, if a phrase is entered frequently, can a code rather than the full phrase be entered?

In addition to a prospective memory feature giving an alarm (with or without an associated message), it is useful to have a general memo facility so that items can be stored which need to be done at some time, but not necessarily on a particular day or at a particular time. In less expensive organisers without such a memo facility, the telephone storage facility can be used instead.

While all electronic organisers have basic text storage devices that allow for both temporary and permanent stores of knowledge, some now come with the facility to offer advanced storage features such as, navigational information, the ability to store pictorial material such as photographs and the ability to link onto information resources on the internet.

Alarm features

Electronic organisers are useful as reminders in the following settings:

1. Instances where events may occur between thinking about doing something and remembering to do it, e.g., deciding in the morning to buy something later in the day. This is particularly important when intervening activities preoccupy the individual.
2. Situations where a long interval separates thinking about doing something and having to do it, e.g., if one makes an appointment for several months in the future.
3. When there is a high premium on very accurate, precise recall and where internal memory aids may be fallible, e.g., remembering to take a cake from an oven at a specific time.
4. Where multiple alarm reminders are required, e.g., having to take tablets several times a day.

There are essentially two types of alarms, those with and those without a verbal/pictorial message. The major virtue of electronic organisers is their ability to display text when an alarm goes off. Therefore, having an alarm with a simultaneous message display, whether this be verbal or pictorial, is a critical feature. This facility can be used for two main purposes: situations where something has to be done on a particular day and at a specific time, and those situations where it is important that certain things are done but which are not necessarily tied to a particular time.

A number of currently available electronic organisers, mobile phones and other types of personal digital assistants, enable pictorial icons to be used within the context of reminder messages. With some devices, it is also possible for recorded speech to be used as a reminder, instead of visual text or pictorial cues, and such a memory aid has been successfully used in one study with five memory impaired patients who had to remember to pass on a message or carry out specific domestic chores (Van den Broek et al., 2000).

Some organisers emit a warning several minutes before the alarm sounds. For certain activities requiring initial preparation, such as having to go to a meeting, this can be useful.

Alarms that can be set to occur at regular intervals, such as daily, weekly or monthly, may be helpful in contexts where activities need to be carried out repeatedly and at specific times.

Turning to research findings with electronic organisers, Azrin and Powell (1969) found that a pill container which sounded a tone at the time medication was to be taken, and which dispensed a tablet at the same time the tone was turned off, was better at inducing patient compliance than a simple alarm timer or a container that made no sound. Fowler, Hart, and Sheehan (1972) used a timer combined with a schedule card to help their patient stick to a daily routine in his rehabilitation programme. Naugle, Naugle, Prevey, and Delaney (1988) worked with a man who consistently forgot to use stationery memory aids such as diaries and log books. They found an "alarm display" watch helped him remember rehabilitation activities. Giles and Shore (1989) used a PSION organiser to help their patient remember to do weekend domestic chores. This was more beneficial than a pocket diary. Kapur (1995) described preliminary data on the use of an electronic organiser to help patients with head injury, multiple sclerosis and epilepsy. In general, an organiser proved to be useful both as a reminder and as a text storage device, but for one patient who was densely amnesic and was living at home, the electronic aid proved to be of little benefit. Van den Broek et al. (2000) found that five memory-impaired patients who were provided with a voice organiser with message-alarm reminder functions had fewer memory lapses in two task settings—passing on a message they had been told nine hours earlier and remembering to carry out specified domestic chores. Kim et al. (2000) reported that most brain injured patients who had been trained to use a palm-top computer during their period of rehabilitation continued to use the device in everyday memory settings several years later. In a single-case study (Kim, Burke, Dowds, & George, 1999), one head injured patient who used this device as an in-patient, was better at remembering to attend therapy sessions and to take medication. Wright et al. (2001) noted that in a group of brain injured patients, high frequency users of organisers tended to prefer a standard keyboard organiser, whereas less frequent users preferred a more novel, penpad input system. In an earlier study involving elderly and younger participants from the general population, Wright et al. (2000) found most participants preferred keyboard data entry to touch-screen data entry, and generally made fewer errors using the keyboard modality.

SPEECH STORAGE DEVICES

As memory aids, speech recording devices are useful when long messages need to be stored. They are also helpful for memory disordered patients who have difficulty using an electronic organiser, possibly due to motor or visual impairment. As well as conventional tape recorders, digital "solid-state" recording devices have recently been introduced that can store up to several hours of speech. The attractive feature of these devices is the ability to store speech in discrete, labelled files which can be rapidly retrieved. Thus, different categories of messages or things to do can be readily stored and accessed.

Some memory-impaired people complain of difficulty in remembering telephone messages, and a few devices are available which automatically tape telephone conversations. Users of such devices should be aware that they need to inform the caller that the conversation is being taped! A few digital voice recorders have alarm features that can be tagged to stored messages, thus enabling the device to be used as an event memory aid.

The main function of these devices is to act as temporary or permanent stores of knowledge. They are of benefit in educational settings such as listening to lectures, and are used for this purpose by many young patients with brain injury. Although at present they are not used as knowledge resources to the same extent as printed or visual electronic media, it is possible that in the future this may change with the enhanced storage and other features of recording devices.

ELECTRONIC COMMUNICATION DEVICES

Electronic communication devices can be classified into fixed devices, such as standard corded phones or free-standing devices such as cordless phones, mobile phones and pagers. Laptop and palm-top computers that can access the internet can also be classified as communication devices, and a number of mobile phones have additional functions similar to those found in electronic organisers and so can be used to send text messages or pictures. Here we focus on phone and paging systems for conveying verbal messages.

Telephones are available that allow storage and easy retrieval of frequently used numbers. Useful features can be found in most phones, e.g., visual display of a number while it is being dialled and the ability to identify the caller. Fixed phones are currently available in some countries with a "photophone" feature—the face of the person to be called can be represented on a button that is programmed with the person's number. Mobile phones and pagers are available with vibration cues instead of a ringing tone. These are useful for people with auditory impairments. Pagers have similar call-signalling facilities, and some pagers are available with in-built alarm features.

Fixed telephones, mobile phones and pagers have a variety of reminder systems associated with them. These range from in-built alarms/message-alarms, which may be pre-set or which can be set to signal at specified intervals or on a fixed date, through to alarm systems dependent on some other resource. Telephone-based reminding systems have in the past been shown to be useful in improving patient compliance with taking medication (Leirer, Morrow, Pariante, & Doksum, 1988; Leirer, Morrow, Tanke, & Pariante, 1991) or keeping appointments (Morrow et al., 1999). In recent years, pagers have been employed to serve as more general reminder memory aids. Commercial paging companies in a number of countries offer reminder services, and a dedicated system for brain-injured patients has also been developed (Hersh & Treadgold, 1994; Wilson, Emslie, Quirk, & Evans, 2001; Wilson, Evans, Emslie, & Malinek, 1997). Phones can also be used to activate devices elsewhere, and thus may help in settings where the individual has to remember to turn on equipment such as domestic appliances.

Most phones have the capacity to store a large number of names and telephone numbers. Those which double-up as organisers have the usual text storage and retrieval facilities of the organisers outlined above. The ability of both fixed and mobile phones to link up to the internet has opened up a cornucopia of information resources that may act as knowledge memory aids.

Pagers can be useful as external memory aids, especially as reminders. Milch, Ziv, Evans, and Hillebrand (1996) found a paging system used in a hospice environment useful in improving compliance among residents in taking medication. In a single-case study, Aldrich (1998) used a dedicated paging system, NeuroPage, to help a head injured patient remember to carry out a range of activities, such as getting up and dressing, making lunch, watching the news headlines, feeding the cat, and taking his medication. The pager led to a significant improvement in performance of these activities. After NeuroPage was withdrawn, some improvement was maintained, but this was task dependent. Similar observations in a further single-case study with NeuroPage were made by Wilson, Emslie, Quirk, and Evans (1999). Wilson et al. (2001) carried out a large-scale study of 143 brain-damaged patients' use of NeuroPage. More than 80% of those who completed the 16-week trial were significantly more successful in carrying out everyday activities such as self-care, taking medication, and keeping appointments. For most patients, this improvement was maintained 7 weeks after returning the pager.

COMPUTER-BASED TECHNOLOGIES FOR KNOWLEDGE ACQUISITION AND UTILISATION

While the distinction between desktop computers, laptop computers, palmtop computers and personal organisers is becoming increasingly blurred as a result of advances in technology, in the following sections we mainly deal with those applications where desktop computers have been used in memory rehabilitation.

Exercises and drills

Although evidence for restoration of function using exercises and drills has not been positive, advances in computer technology and the ready availability of relatively inexpensive hardware have revived interest in such methods (Bradley, Welch, & Skilbeck, 1993). The computer represents an ideal medium for presentation of repetitive exercises, and therapists have been attracted by the time-saving features of computer-delivered services. However, evidence of beneficial effects of memory exercises has not been forthcoming, whether they are delivered by computer or in the more traditional pencil-and-paper format (Skilbeck & Robertson, 1992). A study by Middleton, Lambert, and Seggar (1991), for example, found no specific effects of 32 hours of drill-oriented computer training of cognitive skills, including memory. Chen, Thomas, Glueckauf, and Bracy (1997) found no major differences across a range of neuropsychological measures between two groups of head injured patients, one that received computer-assisted cognitive rehabilitation and another that received more traditional rehabilitation. Skilbeck and Robertson (1992), in their review of computer techniques for the management of memory impairment, concluded that when appropriate controls are included in empirical studies, there is little evidence of positive outcome following computer drills.

Exercises and drills have not proved useful for restoring general memory ability. Nevertheless, repetitive practice is probably essential for memory-impaired patients to improve on any specific task or to learn any specific information, and computers may be a useful medium for the repeated presentation of such materials. Because learning does not appear to generalise beyond the training task, it is important that practice is directed towards something relevant or useful in everyday life. Repetitive practice of meaningless lists of numbers, letters, shapes, or locations plays no beneficial role in memory rehabilitation (Glisky & Glisky, 2002; Glisky & Schacter, 1989b; Wilson, 1991).

External aids

The personal computer has significant potential as an external aid for beneficial use by memory-impaired patients, although its capabilities have not been fully exploited (Ager, 1985; Harris, 1992). As an external aid, the computer has the power to act as a memory prosthesis, storing and producing on demand all kinds of information relevant to an individual's functioning in everyday life. It may also assist directly in the performance of tasks of daily living (see Cole & Dehdashti, 1990), acting as a reminder for activities such as taking medication or meals (Flannery, Butterbaugh, Rice, & Rice, 1997).

A series of successful studies employing microcomputers to assist memory-impaired people with tasks of daily living has been conducted by Kirsch and his colleagues (Kirsch, Levine, Fallon-Krueger, & Jaros, 1987; Kirsch, Levine, Lajiness-O'Neill, & Schnyder, 1992). These investigators used the computer as an "interactive task guidance system" providing a series of cues to guide patients through the sequential steps of real-world tasks such as cookie baking and janitorial activities. In these studies, the computer acts solely as a compensatory device, providing the patient with step-by-step instructions for the performance of a task. Little knowledge of computer operation is required on the part of the subject, who merely responds with a single key-press to indicate that the instructions have been followed.

Another promising line of research was conducted by Cole and colleagues (Cole & Dehdashti, 1990; Cole, Dehdashti, Petti, & Angert, 1993). They designed highly customised computer interventions for brain-injured patients with a variety of cognitive deficits (see also Cole, Dehdashti, Petti, & Angert, 1988). Each intervention tried to help patients perform an activity of daily living they were able to accomplish prior to trauma but were now unable to perform without assistance. For example, a patient with severe memory and attentional deficits was able to use a customised text editor and software to construct things-to-do lists, take notes during telephone conversations, and to carry out home financial transactions (cheque writing, deposits, withdrawals, mailings, etc.), activities that had become impossible since her injury. In this case, the computer was modified to simplify these tasks and to bypass the particular cognitive deficits that were problematic for the patient.

Memory-impaired patients have been able to learn how to use computers as word-processors. For example, Batt and Lounsbury (1990) constructed a simple flowchart with coloured symbols and simple wording that enabled a memory-impaired patient to use a word-processing package. The bypassing of confusing menus and the reduction of memory load, enabled the patient to carry out the appropriate word-processing steps without difficulty and to operate the computer by himself (see also Glisky, 1995; Hunkin & Parkin, 1995; Van der Linden & Coyette, 1995).

In all of these studies, memory-impaired people used the computer to support some important activity of daily life. Hardware and software were modified so that problems were eliminated or reduced and only a few simple responses needed to be learned. The computer essentially served a prosthetic function, allowing brain injured patients to perform activities that were otherwise impossible. These kinds of intervention require no assumptions concerning adaptation of the neural or cognitive mechanisms involved in memory, and in general they make no claims concerning restoration or changes in underlying mnemonic ability. Frequently, however, increases in self-confidence and self-esteem are observed in patients following successful computer experience (Batt & Lounsbury, 1990; Cole et al., 1993; Glisky & Schacter, 1987; Johnson, 1990). Whether these psychosocial changes are specifically attributable to computer use, as opposed to other non-specific features of training, has not been empirically documented.

In the past one of the negative features of these interventions, from a clinical perspective, has been their high cost and limited applicability. Design of customised systems has required time, money and expertise and each design may have been useful for a single patient. With continued development in this area, however, prototypical systems are becoming available that might serve a broader range of patients and be easily administered in the clinic, such as the automated reminder system developed by Mihailidis, Fernie, and Barbenel (2001). Some of these developments are considered elsewhere in this special issue (see, for example, the paper by Mihailidis et al.).

Acquisition of domain-specific knowledge

In an effort to capitalise on the preserved memory abilities of amnesic patients, Glisky, Schacter, and Tulving (1986) devised a fading of cues technique, called the method of vanishing cues, which was designed to take advantage of patients' normal responses to partial cues to teach them complex knowledge and skills that might be used in everyday life. The training technique provides as much cue information as patients need to make a correct response and then gradually withdraws it across learning trials. The microcomputer serves essentially the role of teacher, presenting information and feedback in a consistent fashion, controlling the amount of cue information in accordance with patients' needs and prior responses, and allowing people to work independently at their own pace. Unlike interventions in which the computer is provided as a continuing prosthetic support, the goal of these interventions is to teach people the information that they need in order to function without external support (see Glisky, 1992b).

Using the method of vanishing cues, Glisky and colleagues successfully taught memory-impaired patients information associated with the operation of a microcomputer, and a number of vocational tasks including computer data-entry, microfilming, database management and word-processing (see Glisky & Glisky 2002, for discussion).

There are, however, some caveats concerning the domain-specific learning approach. Although memory-impaired patients are able to learn considerable amounts of complex information, their learning may be exceedingly slow and may result in knowledge representations that are different from those of the general population. In particular, patients cannot always access newly acquired knowledge on demand or use it flexibly in novel situations. In other words, transfer beyond the training context cannot be assumed (Wilson, 1992), although it has been demonstrated under some conditions (Glisky, 1995; Glisky & Schacter, 1989a). It is therefore essential that all information relevant to the performance of a particular functional task be taught directly so that the need for generalisation is minimal (Glisky, Schacter, & Butters, 1994).

The vanishing cues methodology was designed to capitalise on preserved abilities of amnesic patients in order to teach them knowledge and skills relevant in everyday life. Use of intact memory processes to compensate for those that have been disrupted or lost has often been suggested as an appropriate strategy for rehabilitation (Baddeley, 1992; Salmon & Butters, 1987); yet, as Baddeley has pointed out, few interventions of this type, other than the one used by Glisky and colleagues, have been attempted. It is likely that we still lack sufficient knowledge concerning the nature of the processes preserved in amnesia to take optimal advantage of them in rehabilitation. Nevertheless, this approach seems to be a promising one that may gain momentum as basic research provides additional information concerning processes and structures involved in normal memory.

Vocational tasks

One area in which computers might serve a potentially important function is the workplace. Glisky (1992a, 1992b) has suggested that some vocational tasks requiring the use of a computer may present good opportunities for employment for memory-impaired patients for a number of reasons. First, patients are capable of procedural learning; they can acquire a fixed set of procedures such as those required for data-entry or word-processing, and apply them in a consistent fashion over time. Second, computers in general require rather rigid adherence to a set of rules and can be counted on to be highly consistent, unlike their human counterparts. Once patients have learned the rules and their applications, they are less likely to be called upon to make online decisions or respond to novel circumstances. Third, many computer tasks lend themselves rather well to laboratory simulations so that job training can be accomplished before patients enter the workplace. Glisky and colleagues have found that careful step-by-step training in the laboratory of all components of a task facilitates transfer to the real-world environment and allows the patient to enter the workplace with a high degree of confidence and skill (Glisky & Schacter, 1989a).

In general, computer jobs have been overlooked by rehabilitation and vocational specialists perhaps because they seem too high-tech and complex and, therefore, beyond the capabilities of brain injured patients. Yet, even patients with quite severe memory impairments have been able to acquire the knowledge and skills needed to perform computer data-entry and word-processing tasks (Glisky, 1992a, 1995). It is worth keeping in mind, however, that all aspects of a task need to be taught explicitly and directly in order to minimise problems in generalisation. Although transfer of work skills across changes in materials (Glisky, 1992a) and from a training to a work or home environment has been demonstrated (Glisky, 1995; Glisky & Schacter, 1989a), changes in the actual procedures may present serious difficulties.

Another use of computers involves virtual reality technology. As this is dealt with by Rizzo, Schultheis, Kerns, and Mateer, (2004 this issue) we will not discuss it further here.

THE APPLICATION OF MEMORY AIDS IN REHABILITATION SETTINGS

Factors to be considered in the use of memory aids in rehabilitation include general ones applicable to most forms of neuropsychological intervention and memory rehabilitation, and specific ones relating to the particular use of aids to overcome memory difficulties—a form of "compensatory memory training". In a critical review covering a number of areas of cognitive rehabilitation, Cicerone et al. (2000) offered useful guidelines that are relevant for the use of memory aids. They "found evidence for the effectiveness of compensatory memory training for subjects with mild memory impairments compelling enough to recommend it as a Practice Standard. The evidence also suggests that memory remediation is most effective when subjects are fairly independent in daily function, are actively involved in identifying the memory problems to be treated, and are capable and motivated to continue active, independent strategy use" (Cicerone et al., 2000, p. 1605).

General factors

For any intervention to be effective and to be seen to be effective, some criteria need to be satisfied. These include:

1. The intervention needs to bring about meaningful changes in the patient's everyday memory functioning. How one defines "meaningful change" may vary from patient to patient, but the patient should be able to carry out more memory-related activities, with greater ease and success, and with less distress, than before the intervention.
2. The improvement in memory functioning should be permanent.
3. The improvement should have minimal side-effects.
4. The intervention should be cost-effective, both in terms of money and time.
5. The intervention should be easy to administer by a third party.
6. The treatment should be applicable to a large number of patients, ideally across disease categories and severity of memory loss.
7. The intervention should be beneficial over and above any general "placebo" or incidental effects resulting from the treatment.

In individual patients, variables worth considering are:

1. Age, educational level, and premorbid knowledge and skills.
2. Any physical disability, such as sensory or motor loss.
3. The intactness or otherwise of non-memory cognitive functions.
4. Supportive and possible negative influences that the family/carer may bring to bear on the therapeutic programme.

5. Current daily routine and the demands which this places on memory. Many memory functions, and in particular prospective memory, are better earlier than later in the day (Wilkins & Baddeley, 1978).
6. Any behavioural, attentional or motivational problems. On the one hand, memory aids may act as motivational cues to help with problems such as apathy, but the use of memory aids often requires some involvement of executive functions such as initiation of behaviour, planning/organisational skills, problem solving ability, focused attention, etc.

The severity and pattern of memory loss is a major factor, and it is important to pay particular attention to a number of areas:

1. Everyday memory symptoms as reported by the patient and by an informed observer, noting the patient's insight and concern about his memory difficulties.
2. Severity and pattern of anterograde memory loss.
3. Severity and pattern of retrograde memory loss, in particular the extent to which past knowledge and skills have been lost.
4. The extent to which new skill learning and implicit memory are preserved.

Specific factors

There are a number of specific factors to be borne in mind when considering whether to encourage and train patients in the use of memory aids to help everyday memory.

1. How often and which type of memory aid has been used in the past? For example, many elderly people are accustomed to using simple diaries and are reluctant to change to electronic devices, no matter how much more effective they may be. Some patients need to be reassured that using memory aids will not lead to their becoming lazy or their brain wasting away through lack of use. They need to be reassured that using memory aids with other people around is nothing to be ashamed of, perhaps pointing out that such aids are used increasingly by the general population. Memory aids can be seen as status symbols and may enhance the self-esteem of memory-impaired people.
2. Although it is the principal duty of the clinician to find a memory aid simple to use and suitable for a particular patient, the patient should, if possible, be given a choice and be involved in any decisions.
3. A carer/relative needs to be closely involved in the process from the beginning so as to encourage the use of the aid in domestic settings. In particular, if the aid is complicated to use, this person also needs to be taught to use it so that there is someone to turn to if problems arise in operating the aid.

4. Memory aids are often given to patients to use with little further or no intervention from the therapist. If only life were this simple. As Intons-Peterson and Newsome (1992) have pointed out, there are a number of cognitive processes involved in the use of even simple external memory aids. Thus, memory-impaired people need to be trained in the "metamemory" skill of being able to identify situations where a memory aid will be useful, they must motivate themselves to use a memory aid, choose an aid that will be useful for the particular circumstances, and remember how to operate and use the memory aid effectively.
5. Memory-impaired people should be motivated both to learn to use the aid, and to adapt daily routines and habits so as to incorporate the memory aid into such activities. Ideally, they should formulate some of the reminders so that they are seen as self-cues rather than "nagging" from some external source.

For more complex aids such as electronic organisers, a specific training programme should be designed in which stages of learning a particular procedure are broken down into steps. Principles such as spaced rehearsal, graded reduction of support/vanishing cues and error-free learning, feedback and encouragement, and help-cards may be required in the teaching process. The training programme in the clinic should, as closely as feasible, mimic everyday uses of the memory aid, with concrete examples being drawn from the patient's daily routine. Training in the use of electronic organisers usually requires four to six sessions, and if these are provided weekly, homework can be set for the patient. The beginning of a therapy session can test long-term retention of what was learned in an earlier session. Finally, many effective interventions involve a particular combination of environmental, stationery, mechanical, and electronic memory aids, as in the case described by Wilson (1999). The challenge lies with the clinician to use his/her knowledge and experience to suggest and draw up a particular combination of teaching strategies.

An interesting and recent paper by Reason (2002) describes the criteria of good reminders and how these might be used to reduce errors. Although written for people without neurological impairment, Reason's ideas could also apply to the field of memory rehabilitation.

CONCLUSIONS AND FUTURE DEVELOPMENTS

External memory aids are effective in improving everyday memory functioning, and this benefit is particularly evident in the area of prospective memory. Computer-related memory rehabilitation strategies remain largely task-specific in their benefit, but may be useful to the extent that they perform similar functions to external memory aids. The use of environmental cues, either to help navigational memory or to enhance man–machine interaction, is another area which is potentially beneficial to people with memory deficits.

While technological innovations may drive many of the developments in memory rehabilitation, advances in conceptual and clinical spheres are equally important. We do not have a comprehensive conceptual framework to consider the various strategies used to enhance memory functioning. If conceptual and empirical links could be made with other attempts to improve memory functioning, such as pharmacological agents and neural implants, rehabilitation might move forwards, especially if these attempts could be integrated into a theoretical framework that accounts for neural plasticity and recovery of memory function following neurological disease or injury (Robertson & Murre, 1999). In the clinical sphere, there may be a greater refinement in our understanding of which patients will benefit most from memory aids. Ideally, a patient's clinical and neuropsychological profile, together with factors such as specific memory needs should be matched to the features of potential memory aids to inform the clinician of the particular memory aids, or combination of treatments, that will be of maximum benefit to the individual. Careful evaluation of the effectiveness of memory aids will require further advances in memory assessment procedures, in particular those which can reliably assess everyday memory functioning (see Glisky & Glisky, 2002). The cost-effectiveness of memory aids needs to be considered, especially where computer-based aids or expensive electronic devices may perform functions that can be carried out by stationery memory aids or by less expensive electronic memory aids. Advances in technology may allow for the introduction of more sophisticated, cheaper and more user-friendly aids, and some memory aids may emerge that have been purpose-built for memory-impaired individuals. Future developments in external memory aids include:

1. The integration of multiple memory-related functions within a single electronic unit, which will carry out tasks currently performed by devices such as a personal organiser, mobile phone, e-mail/internet facility, reminder/pager, etc.
2. Devices, such as electronic organisers, that more readily accept hand-written input via an adjacent note-pad which permits infrared transfer of impressions made on paper.
3. Memory pens which keep a record of what has been written and which allow this information to be transferred to another storage medium.
4. Reminders that have context-sensitive features, such that a message-alarm will activate when the individual engages in a related activity, or when other critical people are in the vicinity (Lamming et al., 1994).

5. Reminders that include a "task enactment-alarm" link, such that the alarm only turns off when the target activity has been carried out (cf. Azrin & Powell, 1969).
6. Wearable memory aids that integrate more naturally with the dress, habits and routines of patients (cf. Hoisko, 2000).
7. Devices that use wireless (such as the new "bluetooth") technology to convey information about the location of items.

It is too early to say which, if any, of these developments will have a major impact on the application of memory aids in clinical settings. If conceptual, empirical, biological and technological advances across disciplines are harnessed and harmonised in meaningful ways, and if clinicians and researchers focus their attention and resources on the application of resultant devices in clinical settings, there will be undoubted benefits for memory-impaired neurological patients in the years to come.

REFERENCES

Ager, A. (1985). Recent developments in the use of microcomputers in the field of mental handicap: Implications for psychological practice. *Bulletin of the British Psychological Society*, *38*, 142–145.

Aldrich, F. K. (1998). Pager messages as self reminders: A case study of their use in memory impairment. *Personal Technologies*, *2*, 1–10.

Azrin, N., & Powell, J. (1969). Behavioural engineering: The use of response priming to improve prescribed medication. *Journal of Applied Behaviour Analysis*, *2*, 39–42.

Baddeley, A. D. (1992). Implicit memory and errorless learning: A link between cognitive theory and neuropsychological rehabilitation? In L. R. Squire, & N. Butters (Eds.), *Neuropsychology of memory* (2nd ed., pp. 309–314). New York: Guilford Press.

Batt, R. C., & Lounsbury, P. A. (1990). Teaching the patient with cognitive deficits to use a computer. *American Journal of Occupational Therapy*, *44*, 364–367.

Bradley, V. A., Welch, J. L., & Skilbeck, C.E. (1993). *Cognitive retraining using microcomputers*. Hove, UK: Lawrence Erlbaum Associates Ltd.

Chen, S., Thomas, J., Glueckauf, R., & Bracy, O. (1997). The effectiveness of computer-assisted cognitive rehabilitation for persons with traumatic brain injury. *Brain Injury*, *11*, 197–209.

Cicerone, K., Dalhberg, C., Kalmar, K., Langenbahn, D., Malec, J., Bergquist, T., Felicetti, T., Giacino, J., Harley, J., Harrington, D., Herzog, J., Kneipp, S., Laatsch, L., & Morse, P. (2000). Evidence-based cognitive rehabilitation: Recommendations for clinical practice. *Archives of Physical Medicine and Rehabilitation*, *81*, 1596–1615.

Cole, E., & Dehdashti, P. (1990). Interface design as a prosthesis for an individual with a brain injury. *SIGCHI Bulletin*, *22*, 28–32.

Cole, E., Dehdashti, P., Petti, L., & Angert, M. (1988). Prosthesis Ware: A new class of software supports the activities of daily living. *Neuropsychology*, *2*, 41–57.

Cole, E., Dehdashti, P., Petti, L., & Angert, M. (1993). Design parameters and outcomes for cognitive prosthetic software with brain injury patients. *Proceedings of the RESNA International '93 Conference*, *13*, Arlington, VA: RESNA Press.

Flannery, M., Butterbaugh, G., Rice, D., & Rice, J. (1997). Reminding technology for prospective memory disability: A case study. *Pediatric Rehabilitation*, *1*, 239–244.

Fowler, R. S., Hart, J., & Sheehan, M. (1972). A prosthetic memory: An application of the prosthetic environment concept. *Rehabilitation Counselling Bulletin, 16*, 80–85.

Giles, G. M., & Shore, M. (1989). The effectiveness of an electronic memory aid for a memory-impaired adult of normal intelligence. *American Journal of Occupational Therapy, 43*, 409–411.

Glisky, E. L. (1992a). Acquisition and transfer of declarative and procedural knowledge by memory-impaired patients: A computer data-entry task. *Neuropsychologia, 30*, 899–910.

Glisky, E. L. (1992b). Computer-assisted instruction for patients with traumatic brain injury: Teaching of domain-specific knowledge. *Journal of Head Trauma Rehabilitation, 7*, 1–12.

Glisky, E. L. (1995). Acquisition and transfer of word processing skill by an amnesic patient *Neuropsychological Rehabilitation, 5*, 299–318.

Glisky, E. L., & Glisky, M. L. (1999). Memory rehabilitation in the elderly. In D. Stuss, G. Winocur, & I. Robertson (Eds.), *Cognitive neurorehabilitation* (pp. 347–361). Cambridge: Cambridge University Press.

Glisky, E. L., & Schacter, D. L. (1987). Acquisition of domain-specific knowledge in organic amnesia: Training for computer-related work. *Neuropsychologia, 25*, 893–906.

Glisky, E. L., & Schacter, D. L. (1989a). Extending the limits of complex learning in organic amnesia: Computer training in a vocational domain. *Neuropsychologia, 27*, 107–120.

Glisky, E. L., & Schacter, D. L. (1989b). Models and methods of memory rehabilitation. In F. Boller & J. Grafman (Eds.), *Handbook of neuropsychology* (pp. 233–246). Amsterdam: Elsevier.

Glisky, E. L., Schacter, D. L., & Butters, M. A. (1994). Domain-specific learning and memory remediation. In M. J. Riddoch, & G. W. Humphreys (Eds.), *Cognitive neuropsychology and cognitive rehabilitation* (pp. 527–548). Hove, UK: Lawrence Erlbaum Associates Ltd.

Glisky, E. L., Schacter, D. L., & Tulving, E. (1986). Learning and retention of computer-related vocabulary in amnesic patients: Method of vanishing cues. *Journal of Clinical and Experimental Neuropsychology, 8*, 292–312.

Harris, J. E. (1992). Ways of improving memory. In B. A. Wilson, & N. Moffat (Eds.), *Clinical management of memory problems* (2nd ed., pp. 59–85). London: Chapman and Hall.

Herrmann, D., Brubaker, B., Yoder, C., Sheets, V., & Tio, A. (1999). Devices that remind. In F. Durso, R. Nickerson, R. Schvaneveldt, S. Dumais, D. Lindsay, & M. Chi (Eds.), *Handbook of applied cognition* (pp. 377–407). Chichester, UK: John Wiley.

Hersh, N., & Treadgold, L. (1994). NeuroPage: The rehabilitation of memory dysfunction by prosthetic memory and cueing. *Neurorehabilitation, 4*, 187–197.

Hoisko, J. (2000). Context triggered visual episodic memory prosthesis. In *Proceedings of the Fourth International Symposium on Wearable Computers* (pp. 185–186). Atlanta, Georgia: IEEE Computer Society.

Hunkin, N. M., & Parkin, A. J. (1995). The method of vanishing cues: An evaluation of its effectiveness in teaching memory-impaired individuals. *Neuropsychologia, 33*, 1255–1279.

Intons-Peterson, M. J., & Newsome, G. L., III (1992). External memory aids: Effects and effectiveness. In D. J. Herrmann, H. Weingartner, A. Searleman, & C. McEvoy (Eds.), *Memory improvement: Implications for memory theory* (pp. 101–121). New York: Springer-Verlag.

Johnson, R. (1990). Modifying memory function: Use of a computer to train mnemonic skill. *British Journal of Clinical Psychology, 29*, 437–438.

Kapur, N. (1995). Memory aids in the rehabilitation of memory disordered patients. In A. D. Baddeley, B. A. Wilson, & F. N. Watts (Eds.), *Handbook of memory disorders* (pp. 535–557). Chichester, UK: John Wiley.

Kapur, N., Glisky, E. L., & Wilson, B. A. (2002). External memory aids and computers in memory rehabilitation. In A. D. Baddeley, M. D. Kopelman, & B. A. Wilson (Eds.), *Handbook of memory disorders* (2nd ed.). Chichester, UK: John Wiley.

Kim, H. J., Burke, D. T., Dowds, M. M., & George, J. (1999). Utility of a microcomputer as an external memory aid for memory-impaired head injury patient during in-patient rehabilitation. *Brain Injury*, *13*, 147–150.

Kim, H. J., Burke, D. T., Dowds, M. M., Robinson Boone, K. A., & Parks, G. J. (2000). Electronic memory aids for outpatient brain injury: Follow-up findings. *Brain Injury*, *14*, 187–196.

Kirsch, N. L., Levine, S. P., Fallon-Krueger, M., & Jaros, L. A. (1987). The microcomputer as an "orthotic" device for patients with cognitive deficits. *Journal of Head Trauma Rehabilitation*, *2*, 77–86.

Kirsch, N. L., Levine, S. P., Lajiness-O'Neill, R., & Schnyder, M. (1992). Computer-assisted interactive task guidance: Facilitating the performance of a simulated vocational task. *Journal of Head Trauma Rehabilitation*, *7*, 13–25.

Lamming, M., Brown, P., Carter, K., Eldridge, M., Flynn, M., Louie, G., Robinson, P., & Sellen, A. (1994). The design of a human memory prosthesis. *The Computer Journal*, *37*, 153–163.

Leirer, V., Morrow. D., Pariante, G., & Doksum, T. (1988). Increasing influenza vaccination adherence through voice mail. *Journal of the American Geriatric Society*, *37*, 1147–1150.

Leirer, V., Morrow, D., Tanke, E., & Pariante, G., (1991). Elders' nonadherence: Its assessment and medication reminding by voice mail. *The Gerontologist*, *31*, 514–520.

Middleton, D. K., Lambert, M. J., & Seggar, L. B. (1991). Neuropsychological rehabilitation: Microcomputer-assisted treatment of brain-injured adults. *Perceptual and Motor Skills*, *72*, 527–530.

Mihailidis, A., Fernie, G., & Barbenel, J. (2001). The use of artificial intelligence in the design of an intelligent cognitive orthosis for people with dementia. *Assistive Technology*, *13*, 23–39.

Milch, R., Ziv, L., Evans, V., & Hillebrand, M. (1996). The effect of an alphanumeric paging system on patient compliance with medicinal regimens. *American Journal of Hospital and Palliative Care*, *13*, 46–48.

Morrow, D., Leirer, V., Carver, L., Tanke, E., & McNally, A. (1999). Repetition improves older and younger adult memory for automated appointment messages. *Human Factors*, *41*, 194–204.

Naugle, R., Naugle, C., Prevey, M., & Delaney, R. (1988). New digital watch as a compensatory device for memory dysfunction. *Cognitive Rehabilitation*, *6*, 22–23.

Nielsen, J. (1958). *Memory and amnesia*. Los Angeles: San Lucas Press.

Reason, J. (1990). *Human error*. Cambridge: Cambridge University Press.

Reason, J. (2002). Combating omission errors through task analysis and good reminders. *Quality Safe Health Care*, *11*, 40–44.

Rizzo, A. A., Schultheis, M. Kerns, K. A., & Mateer, C. (2004). Analysis of assets for virtual reality applications in neuropsychology. *Neuropsychological Rehabilitation*, *14*(1/2), 207–239.

Robertson, I. H., & Murre, J. (1999). Rehabilitation of brain damage: Brain plasticity and principles of guided recovery. *Psychological Bulletin*, *125*, 544–575.

Salmon, D. P., & Butters, N. (1987). Recent developments in learning and memory: Implications for the rehabilitation of the amnesic patient. In M. J. Meier, A. L. Benton, & L. Diller (Eds.), *Neuropsychological rehabilitation* (pp. 280–293). New York: Guilford.

Schacter, D. L. (2001). *The seven sins of memory*. Boston: Houghton Miffin Company.

Skilbeck, C., & Robertson, I. (1992). Computer assistance in the management of memory and cognitive impairment. In B. A. Wilson & N. Moffat (Eds.), *Clinical management of memory problems* (2nd ed., pp. 154–188). London: Chapman and Hall.

Tulving, E. (1972). Episodic and semantic memory. In E. Tulving & W. Donaldson (Eds.), *Organization of memory* (pp. 381–403). New York: Academic Press.

Tulving, E. (2000). Concepts of memory. In E. Tulving & F. Craik (Eds.), *The Oxford handbook of memory* (pp. 33–43). New York: Oxford University Press.

Van den Broek, M. D., Downes, J., Johnson, Z., Dayus, B., & Hilton, N. (2000). Evaluation of an electronic memory aid in the neuropsychological rehabilitation of prospective memory deficits. *Brain Injury*, *14*, 455–462.

Van der Linden, M., & Coyette, F. (1995). Acquisition of word processing knowledge in an amnesic patient: Implications for theory and rehabilitation. In R. Campbell & M. A. Conway (Eds.), *Broken Memories* (pp. 54–76). Oxford: Blackwell.

Warrington, E. K. (1986). Memory for facts and memory for events. *British Journal of Clinical Psychology*, *25*, 1–12.

Wilkins, A. J., & Baddeley, A. D. (1978). Remembering to recall in everyday life: An approach to absentmindedess. In M. M. Gruneberg, P. E. Morris, & R. N. Sykes (Eds.), *Practical aspects of memory* (pp. 27–34). London: Academic Press.

Wilson, B. A. (1991). Theory, assessment, and treatment in neuropsychological rehabilitation. *Neuropsychology*, *5*, 281–291.

Wilson, B. A. (1992). Memory therapy in practice. In B. A. Wilson & N. Moffat (Eds.), *Clinical management of memory problems* (2nd ed., pp. 120–153). London: Chapman and Hall.

Wilson, B. A (1999). *Case studies in neuropsychological rehabilitation* (ch. 4). Oxford: Oxford University Press.

Wilson, B. A., Emslie, H. C., Quirk, K., & Evans, J. (1999). George: Learning to live independently with NeuroPage. *Rehabilitation Psychology*, *44*, 284–296.

Wilson, B. A., Emslie, H. C., Quirk, K., & Evans, J. (2001). Reducing everyday memory and planning problems by means of a paging system: A randomised control crossover study. *Journal of Neurology, Neurosurgery and Psychiatry*, *70*, 477–482.

Wilson, B. A., Evans, J., Emslie, H., & Malinek, V. (1997). Evaluation of NeuroPage: A new memory aid. *Journal of Neurology, Neurosurgery and Psychiatry*, *63*, 113–115.

Wilson, B. A., & Watson, P (1996). A practical framework for understanding compensatory behaviour in people with organic memory impairment. *Memory*, *4*, 465–486.

Wright, P., Bartram, C., Rogers, N., Emslie, H., Evans, J., Wilson, B. A., & Belt, S. (2000). Text entry on handheld computers by older users. *Ergonomics*, *43*, 702–716.

Wright, P., Rogers, N., Hall, C., Wilson, B. A., Evans, J., Emslie, H., & Bartram, C. (2001). Comparison of pocket-computer memory aids for people with brain injury. *Brain Injury*, *15*, 787–800.

NEUROPSYCHOLOGICAL REHABILITATION, 2004, *14* (1/2), 61–75

Considerations in the selection and use of technology with people who have cognitive deficits following acquired brain injury

Donna Gartland

Oliver Zangwill Centre for Neuropsychological Rehabilitation, Ely, UK

Cognitive deficits are known to be a common sequelae following acquired brain injury. The presence and severity of cognitive deficits is one of several factors that will influence a person's potential for rehabilitation, the type of rehabilitation required for that person, and eventually that person's capability to live independently and be engaged in vocational activity. The use of technology can influence this potential through enabling a person to adapt or compensate for long-term cognitive deficits and thereby reduce the functional consequences of those deficits. Rehabilitation of such individuals therefore needs to address the use of technology to enable the individual to perform at optimum functional ability. Occupational therapists working in the field of cognitive neurorehabilitation would appear to be ideally placed to address such needs.

INTRODUCTION

This paper discusses some of the practical and theoretical considerations when selecting and using technological equipment with the brain injured population, specifically those with deficits in attention, memory and executive skills. The content will be based on the experience of the author and therefore illustration of points will be mainly through experience of the use of electronic memory aids. Different types of technology that are specifically designed for rehabilitation purposes or for the disabled user will be highlighted, such as cognitive prosthetics, tele-rehab, NeuroPage, Smart houses and environmental control systems, with some reference to technology available to all, such as information technology (IT) (word processing,

Correspondence should be addressed to Donna Gartland, Oliver Zangwill Centre for Neuropsychological Rehabilitation, Princess of Wales Hospital, Lynn Road, Ely, Cambs, CB6 1DN, UK.

http://www.tandf.co.uk/journals/pp/09602011.html DOI:10.1080/09602010343000165

Internet, e-mail, route-finding software), mobile phones, navigational hardware, and palmtops. Attention will be focused on considerations for users of the equipment, i.e., the brain injured individual, carers, and the "teachers" (usually therapists). Consideration will also be given to the environments in which the equipment will be used (home, work, and social and rehabilitation settings). Theoretical models of rehabilitation that underpin the use of technology, such as restitution, substitution or compensation, and the use of aids to retrain specific functions as well as those designed to enable compensation for deficits are referred to. The paper considers learning theories in relation to the brain injured population and reflects on other issues, such as cost, keeping pace with change (history and future; time and effort involved), and technical back up requirements.

TYPES OF TECHNOLOGY

The use of technology with clients who have a temporary or permanent disability, whether physical or cognitive, has, I shall argue, increased their potential for independence. For the purposes of this paper, technology may be defined as "the application of scientific knowledge for practical purposes" and the "machinery and equipment based on such knowledge" (*Concise Oxford Dictionary*, 1999).

There are two main types of technological equipment that can be used by rehabilitation providers: that which has been designed for the general population, and that which has been specifically designed for people with "special needs" (Van Schaik, 2000). Technology designed for use by the general population has high face validity for clients because of its normalcy of use, and would include home computers, the Internet, palmtops, mobile telephones and, more recently, the potentially useful global navigational hardware.

There are also types of technological equipment specially designed for people with cognitive deficits to enable them to address specific needs. They include remedial computer software for retraining of individual deficit areas, such as memory, attention, and problem solving skills, based on the restorative model of cognitive rehabilitation. Such computer programs can be useful in identifying change in a person's abilities and suggesting compensatory strategies to improve performance. However, generally there is still little evidence to support the use of such software to retrain specific deficits which then generalise to improved performance in practical tasks (McBain & Renton, 1997).

Compensatory technological equipment would appear to be rather more promising in terms of its usefulness in rehabilitation. An example of this would be NeuroPage, which uses radio-paging technology to send reminders of things to do at pre-determined times in the day. Examples of reminders can be to "take medication", to "feed the dog" or to "go to an appointment". Research has shown that NeuroPage is effective in enabling people to carry out things they need to do during their daily routines (Wilson, Evans, Emslie & Malinek, 1997; Wilson, Emslie, Quirk, & Evans, 2001). It can be useful for people with memory deficits caused by a variety of insults to the brain. When using NeuroPage support needs to be provided to plan the activities a person needs or wishes to complete and then to identify appropriate reminders and appropriate times. These reminders need to be sent through to the paging centre and then the person receives the messages at the allocated time. The person needs to be able to act on the reminders fairly swiftly and therefore needs to have a lifestyle that can be structured around some kind of routine. It can reduce the need for verbal prompting from care staff and family and therefore can alleviate strain on carers as well as reduce the financial burden on social services.

Wilson and Evans (2000) noted one area where they anticipate technology may expand and this is in the development of the use of computers as "Interactive Task Guidance Systems". They report on a computer that provides instructions for guiding patients through multi-stage practical activities to enable the patient to complete a task independently rather than relying on another person to provide those cues. The computer screen can be easily adapted to compensate for additional problems, such as visual disturbance, which is an additional factor.

Smart houses are another recent development, which have been considered in relation to physically disabled or elderly people, but may be suitable for use with people with acquired cognitive difficulties. The term "smart house" refers to "a living or working environment, carefully constructed to assist people in carrying out required activities, using various technical assistive systems and (to) use technology as a tool to facilitate independence" (Allen, 1996, p. 203). They are designed to monitor and control the living environment of the individual by such instruments as alarm systems that alert the individual if a cooker hob is not turned off after a set period of time, or controls to operate electrical devices from a distance (Wilson & Evans, 2000). Environmental control systems have been used for people with severe physical disability or communication difficulties to enable them to retain their independence in their own home, and Smart houses are a logical extension of that process of supporting people with cognitive difficulties.

One interesting development in rehabilitation is that of cognitive prosthetics and tele-rehab. In a presentation to the Oliver Zangwill Centre team, Elliot Cole defined a cognitive prosthesis as being designed specifically for rehabilitation purposes and using computer technology to collect clinically relevant data; it is a rehabilitation compensatory strategy that directly assists individuals in performing their daily activities. This highly customised rehabilitation intervention has been developed in the USA, where it was recognised that many people had access to home computers. It enables therapists to interact with clients from a base some distance away by video link and to review data gathered by the computer to ascertain what clients are doing and how they are progressing in practical activities. It is possible that in the future this facility may extend to the UK, which is encouraging since it enables specialist rehabilitation services to be some distance from a client's home. A study by Brown et al. (1999) identified that telephone groups using teleconferencing technology can offer a method of providing education and support to carers in the community that may be as effective as face-to-face group contact. Thus teleconferencing technology has been demonstrated to enable rehabilitation services to be delivered across a distant location between the clinic and the home of the client and his or her carers. Computer prosthetics such as "Memo Jog" are still in the developmental stages. This particular instrument will be a specially designed palmtop for elderly people with memory difficulties who may find using existing palmtops too difficult (Inglis et al., 2004 this issue). It is anticipated that the development of computer prostheses will be an expanding area as technology advances. (For further discussion of cognitive prostheses, see Arnott, Alm, & Waller, 1999). It raises the issue of closer collaboration between those traditionally involved in the rehabilitation process, i.e., the multi-disciplinary team, with those having knowledge of technology, such as engineers and IT specialists.

Our literature search identified a number of papers that suggest an increasing use within the past five years of virtual reality (VR) technology in the assessment and rehabilitation of clients with cognitive deficits. VR allows the user to "create computer-generated environments within which the user can be immersed, move around and manipulate objects.... In its immersive form, the visual and auditory aspects of the computer-generated environment are delivered to the user via a ... head-mounted display whilst tactile sensations can be delivered via data gloves or a body suit.... In the non-immersive form of VR the visual aspects of the environment are presented to the user on a PC monitor.... The user controls his/her movements by means of a joystick or other control device" (Rose et al., 1999, p. 548). Advantages of using VR include precise control over the environment, close monitoring of patients' responses, adaptation of the environment to their disabilities and allowing patients to be able to operate in safety. One example of this technology in rehabilitation is the use of a computer-simulated kitchen to assess the ability of patients to process and sequence information (Zhang et al., 2001). Zhang noted that clients can use VR with minimal movement, thus creating opportunities to assess the cognitive functioning of people with very severe physical limitations who might otherwise have difficulties with traditional pen and paper tests. VR has also been used to create virtual reality environments to rehabilitate clients by producing simulations of their own environments in order, for example, to learn routes (Schultheis & Rizzo, 2001). Rizzo et al. (1998) argue that VR could limit the weaknesses of both functional and restorative approaches to cognitive rehabilitation. However, it would appear that much more research needs to be done to ascertain whether clients are able to generalise and maintain learning from VR into real-life environments. If this does prove to be the case, VR would be of particular benefit to specialist rehabilitation professionals who are often required to work with an individual at some distance from their locality. A major advantage of VR is that it can set up a form of reality that would be extremely difficult to create in actuality, thus saving time and expense. For example, we might one day be able to create a "virtual" kitchen or even a town centre for shopping in the hospital ward or rehabilitation centre rather than having to set up a real kitchen or take a client into town, both of which would be difficult, time-consuming and even perhaps dangerous.

REHABILITATION MODELS UNDERPINNING THE USE OF TECHNOLOGY

The purpose of rehabilitation will determine how technology may be utilised within the rehabilitation process. Cognitive rehabilitation may involve restitution or remedial intervention, or adaptive, compensatory approaches (McBain & Renton, 1997). It can involve process-oriented rehabilitation, such as attention training; skills-based training, such as pacing or relaxation; or compensatory strategy training, such as the use of a diary (Sohlberg & Raskin, 1996). Generalisation of the use of the technology into everyday use is the desired outcome of technology used for compensatory purposes, while generalisation of restored cognitive skills into daily tasks would be the desired outcome of restitution or substitution-based approaches.

Since the late 1970s computers have been considered as a possible therapeutic tool for people with cognitive problems (McBain & Renton, 1997). The use of Acorn BBC microcomputers within occupational therapy became more widespread following issue of these computers to some departments by the Government in 1983 (McBain & Renton, 1997). Initially, software appeared to be focused on restorative approaches, such as attentional training, or mnemonic exercises for memory retraining. Although the evidence for restoration of cognitive functioning through computer-based training has been less than positive, this area has received new interest with the advancement of technology (Kapur, Glisky, & Wilson, 2002). Attention may be more amenable to computer training than memory, but as yet it is noted that the evidence is "far from persuasive" (Kapur et al., 2002, p. 768). The authors do however note that training using computers to provide repetitive practice is likely to be beneficial to memory-impaired individuals, since the computer provides a level of consistency that humans may not, which would therefore support errorless learning principles. However, they also note that the task should be relevant to everyday life, since learning does not appear to generalise beyond the training task itself.

For people with long-term cognitive deficits, development of compensatory strategies tends to form the basis of intervention, as occurs at the Oliver Zangwill Centre. In pursuit of such strategies, the use of technology should enable the user to complete a practical task more efficiently (timely) and effectively (accurately) than by alternative means. It is already known that computer hardware and software can be adapted in response to the physical or sensory needs of the individual user to enable the bypassing of certain problems that would otherwise prevent them from using a particular device, which may accompany any cognitive deficits. For example, use of a key guard or adapted keyboard for people with co-ordination problems, or voice recognition software. Basic switch operated software or software incorporating bright colours or sounds may be useful for people with more severe attentional or processing problems. Both taped and interactive talking books on CD ROM are available, which enable people with visual attentional difficulties that impact on their ability to read printed words to enjoy books. (Contact AbilityNet on www.abilitynet.org.uk for further details of hardware and software available for people with disabilities.)

CONSIDERATIONS RELATING TO SPECIFIC IMPAIRMENTS

Acquired brain injury may be caused by cerebrovascular accident, trauma, anoxia, tumours, intra-cranial bleeds or infectious processes. It can lead to a wide variety of difficulties affecting movement, sensation, cognitive processes, communication, mood, and behaviour. Any combination of these problems, in conjunction with the person's previous personality, skills, social situation, lifestyle and physical environment can create a unique challenge for rehabilitation professionals.

For someone with severe physical, communicative or cognitive difficulties, interacting with their immediate environment can be challenging and may require the assistance of another person. Through using specialised environmental control systems, with modified input/interface mechanisms, such as touch screen, single switch or blow/suck input mechanisms, they may not require the assistance of another person to cope physically with, for example, opening curtains, switching on the television or answering the front door. In such cases, technology might have much to offer by increasing the quality of life for severely disabled individuals.

Brain injured clients typically present with cognitive deficits in attentional skills; memory skills, particularly prospective remembering; and executive skills, i.e., initiation, planning, problem solving, monitoring, and reduced insight. Functionally, problems may include difficulty concentrating, fatigue, difficulty recalling new information, and being unable to plan an activity or organise information so that it can be referred to when needed. Alerting devices, such as an audible alarm on a palmtop, can prove helpful in bringing a person's attention back on task, or increasing awareness of time passing, or reminding them of something for which they need to take action. In relation to executive difficulties, any device that enables a person to organise and initiate, record and monitor progress and reduce the need to solve problems on the spot can be helpful. The use of files, templates and prompts, such as that found in Microsoft Outlook software, can be helpful to the individual with dysexecutive problems. Palmtops with similar software can also provide the structure needed to aid storage of checklists, to assist in problem solving and retrieving information that an individual is unable to remember. It is suggested therefore that palmtops should be considered for people with dysexecutive problems as well as for memory impaired individuals (Kim et al., 2000).

Inglis et al. (2004 this issue) noted that, for certain cognitively impaired individuals, electronic memory aids had demonstrated an increased independence from carers, and referred to Harris' criteria for considering electronic memory aids, which included their cueing characteristics, capacity, ease of use and functionality. They praised the benefits of specific, timely, active reminders provided by audible alarms as opposed to passive reminders such as diaries, which people have to remember to look at. Wright noted that high frequency users tend to prefer keyboard input electronic organisers, whereas low frequency users tend to prefer touch screen input (Wright et al., 2001). However, portability is a very important criterion for selection by most individuals. Other important factors are insight into memory difficulties and motivation, so involvement of the client in the selection of the aid and functions required is essential.

PRACTICAL CONSIDERATIONS FOR REHABILITATION PROFESSIONALS AND USERS

As medical intervention continues to improve, and more people with severe brain injury survive, the percentage of brain injured people within the population is likely to rise. Specialist multi-disciplinary rehabilitation provision is sparse (Barnes, 1999) and still mainly focused on the acute stages of rehabilitation to facilitate discharge from hospital. However, it is when patients return home and attempt to engage in their previous lifestyle and activities that problems arise. More services are now addressing the longer-term rehabilitation needs of brain injured individuals and rehabilitation is taking place in hospitals, specialist units, in the community, and in people's homes, schools, and working environments. Some professionals are working within specialist teams, others on a more individual basis.

Purpose of technology

Therapists need to consider the most appropriate methods of assessment and intervention to address the presenting deficits and the needs of the client within these different environments. Barnes (1999, p. 929) noted three basic approaches to rehabilitation: "Approaches to reduce the disability, approaches designed to acquire new skills and strategies that will reduce the impact of the disability, and approaches that help alter the environment ... so that a given disability carries as little handicap as possible." These approaches could be used to formulate questions to consider when discussing areas for rehabilitation intervention with clients. The setting of individual client-focused rehabilitation goals to address such needs can enable the professional and the client to identify specifically what the client wishes to be enabled to do and therefore whether the use of technology may assist the individual to attain that goal. Selection of appropriate technology will be unique to each client's needs, and requires interaction between their deficits, lifestyle, goals, support mechanisms, and the physical environment.

Environmental considerations

As previously noted, it is essential that, as part of the rehabilitation process, the client is encouraged to generalise the use of compensatory technology outside the environment in which the rehabilitation has occurred. Teaching and reinforcing use of a new device within the rehabilitation unit needs to be expanded to include training and reinforcement in use of the device in the client's home environment by utilising a multi-context treatment approach (McBain & Renton, 1997). This involves training others as well as the client in the use of the device to ensure consistency of reinforcement. Feedback is frequently used within cognitive neurorehabilitation to facilitate behaviour change (Schlund & Pace, 1999). It can take various forms, but the main benefit is derived if the feedback provided to the individual is consistent and adapted according to the responses of the individual. This is not always possible in rehabilitation because of environmental constrictions placed on the client, professionals and other caregivers. Technology may have a big advantage here because it can offer consistency of feedback across environments.

Access to technology

Technology needs to be made accessible to the user in terms of cost and ease of use. Cost can be a barrier to the use of technology in rehabilitation as the initial outlay can be relatively high. Provision of equipment currently tends to fall under the domain of social services, and health and charitable organisations. Private funding, particularly when a compensation claim is pending, is a route that can be used. However, there are many barriers to overcome in terms of financial restraints, particularly as it is essential that a brain injured client has the opportunity to try out several devices before selecting the one that seems to suit his or her purposes and abilities.

From clinical experience, one of the main issues for the rehabilitation professional would appear to be keeping abreast of new technological developments and the potential for use in the rehabilitation process. The therapist needs to keep up with new developments, or run the risk of advising about a product which in a few months time may be out of date or replaced by a more preferable device. Obtaining knowledge of current issues involving new technology, the reading of specialist journals, surfing the Internet, attending courses and equipment fairs is a time-consuming process. Knowledge of the jargon involved can be a huge barrier to understanding what the equipment can do and why one item may be preferable to another. The therapist needs to be competent and confident in the use of the technology before being in a position to teach the use of computers to clients. As stated earlier, closer collaboration with specialists involved in the design and use of technology may assist this process.

Access to technology can be problematic and potentially expensive. Since loan of items from companies is not always possible prior to purchase, within the Oliver Zangwill Centre a small number of memory aids have been purchased for loan to individuals during their rehabilitation to assist them in making decisions about their needs prior to purchasing a device of their own. However, new products come along rapidly and already a number of barely used aids are obselete and, alongside loss or breakage of devices, this can be a costly process for departments or individual clinicians. Technical advice is helpful but not always readily available, and attempting to contact relevant company helplines can be a frustrating and time-consuming process. In an ideal world, it would be helpful to have technological resource centres within each region, with devices on display and people on hand to offer advice about the products available. Such resource centres are available for general disability equipment and there are regional specialists advising on communication aids and environmental control systems, but as yet not for other more specialist technological devices. This is perhaps a possibility for the future and one that would certainly be welcomed by the author. Therefore it is perhaps more useful and more realistic for individual clinicians to be aware of other organisations which may be better placed to keep up to date with the developing technology available. For example, AbilityNet is an organisation that offers assessment for clients with disabilities regarding hardware and software available to them. REMAP is an organisation that can design and produce custom-made equipment for individuals with special needs in the UK. The Foundation for Assistive Technology (FAST; www.fastuk.org) is a national charity aimed at promoting collaboration between users of assistive technology, service providers, product manufacturers and those involved with research.

The selection of technological equipment for use with people with brain injury and learning difficulties needs careful consideration. One of the most functionally disabling cognitive deficits following brain injury is memory impairment (Rose et al., 1999). "Memory dysfunction may be the primary deficit or secondary to other features such as impaired attention, executive functioning, or depression" (Goldstein & Levin, 1996, p. 204). Functionally, people describe difficulty with remembering peoples' names, things they need to do or where they put something. Use of technology to aid storage and retrieval of such information has expanded dramatically over recent years among the general population with the development of palmtop devices, pagers and mobile telephones with Internet access. Yet the use of such technology within the field of rehabilitation is still relatively patchy and few research articles have demonstrated whether these devices are useful in the rehabilitation of memory impaired individuals in the longer term.

It is possible for people with memory difficulties to learn to operate new devices since their procedural learning following acquired brain injury remains relatively intact (Kapur et al., 2002; Rose et al., 1999; Rizzo et al., 1998). However, the use of errorless learning principles, expanding rehearsal and vanishing cues to aid in the training process needs to be considered, and this can be a time-consuming process as each stage of a task needs to be taught explicitly (Kapur et al., 2002). Donaghy and Williams (1998) refer to Sohlberg and Mateer's protocol for memory journal training for people with severe memory difficulties. The three training phases are acquisition, application and adaptation to naturalistic settings. They also note the importance of capitalising on a memory-impaired person's strengths following acquired injury, usually in the areas of working memory (immediate attention), procedural memory, and old learning. This led them to limit the amount of information given at one time in the training process, to incorporate a method of vanishing cues to aid procedural learning, and use headings in the journal that would be familiar, such as days of the week. These principles could easily be applied to the use of new technology. Wright et al. (2001) noted that devices that present people with unambiguous choices will enable them to use their problem solving skills rather than being reliant on remembering procedures. Education and training of the person's family/carers to enable them to support the person using the device is vital.

In selecting relevant technology, the most important consideration is the client's needs, in relation to their disabilities. For example, at the Oliver Zangwill Centre, when choosing an appropriate palmtop, the client's functional memory needs are clearly ascertained so that the relevant functions on the palmtop can be identified, for example alarmed reminders, voice recording capacity, task list. The behaviours to initially access and subsequently enter information onto the device are supported through use of a loaned device with the relevant functions. Often rewriting the instructions provided needs to be undertaken to support an errorless learning approach. Then, once the client is demonstrating effective use of the loaned device and expressing motivation to use one in the future, he or she is assisted to obtain information about the variety of devices on the market with relevant functions within a price range. Once funding has been secured and the palmtop purchased, the therapist then helps the client to learn how to use the chosen device using the appropriate learning method identified during the initial loan period. The family and/or carers are also involved in this process and the client is supported to identify in writing how he or she will use the device so that there is consistency among all people who are involved. In involving clients and their carers in this process of selection, they can then ascertain when, in the future, their needs are no longer being met by their current device and have a process for selecting a newer model. Otherwise, clients are largely at the will of market forces.

The rehabilitation professional needs to have an understanding of the strengths and weaknesses of the brain injured individual. This can be obtained through a combination of standardised and functional assessments, and discussion with the individual and his or her family. The standardised assessment will enable the therapist to identify specific difficulties with cognitive processes that may influence new learning ability or the conditions which are likely to make a learning process optimally effective. For example, a person with a reduced attention span will need training sessions to be short and free from distractions. A person with reading difficulties may need to use a device with icons and the instructions for the device may need to be made more visual in nature.

Knowledge and understanding of the experience and use of technology by the client prior to the injury is necessary to ascertain previous abilities which could be utilised or identified. A reluctance to use or fear of technology may influence decisions regarding the potential benefit of introducing a technological device. As use of technology becomes more part of everyday life, it would be anticipated that this would become less of a barrier to the use of technology in rehabilitation. Previous experience of using memory aids is known to influence the use of aids after a brain injury, and it would be anticipated that the same would be true for other assistive devices.

Barriers

Barriers to use of technology also need consideration. One of the main barriers is poor insight or motivation, which can be problematic in both acute and post-acute rehabilitation. Burke et al., note that many patients do not recognise their cognitive problems and/or forget when they occur and therefore may resist using a compensatory device that "symbolises the presence of acquired problems" (Burke, Danick, Bernis, & Durgin, 1994, p. 72). Motor and sensory deficits will impact upon the ability of the client to use a device, as will cognitive deficits, including poor initiation, difficulty following through plans, or communication deficits. Therefore, consideration should be given to such needs by, for example, providing cues to help people with a short attention span or supplying iconic prompts to people with dysphasia. It is important to select the right software to enable the individual to focus on the desired task without hindrance from other cognitive deficits. Social factors may also prove problematic; for example, carers may attempt to do things for clients and therefore unwittingly undermine therapists' attempts to encourage clients to do things for themselves through the use of technology. Emotional factors may include adjustment issues and self-identity and are likely to need involvement of a psychologist to enable clients to come to terms with these areas (Burke et al.,1994).

User requirements

Besides initial cost of acquisition and further costs involved in maintenance, there are a number of practical considerations for the brain injured user of technology. Studies indicate that, somewhat surprisingly, relatively few people are using electronic external memory aids in preference to more traditional memory aids, such as watches, calendars and diaries (Evans et al., 2003). Generalisation of use of technology is a consequence of factors "specific to the individual (deficits, skills, goals, awareness), and those external to the individual, such as environmental constraints, support, and training technique". (Sohlberg & Raskin, 1996, p. 66). In terms of training a client in the use of a compensatory aid, the authors suggest that the therapist needs to use the assessment process to identify "the individual's cognitive, physical and environmental profile" and "select a system ... consistent with the culture of the individual" (Sohlberg & Raskin, 1996, p. 72).

The ease of use of any particular technological device is a significant factor. Customisation should be considered for the individual when technical support is available to facilitate this (Wright et al., 2001). In using remedial software with people, McBain and Renton note that "many programs have rather too few variable factors, which does not allow the operations to be tailored to suit individual patients" (McBain & Renton 1997, p. 203). However, as technology advances, equipment tends to become more user friendly and therefore facilitates learning how to use the device for someone who has cognitive difficulties affecting their memory, concentration and problem solving processes. The use of icons on palmtop devices is an example, where one touch on an icon that looks like a diary will bring up the diary function on screen. Portability will influence the use of most external memory aids and the storage potential of palmtops frequently makes them more preferable to bulging filofaxes or diaries. For the person with dysexecutive difficulties, the ability to store information in relevant sections can be extremely useful to aid their organisation and retrieval of essential information. The newer digital dictaphones enable users to file voice messages in different sections to assist this process, rather than spool through a tape to find the message they want. Voice activated software is still being developed but carries enormous potential for people with communication or physical deficits. The look of the device can also influence its use. As well documented, the majority of traumatic brain injuries occur to young male adults and it is the experience of the author that they are concerned with how they will look to their peers when using a device, which can influence their choice.

Glisky noted that the use of computers may provide employment opportunities for people with cognitive difficulties. Since they involve procedural learning, this group of people can learn the components prior to entering the work environment. Also, "they require rather rigid adherence to a set of rules and can be counted upon to be highly consistent... Once patients have learned the rules and their applications, they are less likely to be called upon to make online decisions or respond to novel circumstances" (Glisky, 1996, p. 568). For clients with dysexecutive difficulties, this can be particularly helpful. Funding via access to work schemes through the employment service may enable a person to purchase a specific device for use in the work environment. As technology becomes increasingly widespread in everyday life, opportunities to study may increase, and vocational opportunities through application of technology may provide increasing opportunities for those with cognitive difficulties. This is an area that is likely to need the involvement of rehabilitation professionals.

THE FUTURE

In future, the use of videophones, tele-conferencing, computerised shopping, smart cards, voice-operated environmental controls in homes, interactive television, and increasingly sophisticated mobile phones are likely to become more widespread. What will this mean for the brain injured population? For those with physical deficits, there are obvious benefits to being able to readily access information and people from home, and operate devices within the home without excessive physical effort. For the person with cognitive deficits, being able to access information and contact people or products more speedily and easily will also clearly be beneficial. Alerting reminders can assist people with poor attentional skills. Technological advances can result in a product becoming more user friendly. Through redesign of the interface of a particular device, a person with cognitive deficits may be helped to find solutions to problems or store things to be remembered. Smaller, more portable devices may increase use and/or reduce the incidence of losing a device because it can be more easily transported. However, without information and financial resources, people who could benefit from using technology may miss out on an opportunity to develop their independence and improve their quality of life.

In their article, McBain and Renton (1997) note that clinicians need to be more involved in the development of software for computers used in cognitive rehabilitation. They recommend (McBain & Renton, 1997, p. 207) more collaboration between clinicians and programmers. "Ideally, a programmer who has the knowledge and experience to exploit the capabilities of the hardware used and implement an effective program should work with a therapist who would guide the theoretical and clinical application aspects of the software." This recommendation could also be applied to designers of all different types of new technology. They also recommend training at undergraduate level in the therapeutic value of information technology.

CONCLUSION

As technology develops apace, clinicians involved in the rehabilitation of people with cognitive deficits following acquired brain injury face an exciting challenge. More research needs to be undertaken to determine the effectiveness of using different types of technology in the short, medium and longer term as part of the rehabilitation process of brain injured clients. Appropriate teaching methods need to be identified and easier access to people with knowledge of products should be encouraged, and of course financial resources to fund the provision of technology should be made available. As the future will continue to be full of change, clinicians involved in brain injury rehabilitation need to be increasingly flexible in the way they address the needs of their clients in order that opportunities for optimising the independence of their clients increase at a rate that matches the development of new technology.

REFERENCES

Allen, B. (1996). An integrated approach to Smart House technology for people with disabilities. *Medical Engineering and Physics*, 18(3), 203–206.

Arnott J., Alm, N., & Waller, A. (1999). Cognitive prostheses: Communication, rehabilitation and beyond. *Proceedings of the IEEE International Conference on Systems, Man and Cybernetics*, Tokyo, Japan 12–15 October.

Barnes, M. P., (1999). Rehabilitation after traumatic brain injury. *British Medical Bulletin. Trauma*, *55*(4), 927–943.

Brown, R., Pain, K., Berwald, C., Hirschi, P., Delehanty, R., & Miller, H. (1999). Distance education and caregiver support groups: Comparison of traditional and telephone groups. *Journal of Head Trauma Rehabilitation*, *14*(3), 257–268.

Burke, J. M., Danick, J. A., Bemis, B., & Durgin, C. J. (1994). A process approach to memory book training for neurological patients. *Brain Injury*, *8*(1), 71–81.

Donaghy, S., & Williams, W. (1998). A new protocol for training severely impaired patients in the usage of memory journals. *Brain Injury*, *12*(12), 1061–1076.

Evans, J., Wilson, B. A., Needham, P., & Brentnall, S. (2003). Who makes good use of memory aids? Results of a survey of people with acquired brain injury. *Journal of the International Neuropsychological Society*, *9*, 925–935.

Glisky, E. L. (1996). Computers in memory rehabilitation. In A. Baddeley, B. A. Wilson, & F. N. Watts (Eds.), *Handbook of memory disorders*, (pp. 557–585). Chichester, UK: John Wiley.

Goldstein, F. C., & Levin, H. S. (1996). Post-traumatic and anterograde amnesia following closed head injury. In A. Baddeley, B. A. Wilson, & F. N. Watts (Eds.), *Handbook of memory disorders*, (pp. 187–209). Chichester, UK: John Wiley.

Inglis, E. A., Szymkowiak, A., Gregor, P., Newell, A. F., Hine, N., Wilson, B. A., Evans, J. J., & Shah, P. (2004). Usable technology? Challenges in designing a memory aid with current electronic devices. *Neuropsychological Rehabilitation*, *14*(1/2), 77–87.

Kapur, N., Glisky, E. L., & Wilson, B. A. (2002). External memory aids and computers in memory rehabilitation. In A. D. Baddeley, M. Kopelman & B. A. Wilson, (Eds.) *Handbook of memory disorders* (2nd ed., pp 757–784). Chichester, UK: John Wiley.

Kim, H. J., Burke, D. T., Dowds, M. M., Robinson Boone, K. A., & Parks, G. J. (2000). Electronic memory aids for out-patient brain injury: Follow-up findings. *Brain Injury*, *14*(2), 187–196.

McBain, K., & Renton, L. M. B. (1997). Computer-assisted cognitive rehabilitation and occupational therapy. *British Journal of Occupational Therapy*, *60*(5), 199–204.

Rizzo, A. A., Buckwalter, J. G., Neumann, U., Kesselman, C., & Thiebaux, M. (1998). Basic issues in the application of virtual reality for the assessment and rehabilitation of cognitive impairments and functional disabilities. *CyberPsychology and Behaviour*, *1*(1), 59–78.

Rose, F. D., Brooks, B. M., Attree, E. A., Parslow, D. M., Leadbetter, L. G., McNeil, J. E., Jayawardena, S., Greenwood, R., & Potter, J. (1999). A preliminary investigation into the use of virtual environments in memory retraining after vascular brain injury: Indications for future strategy? *Disability and Rehabilitation*, *21*(12), 548–554.

Schlund, M. W., & Pace, G. (1999). Relations between traumatic brain injury and the environment: Feedback reduces maladaptive behaviour exhibited by three persons with traumatic brain injury. *Brain Injury*, *13*(11), 889–897.

Schultheis, M. T., & Rizzo, A. A. (2001). The application of virtual reality technology in rehabilitation. *Rehabilitation Psychology*, *46*(3), 296–311.

Sohlberg, M. M., & Raskin, S. A. (1996). Principles of generalisation applied to attention and memory interventions. *Journal of Head Trauma Rehabilitation*, *11*(2), 65–78.

Van Schaik, P. (2000). Adapted technology for people with special needs: The case of Smart Cards and Terminals. *British Journal of Occupational Therapy*, *63*(3), 111–114.

Wilson, B. A., Emslie, H., Quick, K., & Evans, J.J. (2001). Reducing everyday memory and planning problems by means of a paging system: A randomised control crossover study. *Journal of Neurology, Neurosurgery and Psychiatry*, *70*, 477–482.

Wilson, B. A., & Evans, J. J. (2000). Practical management of memory problems. In G. E. Berrios, & J. R. Hodges (Eds.). *Memory disorders in psychiatric practice* (pp. 219–310). Cambridge: Cambridge University Press.

Wilson, B. A., Evans, J. J., Emslie, H., & Malinek, V. (1997). Evaluation of NeuroPage: A new memory aid. *Journal of Neurology, Neurosurgery and Psychiatry*, *63*, 113–115.

Wright, P., Rogers, N., Hall, C., Wilson, B., Evans, J., Emslie, H., & Bartram, C. (2001). Comparison of pocket-computer memory aids for people with brain injury. *Brain Injury*, *15*, 787–800.

Zhang, L., Abreu, B. C., Masel, B., Scheibel, R. S., Christiansen, C. H., Huddleston, N., & Ottenbacher, K.J. (2001). Virtual reality in the assessment of selected cognitive function after brain injury. *American Journal of Physical Medicine and Rehabilitation*, *80*(8), 597–604.

NEUROPSYCHOLOGICAL REHABILITATION, 2004, *14* (1/2), 77–87

Usable technology? Challenges in designing a memory aid with current electronic devices

E. A. Inglis, A. Szymkowiak, P. Gregor, A. F. Newell, N. Hine, B. A. Wilson, J. Evans, and P. Shah

University of Dundee, Dundee, Scotland

Electronic devices such as personal digital assistants have been used successfully as aids for people with memory problems. However, limitations of currently available technology can create difficulties in the day-to-day use of such devices, particularly for memory impaired and older users. These limitations are discussed in terms of both the software and hardware issues, and are set into the context of challenges raised in the current study, which is to design a new interactive memory aid. It is concluded that a specific, customisable software interface is needed to meet the dynamic requirements of the user groups. This would also go some way to compensate for the hardware limitations until available technology becomes more usable.

INTRODUCTION

Many electronic devices, such as personal digital assistants (PDAs), dictaphones, pagers, and mobile phones have been used as memory aids in the rehabilitation of memory impaired people (Kim, Burke, Dowds, & George, 1999; Kim et al., 2000; Van de Broek et al., 2000; Wade & Troy, 2001; Willkomm & LoPresti, 1997; Wilson, Emslie, Quirk, & Evans, 2001; Wright et al., 2001). These trials have proved to be successful, with the reminders issued from the compensatory aids enabling the user to carry out daily activities, such as attending appointments or taking medication, with little or no input from carers or family. In particular, a small pager device has been evaluated with great success. The "NeuroPage" system, which provides the user

Correspondence should be addressed to Elizabeth Inglis, Applied Computing, University of Dundee, Dundee DD1 4HN. Tel: 01382 344153, Fax: 01382 345509.
Email: einglis@computing.dundee.ac.uk

http://www.tandf.co.uk/journals/pp/09602011.html DOI:10.1080/09602010343000129

with scheduled prompts, was developed by Hersh and Treadgold (1994) and evaluated by Wilson et al. (1997, 2001). The aid was found to be very successful, in particular with people exhibiting severe memory, attention and organisational problems. As memory problems can severely disrupt daily life and put a huge strain on carers (Wilson, 1995), the use of electronic devices as memory aids can be seen to improve the quality of life of not only the client, but also of the people immediately surrounding the client.

Memory problems are one of the commonest effects of brain injury, and are also associated with the ageing process. A study is currently being undertaken to develop a memory aid which will be usable by both of these user groups, with particular focus on older people. Based on the success of the NeuroPage system, it is hoped to develop an electronic memory aid which will maintain the basic functionality of the pager system, while enhancing the service in terms of interactivity and functionality. Two-way communication between a memory aid device and a base station will enable carers to be contacted if the user does not respond to critical prompts from the memory aid. It is hoped this will provide the reassurance to relatives and carers which is required to reduce their workload and worry and increase the independence of the user of the system.

Increasing the functionality of a simple pager system presents both usability and technological design challenges. This paper discusses the limitations of the currently available technology both in terms of the usability of the software interface and the practicalities of carrying an electronic memory aid as a daily companion.

MEMORY LOSS

At the beginning of this research, a participant who lives with memory loss attempted to explain what he wanted in a memory aid. "Imagine a memory which is outside you and responsive to you but doesn't control you." This was the challenge: To design an effective aid which would be a natural extension to the memory which most of us do not realise just how much we depend upon.

Memory loss can take many forms and affect many people, although it is a decline in prospective memory, the ability to "remember to remember", which is particularly relevant to the design of a memory aid. Prospective memory is known to deteriorate in relation to age (McDaniel & Einstein, 1993) and is one of the most common forms of impairment following brain injury. Brain injured people characteristically have difficulty remembering most kinds of new information, including future events, although they have normal to near normal immediate memory (Wilson, 1995). One way to gauge the extent to which these problems can affect the everyday life of these people is to look at the messages which users programmed into the NeuroPage memory aid system. Wilson et al. (1997) report that the most common messages used on this system were "good morning, it is 'day and date'", "take your medication now", "fill in your diary", and "make your packed lunch". These messages reveal an underlying deficiency in basic memory functioning that has serious implications for day-to-day living.

Older people suffer similar problems. In normal ageing, different degrees of impairment affect different forms of memory. In a population-based study of almost 12,000 older participants (aged 65 years and over), Huppert, Johnson, and Nickson (2000) found that only 54% of the subjects successfully completed an event-based prospective memory task. Participants were recruited from five centres across the country through their local GPs, with care being taken that the "very old" (75 years and over) were equally represented in the sample. The memory task involved participants being given an envelope and being told that later on they would be asked to write a name and address on the envelope, at which time they should also remember to seal it and write their initials on the back. Ten minutes elapsed between these instructions being given and the task enactment being carried out. Success in this task was strongly and linearly related to age, which is illustrated by highlighting the results in the youngest age group (65–69 years), where 68% succeeded, against the oldest age group (90 years and over) where only 19% performed the task successfully. The underlying significance of this research is that just under half the population of adults over the age of 65 in the UK suffer from some form of prospective memory impairment, and that, as a consequence, the safety and well-being of many older people may be at risk. A device to aid memory therefore has huge potential. The reluctance of many older people to use new-technology suggests that a memory aid device may prove even more effective if taken up by the "young-old" to aid them in later life.

REVIEW OF CURRENT ELECTRONIC MEMORY AIDS

Despite the prevalence of prospective memory problems among older people, the vast majority of research in this area has focused on the rehabilitation of individuals from brain injury. A number of ways of improving lost memory functions have been investigated and applied (Harris, 1992). These include strategies such as artificial mnemonics and repetitive practice (a restorative approach to improving memory) and the use of external aids such as calendars and diaries (a compensatory approach). While some restorative methods have been successful (Raskin & Sohlberg, 1996), it is the compensatory approach which shows greater potential, with prospective memory deficits being "replaced" by prompting the user to carry out tasks and appointments with an external aid.

It is in this area that technology has been used as an aid to memory. The following review of current electronic memory aids highlights a number of successful studies. However, there are many potential problems with using electronic devices as memory aids, and these technological limitations are also discussed.

Current personal digital assistants (PDAs) and palmtop computers provide time management software which has the potential to be used as a diary/alarm system for people with memory impairment. Kim et al. (1999) introduced a Psion Series 3a palmtop computer to a 22-year-old man whose memory skills were poor and who was currently undergoing rehabilitation for a closed head injury. Staff at the rehabilitation centre programmed alarms to remind him to attend therapy sessions and ask for medication and the patient was able to carry out all tasks without further cues. In an additional study, Kim et al. (2000) report on a trial involving 12 brain injured patients using a Psion Series 3a computer to assist with memory-dependent activities in their day-to-day lives. In a follow-up interview 9 of the 12 participants judged the device to be useful to them on a daily basis, while all patients recommended that the palmtop should be continued to be used in outpatient therapy for brain injured patients.

Further studies by Van de Broek et al. (2000) and Willkomm and LoPresti (1997) have evaluated the use of a voice organiser device as a memory aid. The voice organiser is a handheld dictaphone which can be programmed to replay messages at times specified orally by the user. The user is alerted to a message by an alarm, and on pressing a button the message is replayed. Van de Broek asked five subjects with significant acquired prospective memory impairment to perform prospective memory tasks, both with and without the voice organiser, over a period of three weeks for each phase. All subjects improved during the introduction of the voice organiser, with three subjects establishing a routine which persisted to a certain extent following removal of the device. Similar results have been obtained by Wilson, Emslie, Quirk, and Evans (1999), who report that a severely memory impaired user of NeuroPage improved on time-based tasks, such as preparing a meal, from a 50% success rate pre-pager to 100% during use of the NeuroPage device. For some tasks, the higher success rate was maintained once the pager had been removed due to the establishment of a routine.

Ordinary mobile phones have also been used and evaluated as memory aids. In a study by Wade and Troy (2001), an outside company was approached to develop a computerised system to send reminders to a mobile phone. When the user answered the phone a short spoken message indicating a reminder was heard, followed by the message delivered in a voice of the user's choice. If the phone was in use when a reminder was sent then it was sent repeatedly until it got through. In the event that a high priority reminder call remained unanswered, the call was transferred to a carer who could take appropriate action. The evaluation of the mobile phone showed that users generally achieved independence from carers. However, its function as a phone was overused, which proved problematic as the engaged tone meant reminder messages did not always get through. This suggests that the existing functionality of a device can be an important factor in both its success and acceptance as a new memory aid.

LIMITATIONS OF CURRENTLY AVAILABLE TECHNOLOGY

The reviewed literature clearly shows the broad range of electronic devices that have been employed and evaluated as memory aids (Kim et al., 1999, 2000; Van de Broek et al., 2000; Wade & Troy, 2001; Willkomm & LoPresti, 1997; Wilson et al., 2001; Wright et al., 2001). However, the average day-to-day use of such devices reveal problems in design which can only be exacerbated when used by older or memory impaired people. The limitations of current technology are therefore an important consideration in the successful application of an electronic device as a memory aid.

These limitations can be classified into two distinct groups: The design of the software interface which is presented to the user and the design of the hardware on which the software itself runs.

Software limitations

Current time-management software running on PDAs requires basic training for an average users to familiarise themselves with the system. The software contains computer terminology and conventions which are "hidden unknowns" to an inexperienced computer user. Although the ease of use of such software applications varies across the range of devices available and the platform on which they run (PalmOS/PocketPC/EPOC), it is clear they are not designed for people unfamiliar with computers, or for people with memory problems.

Wilson and Moffat (1984) found that learning to use electronic organisers produces great problems for memory impaired people, and reports from Kim et al. (2000) detailing subjects requiring supervised training twice a week suggests that the level of training required is not diminishing as the technology advances. When this is considered in conjunction with recent research (Clare et al., 2000; Wilson & Evans, 1996), which shows that memory impaired people benefit from errorless learning techniques, it is clear that the training required to learn how to use electronic memory aids should be minimal and produce as few errors as possible.

"Memory management" software designed for error-free learning could therefore be a huge benefit to people with memory problems. Wright et al. (2001) conducted a study in which an interface specifically designed for brain injured users was employed on two styles of PDAs. It was found that users who had suffered traumatic brain injury could use the PDAs successfully as memory aids, pointing to the need for a custom-designed error-free interface for both brain injured and older users.

Furthermore, a custom-designed software interface would support the varying characteristics of memory-impaired older users. An identified user group is not likely to be homogeneous—older people are not a group but are different, ranging from "fit older people" to "frail older people" (Gregor & Newell, in press), which has an impact on their demands and ability to interact with a memory aid. Large text, clear fonts, good contrast maintained through the correct use of colours (as suggested by Hawthorn, 2000), and intuitive usability which avoids computer conventions would make memory aid software acceptable to a wide range of older users.

Older people with memory loss could also benefit from a software interface which minimises the load on working memory as the ability to process items in working memory has been shown to decline with age (Salthouse, 1994). Zajicek and Morrissey (2001) highlight this point by suggesting that memory impairment reduces the ability of users to build conceptual models of the working interface. The design of software for a memory aid would need to take this into account by reducing the functionality of the system and ensuring that the structure of the system is clearly visible at all times. This needs to be achieved within the context of the small screen space available on a PDA and other electronic devices. A parallel report on WAP usability (the technology used to access the internet from mobile phones) by Ramsey and Nielsen (2000) gives detailed evidence of the problems of creating usable systems for small screen space such as mobile phones and PDAs. Scrolling pages, screen layout and the use of images and text all contribute to a difficult usability problem which must be overcome if these technologies are to successfully employed as external memory aids.

Hardware limitations

The second distinct category of current technological limitations is the hardware on which the memory aid software runs. In the context of carrying out the current research to develop a new memory aid, focus groups, informal discussion and interviews with older and memory impaired people have been conducted (Inglis et al., 2002). This has enabled the characteristic requirements of the user groups to be identified in specific relation to the hardware available.

The chosen hardware would need to address the issues of coping with the following:

Carrying a memory "outside you". A typical behaviour of people with memory impairment is the need to "carry" their memory with them. A participant in the current research who carries a bulky lever-arch file around with him expressed a desire to keep a record of all his information entered into an electronic memory aid device, as well as a hard copy as a backup. Although this is ultimately unrealistic, clearly a PDA (which at the time of writing could store the equivalent of two music CDs) would go some way to resolving this problem. Backup copies of older data could also be made and stored on a local PC.

Carrying a memory everywhere with you. For an external aid to be of use to memory impaired people, it must be carried everywhere with them. It is here that the pager system NeuroPage excelled as the small device could be carried easily in a pocket or clipped to a belt, and was seen as prestigious rather than an embarrassment (Wilson et al., 1999). Wade and Troy (2001) also report that using a mobile phone as a memory aid was considered highly socially acceptable to young people. Larger devices such as a PDA may also prove prestigious, although the additional functionality can cause problems such as unwittingly pressing controls while a device is carried in a pocket or bag. For example, a recording being made accidentally while a button was pressed led to a digital recording of approximately four floppy discs—enough to cripple a system with low memory capacity. A scenario like this could also lead to all the data on the device being lost if the "power on" button was pressed. Currently PDA devices incorporate lithium batteries which need to be charged by external power on average every 10 hours, and hence would run down quickly in this situation. Clearly this could be a real issue for memory impaired users.

Declining vision. For older people, changes in vision, including declining visual acuity, contrast sensitivity and reduced sensitivity to colour, particularly blue-green tones (Hawthorn, 2000) make the small screens of phones, pagers and PDAs difficult or impossible to see. Mobile phones and handheld dictaphones can partially overcome this problem through the use of spoken messages, although this assumes the user's hearing is good (Wade & Troy, 2001; Van de Broek et al., 2000). PDAs have relatively large colour screens which facilitate large text and acceptable contrast, while also having the potential to provide a voice interface with digital recordings. However, this would not be feasible at present due to the small memory capacity of PDAs.

Declining dexterity. Older people also experience declining abilities in control of fine movement (Vercruyssen, 1996) which would have an impact on the ability to manage a small device with small buttons. A touchscreen PDA would help this by providing a flexible interface with large buttons on screen which could be operated with a forefinger. This would also remove the need to use and lose any stylus provided with the device. However, a disadvantage to this approach is the reduced feedback which is provided by a touchscreen in comparison to traditional buttons. The aid would also need to be robust, with a high probability of a small device being dropped or knocked while in day-to-day use. Special PDA models made for use in a warehouse environment may be of use to older people in this scenario.

A memory being responsive to you but not controlling you. A device being responsive to individual users clearly suggests the need for customised interfaces, as discussed above. This is a software requirement which very much depends on the available hardware—for this to be realistic the device must feature an operating system which is accessible for the development of such custom software. PDA's are particularly useful here as they can be programmed to perform certain functions with the support of the open development policies of the major PDA companies. This ability to develop a more flexible system could also help to achieve a memory which "does not control you".

POTENTIAL OF NEW TECHNOLOGIES

Despite the limitations discussed above, PDAs seem to represent the best currently available technology on which to develop a functioning prototype memory aid. The flexibility of using what is essentially a small computer allows software to be developed which can to some degree overcome the limitations presented by the hardware design. A customised interface which supports large text, large touchscreen buttons and a usable and intuitive system model can remove some of the problems of interacting with a small device. Voice recognition will enhance this interaction as the memory capacity of devices improves.

In the future, portable software, which could be web-based and if necessary downloaded from the internet, would allow a memory aid to be maintained on any device which would support this protocol. As mobility of information is now the main focus of the development of PDAs and mobile phone technology, this would provide a truly flexible and adaptable system designed to maximise the potential of these future technologies.

A whole new dimension is added by the current integration of mobile phone and PDA technologies. The potential for the use of this technology within a memory aid is enormous, and it is the primary goal of the current research to develop a memory aid which incorporates this remote communication. Remote access to the memory aid device could be provided through a mobile telephone link to a base station server. This in turn could be accessed remotely from any PC which was live on the internet, allowing reminder messages to be entered into the system from a large number of suitable locations at any time of day. The device could therefore be accessed not only by the user, but also by carers. This has the potential to alleviate some of problems discussed above relating to dexterity and vision which make data entry so difficulty for older people on such a small device. The chain of communication created by the mobile telephone link would download the new reminders to the device, keeping the user and carer in touch and removing the necessity of a manned "call centre" for a functional system. This would provide greater peace of mind and flexibility to carers, and improved ease of use for users.

For this to approach a failsafe system, the ability to connect to a remote base station at any time and stay in range of a mobile network are critical. The emerging availability of faster and more efficient mobile networks (General Packet Radio Service or GPRS), where the mobile device is more likely to be connected at all times has the potential to provide greater reassurance than the current mobile network technology (Global System for Mobile communication or GSM). Expanding these technological developments beyond the targeted professional sector can only benefit the non-ordinary user of a memory aid system.

CONCLUSION

Technology has been used and proved to have a positive effect on helping memory impaired people. However, usability and technological difficulties have limited the potential in terms of the number of people who can benefit from these aids. Older people whose memory has declined through the process of ageing are among those who could be excluded by small, difficult to use devices. These difficulties have also limited the extent to which the aids can contribute to longer lasting independence and safety of users.

Both the software and hardware of available technology need to be improved in order to be used easily as a memory aid. However, within the current limitations of the range of devices available, a PDA seems to best meet the requirements of memory impaired and older users. A study is currently being undertaken to develop a new aid which aims to overcome some of these limitations through the design of a customised interface which could be adapted for individual users. The development of such software would go some way to compensate for the hardware limitations, in particular when interacting with the device.

Ideally the new memory aid software would be web-based and portable, allowing it to be used on any current or future device which supports web protocol. As technology becomes more usable, hardware restrictions will be diminished and the enhanced usability of the device will complement the customised, user-friendly memory aid software.

REFERENCES

Clare, L., Wilson, B. A., Carter, G., Breen, K., Gosses, A., & Hodges, J. R. (2000). Intervening with everyday memory problems in dementia and Alzheimer type: An errorless learning approach. *Journal of Clinical and Experimental Neuropsychology, 22*, 132–146.

Gregor, P., & Newell, A. F. (in press). Designing for dynamic diversity—making accessible interfaces for older people. In *Proceedings of the NSF/EC Workshop on Universal Accessibility and Ubiquitous Computing*, 2001, Alcacer Do Sal, Portugal, ACM Press.

Harris, J. E. (1992). Ways to help memory. In: B. A. Wilson & N. Moffat (Eds.), *Clinical management of memory problems* (2nd ed, pp. 50–85). London: Chapman & Hall.

Hawthorn, D. (2000). Possible implications of aging for interface designers. *Interacting with Computers, 12*, 507–528.

Hersh, N. A., & Treadgold, L. G. (1994). NeuroPage: The rehabilitation of memory dysfunction by prosthetic memory and cueing. *Neurorehabilitation, 4*, 187–197.

Huppert, F. A., Johnson, T., & Nickson, J. (2000). High prevalence of prospective memory impairment in the elderly and in early-stage dementia: Findings from a population based study. *Applied Cognitive Psychology, 14*, S63–S81.

Inglis, E. A., Szymkowiak, A., Gregor, P., Newell, A. F., Hine, N., Wilson B. A., & Evans, J. (2002). Issues surrounding the user-centred development of a new interactive memory aid. In S. Keates, P. Langdon, P. J. Clarkson, & P. Robinson (Eds.), *Universal access and assistive technology*. London: Springer-Verlag.

Kim, H. J., Burke, D. T., Dowds, M. M., & George, J. (1999). Utility of a microcomputer as an external memory aid for a memory-impaired head injury patient during in-patient rehabilitation. *Brain Injury, 13*, 147–150.

Kim, H. J., Burke, D. T., Dowds, M. M., Robinson Boone, K. A., & Park, G. J. (2000). Electronic memory aids for an outpatient brain injury: Follow-up findings. *Brain Injury, 14*, 187–196.

McDaniel, M. A., & Einstein, G. O. (1993). The importance of cue familiarity and cue distinctiveness in prospective memory. *Memory, 1*, 23–41.

Ramsey, M., & Nielsen, J. (2000). *WAP usability déjà vu: 1994 all over again*. California: Nielsen Norman Group.

Raskin, S. A., & Sohlberg, M. M. (1996). The efficacy of prospective memory training in two adults with brain injury. *Journal of Head Trauma Rehabilitation, 11*, 32–51.

Salthouse, T. A. (1994). The ageing of working memory. *Neuropsychology, 8*, 535–543.

Van de Broek, M. D., Downes, J., Johnson, Z., Dayus, B., & Hilton, N. (2000). Evaluation of an electronic memory aid in the neuropsychological rehabilitation of prospective memory deficits. *Brain Injury, 14*, 455–462.

Vercruyssen, M., (1996). Movement control and the speed of behaviour. In A. D. Fisk & W. A. Rogers (Eds.), *Handbook of human factors and the older adult*. San Diego, CA: Academic Press.

Wade, T. K., & Troy, J. C. (2001). Mobile phones as a new memory aid: A preliminary investigation using case studies. *Brain Injury, 15*, 305–320.

Willkomm, T., LoPresti, E. (1997). Evaluation of an electronic memory aid for prospective memory tasks. *Proceedings of the RESNA 1997 Annual Conference* (pp. 520–522). Arlington, VA: RESNA Press.

Wilson, B. A. (1995). Management and remediation of memory problems in brain-injured adults. In A. D. Baddeley & F. N. Watts (Eds.), *Handbook of memory disorders* (pp. 451–479). Chichester, UK: John Wiley.

Wilson, B. A., & Moffat, N. (1984). Rehabilitation of memory for everyday life. In J. E. Harris, & P. E. Morris (Eds.), *Everyday memory, actions and absent-mindedness* (pp. 207–233). London: Academic Press.

Wilson, B. A., Emslie, H. C., Quirk, K., & Evans, J. J. (1999). George: Learning to live independently with NeuroPage. *Rehabilitation Psychology*, *44*, 284–296.
Wilson, B. A., Emslie, H. C., Quirk, K., & Evans, J. J. (2001). Reducing everyday memory and planning problems by means of a paging system: A randomised control and crossover study. *Journal of Neurology, Neurosurgery and Psychiatry*, *70*, 477–482.
Wilson, B. A., & Evans, J. J. (1996). Error-free learning in the rehabilitation of people with memory impairments. *Journal of Head Trauma Rehabilitation*, *11*, 54–64.
Wilson, B. A., Evans, J. J., Emslie, H. C., & Malinek, V. (1997). Evaluation of NeuroPage: A new memory aid. *Journal of Neurology, Neurosurgery and Psychiatry*, *63*, 113–115.
Wright, P., Rogers, N., Hall, C., Wilson, B., Evans, J., Emslie, H. C., & Bartram, C. (2001). Comparison of pocket-computer memory aids for people with brain injury. *Brain Injury*, *15*, 787–800.
Zajicek, M., & Morrissey, W. (2001). Speech output for older visually impaired adults. In A. Blandford, J. Vanderdonckt, & P. Gray (Eds.), *People and computers—Interaction without frontiers: Proceedings of HCI-IHM 2001* (pp. 503–513). London: Springer-Verlag.

NEUROPSYCHOLOGICAL REHABILITATION, 2004, *14* (1/2), 89–116

An electronic knot in the handkerchief: "Content free cueing" and the maintenance of attentive control

Tom Manly[1], Joost Heutink[1,3], Bruce Davison[1], Bridget Gaynord[1], Eve Greenfield[1], Alice Parr[1], Valerie Ridgeway[1], and Ian H. Robertson[2]

[1]*MRC Cognition and Brain Sciences Unit, Cambridge, UK;*
[2]*Psychology Dept. Trinity College, Dublin, Ireland;*
[3]*University of Groningen, Department of Psychology, Neuropsychology and Gerontology Unit, Academic Hospital Groningen, The Netherlands*

Rapid changes in consumer technology mean that many of us now carry a range of automated cueing devices. The value of organisers and pagers in cueing specific to-be-remembered items, particularly for people with memory deficits, is clear. Here we investigate whether cueing can serve a more general purpose—not in reminding us of a particular event or action, but in helping us to periodically take a more "executive" stance to our activities. In these studies we use a highly reduced "model task", the Sustained Attention to Response Test (SART)—designed to provoke "absentminded" lapses in action. Seven patients with right hemisphere stroke and who experienced difficulties in maintaining attention completed the task under two conditions. Periodic auditory cues that carried no content other than by association with the patient's remembered goal and which had no predictive value for events in the task were, nevertheless, associated with significant improvements in accuracy compared with an un-cued condition. A second experiment suggests that these improvements are not necessarily accompanied by an overall slowing in performance or a generally decreased tendency to make responses. We speculate that the transient hiatus in responses observed immediately following a cue

Correspondence should be addressed to Dr Tom Manly, MRC Cognition and Brain Sciences Unit, Box 58 Addenbrooke's Hospital, Hills Road, Cambridge, CB2 2QQ, UK. Email: tom.manly@mrc-cbu.cam.ac.uk
The research was supported by the UK Medical Research Council.

http://www.tandf.co.uk/journals/pp/09602011.html DOI:10.1080/09602010343000110

serves a role in disrupting automatic, stimulus-driven responding and allows a more attentive stance to be re-established. Consistent with this view, in a final study we show that disruption to responses is substantially greater in a variant of the task designed to maximally encourage "unsupervised" action. We suggest that interruption to current activity can—at times—be a useful aid to keeping track of one's overall goals. The potential role of such cueing in helping dysexecutive patients to generalise training from the clinic to everyday settings is discussed.

INTRODUCTION

Recently, one of the authors was replacing a damaged sink outflow. One stage in this process is to discard the water trapped in the "U" shaped section of pipe. Being personally and academically familiar with human error, he knew that there was a reasonably high risk of tipping this unwanted water back into the sink—which, given that he was holding the removed outflow pipe, would not only be pointless but could also lead to wet shoes. Through continuous attention, this mistake was avoided. Having safely tipped the water into a nearby jug, however, he then proceeded to rinse his hands ...

Since William James' seminal discussion on habit (James, 1890), the occurrence of such "slips-of-action" (where a routine response is absent-mindedly produced despite the "knowledge" that it is contrary to current goals) has informed a view that response selection is subject to different levels of control. Norman and Shallice (1980) argued that routine responses are triggered in a relatively automatic fashion by strongly associated contextual cues. Via this route, even complex sequenced activities can be performed effectively without the need for continuous, conscious control. However, in novel circumstances (where there is no "pre-packaged" response option), or when the triggered response is inappropriate to an overall goal, a separate supervisory system was postulated to intercede and modulate automatic response selection. The parallels between the predicted consequence of damage to such a "supervisory attentional system" (in particular, getting caught up in a routine and failing to adapt behaviour to changed circumstances) and deficits shown by some neurological patients (notably, those with anterior lesions)—have made this framework highly influential in the clinical field (Burgess, 1997; Burgess & Shallice, 1996a, 1996b; Shallice, 1988; Shallice & Burgess, 1991, 1993).

The presence of "dysexecutive" deficits, including in response control, represents a major challenge to functional recovery following brain injury. Evidence suggests that, even for brain injured people with well-preserved memory, language and other capacities, problems in the higher level co-ordination of behaviour can lead to disastrous levels of disorganisation in everyday life—a level that prevents the *useful* expression of those other retained abilities (Shallice & Burgess, 1991). Given that the very skills required to flexibly adapt behaviour are compromised, it is not surprising that rehabilitation in this area is an inherently difficult process. To date, the most carefully evaluated neuropsychological interventions for this type of deficit have followed an educational/re-training model. Von Cramon, Matthes-von Cramon, and Mai (1991), for example, provided "problem solving training" groups. Here patients received education about commonly experienced executive difficulties and training in step-by-step procedures for assessing novel problems, weighing up different potential solutions and evaluating the effects of actions. Levine et al. (2000) adopted a somewhat similar approach using "goal management training". This encouraged patients to regularly engage in an iterative, systematic process including: periodically stopping whatever activity they were currently engaged in; thinking about their overall aims; breaking main goals into sub-goals; and re-prioritising what they were to do next as necessary.

An important issue for this type of approach is whether the patient's *knowledge* of the procedures, and his or her ability to carry them out in a structured clinic setting, readily generalise to complex real-world situations. There are often considerable barriers to such spontaneous application. A patient may find it difficult, for example, to disengage from current activity, to recognise that a situation is challenging or contains a novel problem that needs solving, and, as referred to above, may show a dissociation between a stated plan/knowledge and actual behaviour (Duncan, 1993). Von Cramon and Matthes-von Cramon (1992) provide the illustrative example of a doctor who, following a brain injury, became somewhat impulsive in his diagnoses. They note that, while training in applying systematic analysis improved his diagnostic performance, little generalisation to other aspects of his life was observed.

It is important to note, however, that patients' deficits are often neither absolute (in the sense that they will invariably show *some* ability to plan, monitor their own behaviour and so on), nor entirely stable (in the sense that performance at one time or in one circumstance will be better than another). If factors can be identified that facilitate the expression of residual function—and these can be contrived to occur with increased frequency—this may have value as part of neuropsychological rehabilitation. The question we address here is whether patients may be assisted in generalising training and expressing executive function if they are given periodic environmental cues to do so. Clearly, this is a far from novel approach. Professional carers or family members often operate in precisely this manner, asking patients to think about what they need to be doing. Of particular relevance to this special issue are the now numerous portable electronic devices that, in principle, can improve the independence and relationships of brain damaged people by taking up some of that load. Some systems (e.g., those that allow stored text to be presented in conjunction with a timed alarm or those that can receive text/voice from another source—see, for example, Wilson, Emslie, Quirk, & Evans, 1997a, 1999; Wilson, Evans, Emslie, & Malinek, 1997b) can have a hugely valuable role in cueing specific "to-be-remembered" events. An obvious limitation is that those events and the timing of relevant behaviour have to be precisely anticipated. A different approach, that many of us with or without a neurological injury adopt, is to contrive reminders to engage in "executive" reviews. These can include tying a knot in a handkerchief or leaving incongruous objects by the front door as a marker that *something* needs to be remembered. These examples are interesting in that the cues themselves often carry no information about the content of the plan. Their role is to attract the individual's attention from time to time (when emptying one's pockets or leaving the house) and provoke a process of stopping and thinking. A clear disadvantage of such techniques is that they rely on us having a clear memory of what we intended to do, a memory that may elude people, particularly in the context of brain injury. A major advantage is that the process is entirely flexible to any goal and to changes in one's goals as events unfold. If it is the case that, in the absence of a severe memory deficit, many "dysexecutive" patients do have an adequate memory/plan for what they *should be* doing (Duncan, 1993; Shallice & Burgess, 1991), or if prompted can plan and adjust behaviour (Manly et al., 2002), such cues may have a role in making these "mental reviews" more likely. Here we investigate whether periodic, intrusive auditory "beeps"—an electronic equivalent of the knot in the handkerchief—can be useful within the context of a specific, highly controlled test.

Precise assessment of "executive" behaviours in complex real-world situations is difficult—particularly when patients may have a number of other deficits that can affect performance. In these preliminary studies, our aim was to consider the effect of cueing on a highly reduced analogue computer task designed to provoke "absentminded" lapses. In the Sustained Attention to Response Test (SART; Robertson et al., 1997), participants are asked to watch a random sequence of single digits presented on a computer screen at a regular, rhythmic rate. The instruction is to press a single response key as each digit appears, with the exception of the number 3, to which no response should be made. Through the simplicity of the task, the repetitive requirement to respond, and the rarity of the "no-go" digit, the SART was designed to encourage a rather automatic, inattentive ("stimulus–press, stimulus–press") response set. If lapsing attention allows responses to be triggered by the onset of each trial, errors of commission (pressing for no-go trials) become much more likely. In this manner, the accuracy score forms a useful index of participants' ability to actively maintain supervisory attentional control over their responses. In line with this prediction, poor performance on the SART has been previously reported in a group vulnerable to frontal injury and executive impairment—survivors of traumatic brain injuries (TBI; Robertson et al., 1997). Error propensity on the task has also been shown to be associated with the frequency of everyday cognitive slips (as indexed by Broadbent, Cooper, FitzGerald, & Parks, 1982, Cognitive Failures Questionnaire) in both TBI and neurologically healthy participants (Robertson et al., 1997; Manly, Robertson, Galloway, & Hawkins, 1999).

Previous studies with the SART have identified patterns of drift in reaction times to "go" trials as useful markers of increasingly error prone responding (Robertson et al., 1997; Manly et al., 1999—although see Manly et al., 2000). In the first study we describe here, our aim was to maximise the effect of auditory reminders to "pay attention" by synchronising their presentation with postulated periods of maximal attentional lapse. To this end, seven patients who had experienced a right hemisphere stroke (and who had difficulties in maintaining attention in everyday situations) were asked to perform a standard version of the SART. For each individual, the mean correct reaction times to "go" trials in the task were then calculated. In the subsequent experimental condition, speeding in reaction time from this individual mean, as an approximate on-line index of attention, was used as the criteria for triggering an auditory cue. The cue was a simple tone that carried no content other than by association with the patients' own goals and served no predictive purpose for the presentation of a no-go trial. It was hypothesised, however, that this periodic cueing, in helping patients to maintain their attention over responses, would be associated with reduced errors of commission in comparison with the un-cued condition.

EXPERIMENT 1

Method

Participants

Seven patients with right hemisphere lesions from cerebrovascular accidents (CVA) took part in the study. The patients, who had all been seen at Addenbrooke's Hospital at the time of their CVA, were selected on the basis of current self- or informant-reports of attention difficulties in everyday life based on a semi-structured interview. The five men and two women were of mean age 63.0 (SD 10.50) and were seen at a mean of 41.0 (SD 12.92) months post-stroke. Lesion site and extent varied considerably (see Table 1 for details).

As part of an initial assessment, six of the patients completed the Telephone Search (speeded visual search) and Lottery (auditory vigilance level task) subtests of the Test of Everyday Attention (TEA; Robertson, Ward, Ridgeway, & Nimmo-Smith, 1994, 1996—see measures). The results, shown below in Table 1, show generally poor performance across both

TABLE 1
Age, sex, lesion details and performance on two tests of attention (percentile levels) among the 7 patients taking part in Experiment 1

	Age	*Sex*	*Lesion details*	*Telephone search*	*Lottery*
1	59	F	Right CVA, occipito-parietal	20th–31st	1st–3rd
2	72	M	Right CVA, residual effects unclear from scan	3rd–7th	7th–12th
3	73	M	Right CVA, striatal lesion affecting right lentiform nucleus and corona rediata	20th–31st	7th–12th
4	55	M	Right CVA, tempero-parietal damage	31st–43rd	7th–12th
5	49	M	Right CVA, extensive tempero-parietal lesion extending into subcortical regions	57th–69th	<1st
6	76	F	Small poorly demarcated area of low attenuation in the right subinsular region extending into the parietal lobe. Appearences in keeping with an area of infarction	7th–12th	7th–12th
7	57	M	Right CVA, temporal lobe lesion	See text	See text

measures, relative to age norms. As might be expected in the context of right hemisphere lesions (Cohen & Semple, 1988; Pardo, Fox, & Raichle, 1991; Rueckert & Grafman, 1996; Wilkins, Shallice, & McCarthy, 1987), the sustained attention task was performed particularly poorly. Due to later recruitment and a difficulty in completing long testing sessions, the seventh patient did not complete these measures. Previously, however, he had completed a tone counting task using items from the TEA Elevator Counting subtest. His score (11/20 items) on this task—which usually attracts ceiling scores even in older adults (Robertson et al., 1994)—is consistent with a considerable difficulty in self-maintaining attention to task.

Seven neurologically healthy age-matched participants, recruited from the MRC Cognition and Brain Sciences Unit Volunteer panel (mean age 61.57: SD 9.37, 4 men, 3 women) also participated in the study.

Background measures of attention

Subtests of the Test of Everyday Attention (Robertson et al., 1994; Robertson et al., 1996) were performed.

Telephone Search. In this measure, participants are asked to search though a visually "noisy" A3 sheet designed to emulate a telephone directory page. Four columns of company names, slogans, telephone numbers and symbol-pairs are presented. Participants are given a pen and asked to find and mark any instance where both symbols in any pair are identical. Twenty targets are presented. Time taken and accuracy of search are taken into account in a "time-per-target" score.

Lottery. This is an auditory vigilance level measure of sustained attention. Participants are asked to listen to a 10-min audiotape of an announcer reporting winning lottery tickets. Each ticket is represented by two letters and three digits. Participants are asked to listen out for any tickets ending in the digits 55, and to write down the two letters beginning that ticket sequence. Ten targets are presented. Correct reporting of either the first or second letter of each target scores a point.

Elevator Counting. In this well-validated measure of sustained attention, participants are asked to listen to slowly presented strings of identical tones and to report the total presented at the end of each item.

Experimental measures

A version of the Sustained Attention to Response Test was used to establish reaction time criteria.

Shortened version of SART. In this version of the standard SART (see Robertson et al., 1997), 112 single digits (1–9) were presented sequentially in the centre of a computer monitor. In each trial, the digit (presented in white against a background) appeared for 250 ms and was followed by a masking pattern (white circle with diagonal white cross) for 900 ms—giving a total trial duration of 1150 ms. The digits were presented in a random sequence with each digit being selected equally over the duration of the test. Participants were asked to press a single response key (the button on the computer mouse), using the index finger of their preferred hand, as soon as possible after the presentation of each digit. The exception was for the nominated no-go digit (3), to which no response should be made. Twelve no-go digit presentations occurred across the test (10.7% of trials). Errors of commission (pressing on a no-go trial), errors of omission (not pressing on a go trial), and reaction times relative to the onset of each trial, were recorded.

Cued SART condition. This task was identical to that described above with the exception that, if reaction times below an individually established threshold (see below) were detected, an auditory cue was presented over the built in computer speakers. The cue comprised a single alternation two-tone (523.3 and 659.3 Hz) "siren" of 30 ms. duration and approximately 62 dB intensity.

Standard un-cued SART condition. The control condition was identical to the cued condition with the exception that no auditory cues were presented. The tasks were programmed using Psyscope experimental software (Cohen, MacWhinney, Flatt, & Jefferson, 1993) and presented on a Macintosh laptop computer (monitor size 215 mm × 135 mm).

Procedure

Patients were tested in their own homes. The majority of control participants were tested in a quiet room at the research unit or at home.

The participants were initially given the standard SART instructions, namely to press the mouse key as quickly as possible following each digit with the exception of the nominated no-go target. Following 18 practice trials, participants then performed the shortened standard version of the task. The mean correct reaction time (and standard deviation) to go trials was then calculated.

Previous studies suggest that speeding in SART reaction time (RT) equivalent to approximately one half of a standard deviation of an individual's mean RT is associated with increased errors of commission (Manly et al., 1999; Robertson et al., 1997). Accordingly, for each participant, the experimenter subtracted half a standard deviation from the mean and entered this as the threshold for the subsequent experimental conditions.

A total of 450 trials (including 50 no-go trials) were run in each of the two conditions (cued and un-cued). These were divided into four sub-blocks of 112 trials each. The ordering of sub-blocks was such as to allow a covert change between the cued and un-cued conditions during continuous performance, with rest breaks occurring within-condition (e.g., CU–UC–CU–UC; where C = cued sub-blocks, U = un-cued sub-blocks and – = rest). Order of initial condition varied between participants. Total task duration (approximately 40 min) varied slightly depending on the length of inter-block rest periods.

In this study, following the initial criteria setting version of the test, the link between the presentation of the tone and speeding in reaction times was made explicit. After a discussion about attention wandering from the task and responses speeding up, participants were told: "To help you avoid this, the computer will play you a sound to warn you if you are pressing too quickly." The participants were not told that the auditory cue would only be present within blocks on half of the trials.

Results

Criterion setting and practice performance

In the initial criteria setting version of the task (i.e., prior to any explicit instruction on attention wandering and speeding)—and in line with their more general attentional deficits—the patients made significantly more errors of commission (responding to no-go trials) than the control participants; Patient errors of commission = 6.0 (SD 2.58), control participants = 2.86 (SD 2.54); $F(1, 12) = 5.261, p < .05$.

Correct reaction times to go trials did not differ between the two groups: patients = 408 ms (SD 98), control participants = 394 ms (SD 41); $F(1, 12) = 0.12$, $p = .75$. This is consistent with previous clinical findings suggesting that, while within-subject RT speeding was associated with increased errors, group differences in overall response times were insufficient to account for the increased error rates (Manly et al., 1999; Robertson et al., 1997). As a consequence of the equivalence in RT, the calculated thresholds (half a standard deviation below individual means) did not significantly differ between the groups: mean threshold for patients = 320 ms (SD 68, range 204–398); mean threshold for control participants = 364 ms (SD 42, range 287–431); $F(1, 12) = 2.14, p = .169$.

Exposure to tones in the cued condition

Perhaps due to the individual tailoring of the reaction time criterion for presentation of the auditory cue, there was remarkable consistency between the patient and control groups in the number of auditory alerts presented in the across the cued condition sub-blocks: patient group = 189.43: SD 80.68; control group = 188.71 SD 120.48; $F(1, 12) = 0.00$, $p = .990$. This fortunately rules out differential exposure to the tone as a factor in determining any performance differences between the groups.

Comparison of performance under cued and un-cued conditions

Errors of commission (responding on no-go trials). The potential improvements caused by the tone were examined in a repeated measures ANOVA with condition (cued vs. un-cued) as the within-subject factor, status (patient vs. control group) as the between-subjects factor, and errors of commission as the dependent variable.

Both main effects of status, $F(1, 12) = 5.91$, $p < .05$, and condition, $F(1, 12) = 5.73$, $p < .05$, were statistically significant. The patients performed the task more poorly than control participants, and showed significant improvements in withholding accuracy during the cued blocks. The lack of a significant interaction, $F(1, 12) = 1.95$, $p = .188$, indicates that both patient and control groups benefited from the cueing. As can be seen in Figure 1, with the cues, the patients' mean error score dropped by approximately 30% from 22.57 (SD 10.95) to 14.43 (SD 9.36) errors of commission. For the control participants, the error scores fell by approximately 24% from a mean of 10.0 (SD 5.72) to 7.86 (SD 6.44).

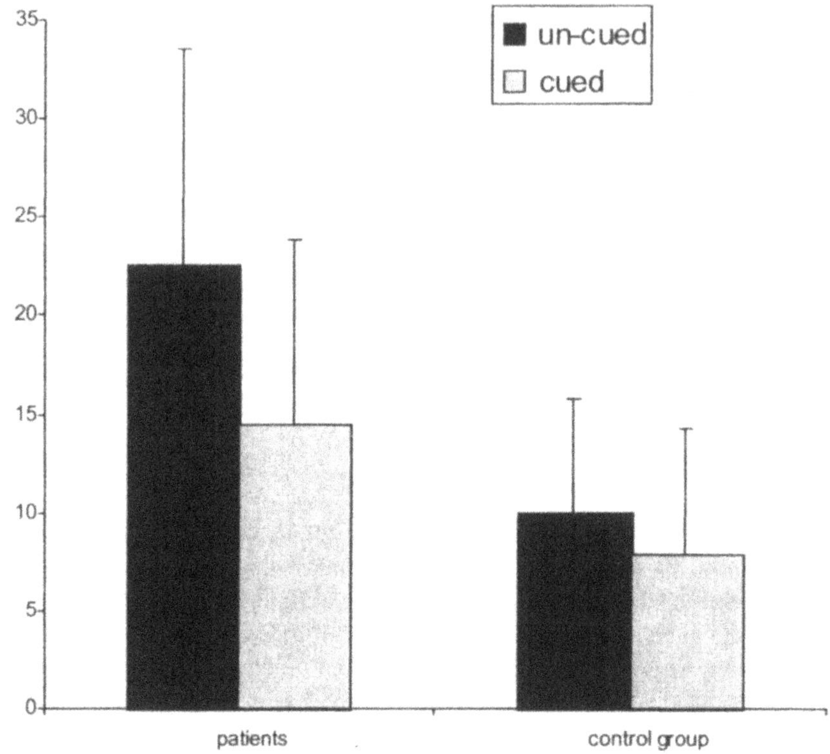

Figure 1. Errors of commission made on the SART under cued and un-cued conditions for right hemisphere patients and age-matched controls (error bars = standard deviation).

Errors of omission (not responding on go trials). Failure to make responses during go trials was examined using a repeated measures ANOVA with condition and status as factors. The patients failed to press for significantly more go trials than did the neurologically healthy control group, $F(1, 12) = 18.86$, $p < .01$; patient errors of omission in un-cued condition = 23.28: SD 12.86; in cued condition = 35.57: SD 23.36; Control group errors of omission in un-cued condition = 0.29: SD 0.49, in cued condition = 1.29: SD 1.38. There was no significant effect of condition, $F(1, 12) = 2.44$, $p = .14$, nor a significant interaction between status and condition, $F(1, 12) = 1.76$, $p = .21$. In summary, failing to press on go trials was relatively rare—although more common among the patients (errors of omission accounting for 4.6% of all go trials for the patients and 2.23% of go trials for control participants). The significant reduction in errors of *commission* reported above is therefore unlikely to stem simply from a reduced tendency to make responses in general.

Reaction times

Correct reaction times (i.e., responses during go-trials) were examined across conditions. In the un-cued, standard condition, the patients' responses were made at a mean of 429 ms (SD 93) after digit onset. In the cued condition, this increased to 465 ms (SD 89). For the control participants, the un-cued condition reaction time of 436 ms (SD 68) increased to 464 ms (SD 62). In a repeated measures ANOVA with condition and status as factors, the main effect of condition was significant, $F(1, 12) = 11.92, p < .01$, but there was no significant effect of status, nor status–group interaction. Patients did not differ from control participants in their response times, and both produced significantly slower responses during the cued condition.

Stability of performance

In order to examine the stability of the SART as a measure across a long period of task performance, and the possible carry-over effects of cueing, the first 225 trials of the un-cued condition were compared with the last 225 trials of the un-cued condition. A repeated measures ANOVA with time (first 225 trials vs. last 225 trials) and status (patient vs. control) as factors, and errors of commission as the dependent variable, revealed the expected significant main effect of group, $F(1, 12) = 7.25, p < .05$, with patients performing more poorly than controls, but no effect of time, $F(1, 12) = 0.13, p = .729$, and no significant interaction between status and time, $F(1, 12) = 0.13, p = .729$. There was a high degree of consistency in performance over time for both groups. The right hemisphere patients made a mean of 11.71 errors of commission (SD 5.91) on the first 225 trials, and 10.86 (SD 5.96) on the last. The control participants made a mean of 5.00 errors (SD 2.89) on the first block and 5.00 (SD 4.24) on the last.

Discussion

The results of this experiment show that a group of patients with right hemisphere damage and reported everyday attentional difficulties, as predicted, performed significantly more poorly on the standard SART than age-matched controls. It should be noted that the comparison is not with left hemisphere lesioned patients, and specificity of the task to right hemisphere damage is not informed by this design.

The results show that the presentation of the alerting tone produced significant improvements, reducing the patients' commission error rates by around 35% and those of the control participants by approximately 22%. These improvements cannot be accounted for by a generally reduced tendency to make responses (as might be predicted if the tones were highly distracting) as no change in omission error rates was observed.

Speed of response did, however, significantly increase for both groups under the cued condition. Although this slowing is consistent with participants allocating more attention or supervisory control to their actions, the explicit link between cue presentation and speeding in responses makes clear interpretation difficult. This question is re-examined in the subsequent experiments.

The stability of performance in the un-cued condition for both patient and control groups over the duration of the testing session is consistent with previous reports showing modest or absent practice effects on the task. It also suggests that, whatever the mechanisms underpinning the improvement, it was apparently dependent on the tone *actually being presented* rather than instructional set alone (this was constant across the task and changes between conditions occurred covertly).

Previous studies have shown that neurologically healthy participants, as here, are often far from perfect in their SART performance—and there are reasonable grounds to believe that errors are quantitatively rather than qualitatively different to those of patients. This finding allows more in-depth analysis of the effect of cueing in neurologically healthy as well as impaired groups.

In Experiment 1, our aim was to present cues at the moment of "most need"—at least as indexed by speeding in reaction times. In Experiment 2, we first examine whether it is necessary, if we are to see these benefits, to make the link between errors, RT and cues explicit for participants. Second, we examine whether the provision of cues that are wholly unconnected to changes in RT may also produce performance gains. Here, we simply ask participants to use the tone as a cue to "think about what you are doing".

EXPERIMENT 2

Method

Participants

Thirty neurologically healthy participants, recruited from the MRC CBU subject panel, volunteered to take part in this study. The group were of mean age 39.0 (SD 15.2) and comprised 18 women and 12 men.

Measures

Standard un-cued SART. The standard control condition was identical to that described for Experiment 1 with the exception that 135 trials (including 15 no-go trials) were run in each continuous block (see below).

Contingent cue condition. The contingent alert condition was identical to the standard condition with the exception that a response below an individually set threshold triggered the presentation of a tone (a 200 ms, 400 Hz tone at approximately 58 dB). As with Experiment 1, the reaction time criterion for tone presentation was established by first calculating the mean and standard deviation of correct reaction times in the standard condition. The threshold was then set at one half of a standard deviation below the mean for each subject individually.

Random cue condition. In this condition, tones were also presented, but at points randomly selected by the computer program. In order to equate tone exposure between this and the contingent cue condition, the same number of tones were presented as had been triggered by the participant in the pervious RT contingent-cue block.

Two blocks of each condition were presented within the task session. This yielded 270 trials (including 30 no-go trials) in each condition. The procedure of using the control condition to calculate the RT criterion for the contingent cue condition—and the number of tones presented in the contingent cue condition to determine the number in the random cue condition—imposed constraints on the block order. The task was therefore run in the fixed sequence that controlled for order effects—UCRRCU—where U was the un-cued control condition, C the contingent cue condition and R the random cue condition.

Procedure

Participants were tested in a quiet office. They were asked to press for each number as quickly as possible while trying to avoid making a response to the digit 3. Responses were made by pressing the mouse key with the index finger of the preferred hand. The participants were told that they might periodically hear a tone. They were asked to use this as a reminder to try and be *"very aware of what you are doing in the task"*.

Results

Errors of commission (responding during no-go trials)

It was predicted that the presentation of cue tones would improve the participants' capacity to avoid errors of commission on the task. The participants made a mean of 7.3 errors of commission under the un-cued SART condition (SD 5.17). Under the contingent and random cued conditions this was reduced to 5.5 (SD 5.79) and 5.7 (5.29), respectively. A repeated measures ANOVA with errors of commission as the dependent variable, and condition (un-cued, contingent cue and random cue) as levels of the factor revealed a statistically significant effect of condition, $F(2, 58) = 5.09$, $p < .01$. Post hoc analysis using Tukey's HSD showed that the difference between the un-cued and the contingent cue condition, and between the un-cued and the random cue condition, were statistically significant at $p < .05$. The difference between the contingent and random alerting conditions did not reach statistical significance. The presentation of cues therefore improved performance whether they were contingent upon speeding in RT or presented at random points in the task.

Errors of omission (not responding during a go trial)

Failure to respond during go trials was examined across the three conditions using repeated measures ANOVA. There was no statistically significant effect of condition, $F(2, 58) = 1.13$, $p = .33$. As previously observed, SART omission error rates were low accounting for 0.71% of go trials in the un-cued SART condition (SD 1.95%), 1.7% in the contingent cue condition (SD 4.96%), and 1.6% in the random cue condition (SD 7.92%). As with experiment 1, therefore, the reduction in errors of commission under cued conditions was not accompanied by a generally reduced tendency to make responses.

Reaction times

Correct RTs during go trials were considered across the three conditions in a repeated measures ANOVA. As shown in Figure 2, in the un-cued condition, responses were made at a mean of 400 ms (SD 77). In the contingent and random cue conditions the values were slightly higher at 423 ms (SD 97) and 413 ms (SD 85), respectively. The combined ANOVA reached statistical significance, $F(2, 58) = 3.2$, $p < .05$.

Post-hoc analysis (Tukey's HSD) revealed that the difference between un-cued and RT contingent cue conditions was significant at $p < .05$. There was, however, no statistically significant difference between un-cued and random cue conditions.

The number of tones presented and the effect of the tone on reaction times

We have argued in the introduction that interruption of ongoing automatic behaviour may be useful in subsequently regaining more attentive, goal-directed control. In the case of the SART, overt on-going behaviour is the production of responses. As described above, the mean reaction times for the un-cued and random cue conditions did not significantly differ. However, this may mask potentially informative changes around the time of cue presentation. To consider this we compared RTs of responses that immediately followed the presentation of a tone with those that immediately preceded one

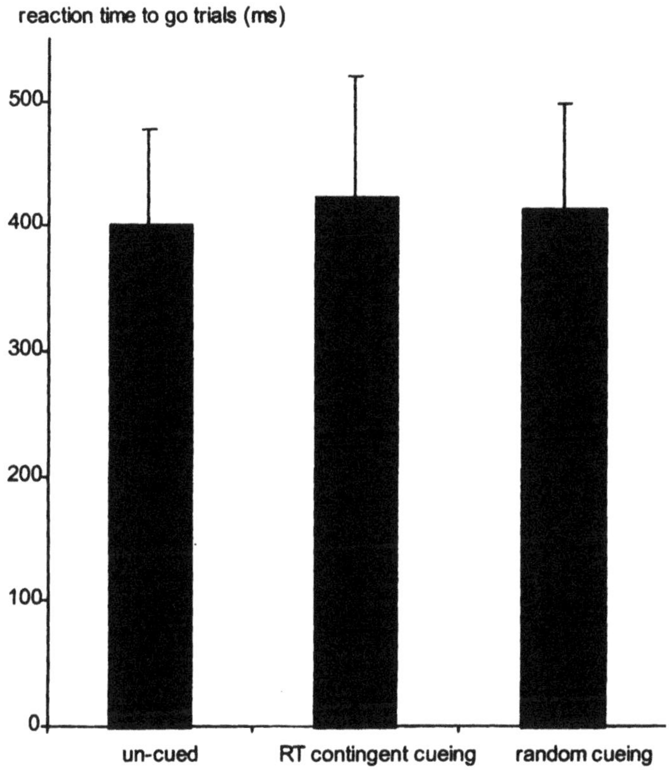

Figure 2. Mean correct reaction time (ms) to go trials across the three conditions of Experiment 2 (error bars = standard deviation).

in the random cue condition.[1] Additional criteria for trial selection were that a response to a trial preceding a tone should not itself have been preceded by a tone for at least four trials. Trials that followed the presentation of a tone should not, themselves, have coincided with a tone presentation.

Mean reaction time values were calculated for each trial type for each subject and compared in a repeated measures ANOVA. Pre-tone reaction times were made at 414 ms (SD 88). After a tone this was significantly increased to 445 ms (SD 104), $F(1, 27) = 8.99, p < .01$.

[1]In the contingent condition, such a comparison would be fatally confounded. Tones are triggered by fast responses. If a subsequent response was as fast or faster, it would also trigger a tone and, therefore, be excluded from the analysis. Using these criteria, slowing following a tone would be inevitable.

Tone novelty and reaction time slowing

The number of tones presented to each subject in the random condition varied according to the number presented in the contingent condition.

In order to address the question of whether the rarity or novelty of the tone had an effect, correlations were performed between the number of tones presented and the average magnitude of the slowing effect for each participant. The slowing effect was calculated by subtracting reaction times immediately following a tone from those immediately preceding a tone and expressing the difference as a proportion of the former. Using this proportionate, rather than absolute, slowing reduces the risk of a confounding the effect of tone rarity with general differences in reaction times.

There was a relationship (Pearsons $r = -.59$, $p < .01$). The rarer the presentation of the cue, the greater the proportionate impact on reaction time.

Discussion

The results of this study support and add to those of Experiment 1. The presentation of auditory cues to pay attention contingent upon speeding significantly reduced error rates in the task. The percentage improvement seen in healthy participants in both studies was broadly equivalent (22% vs. 24%). This suggests that the explicit link between response times and tone presentation in the instructions for Experiment 1 was *not* fundamental to producing the effect.

As before, the reductions in errors of commission cannot be related to a generally reduced tendency to make responses. Failure to press the mouse key for go trials was at a very low level and was not modulated by condition.

The absence of a significant difference between the contingent and random cue conditions suggests that it is the presence of cues more generally—rather than their relationship to current reaction time—which underpins the bulk of the observed improvements. From the point of view of informing potential rehabilitative interventions, this result is important. It suggests that the provision of cues that are both *irrelevant to the task being performed* (in the sense of not predicting the appearance of a no-go trial), and *independent of any marker of the subject's current "attentive" state*, may still serve to improve the maintenance of control.

In removing the explicit link between reaction time and cues, these results also clarify the nature of the effect. No significant differences in overall reaction time were observed between the un-cued and random cue conditions, indicating that the performance benefits did not simply stem from participants slowing down. In order to account for the improvements it is therefore necessary to posit a change in an "internal" state under which control over responses is better maintained.

While the presentation of the tones did not cause an overall slowing of responses in the random cue condition, significant and short-lived increases in response time were observed immediately after a tone. The magnitude of this slowing was related to the rarity of the tone. Although the results do not conclusively establish a link, they are consistent with temporary disruption to ongoing responses having value in the subsequent re-assertion of control. As will also be considered in more detail in the general discussion, within Norman and Shallice's supervisory attention system framework, the detection of novel circumstances is argued to favour supervisory control over routine response production (Shallice, 1988; Shallice & Burgess, 1993, 1996). A reasonable prediction from this position is that the effect of a novel event (if detectable) will be greater on the production of routine responses than on more controlled performance. If it is possible to manipulate the likely degree of "automatic" or "controlled" response production in the SART, this position can be investigated. Experiment 3 attempts this through using both the usual random digit sequence of the SART and a version in which the sequence is fixed such that the occurrence of the no-go trial becomes highly predictable. In the random condition an ideal participant should maintain a high degree of control over his or her responses—as a no-go trial might occur at any time. In a fixed version, where the no-go trial occurs predictably every nine trials, such control may be appropriately delegated to a more "task driven" response set across the intervening trials.

EXPERIMENT 3

Method

Participants

Thirty neurologically healthy participants, recruited from the MRC Cognition and Brain Sciences Unit, volunteered to take part in this study (mean age 46.5 years: SD 18.8; 18 women and 12 men).

Measures

Cued random sequence SART. This version of the task was as previously described, that is digits between 1 and 9 were presented within a random sequence with participants being asked to respond to each digit with the exception of a nominated no-go target. A total of 270 test trials (including 30 no-go trials) were administered. Ten cue tones were presented during the task. In order to ensure a reasonable distribution of the tone effects, their presentation was determined to occur at a random point within each cycle of 26 trials.

Cued fixed-sequence SART. In this condition, the structure of each trial was identical to that of the standard SART. Rather than using a randomly generated sequence of digits, this task presented successive digits (1–9) in the conventional, ascending order (1, 2, 3 … 9). In this task the cue tones were set to occur at random points within the sequence 5–6–7–8–9—that is well before the no-go target 3. A total of 199 trials, including 21 no-go trials were run in this condition.

Procedure

The participants were tested in a quiet office. For each condition, the nominated no-go digit was 3. The instructions were identical for each condition, with participants being asked to press for each number as quickly as possible with the exception of 3. They were told that they might hear an occasional "bleep" and to use this as a reminder to *"try and be aware of what you are doing in the task"*.

Condition order was balanced across subjects.

Results

The effects of cues on reaction times

Reaction times from the two conditions were examined for the effects of the cue. As in the previous study, statistically significant slowing in responses was observed in both conditions following tone presentation. In the random-sequence condition, trials before tones were responded to at a mean of 327 ms (SD 67 ms). Following a tone this increased to 349 ms (SD 66); $F(1, 29) = 14.32, p < .01$. In the fixed-sequence condition, the trials prior to a tone attracted a mean RT of 180 ms (SD 126). This increased to 256 ms (SD 121) following the tone, $F(1, 29) = 105.15, p < .001$, see Figure 3.

While the random presentation of tones should ensure that the pre-tone trials are representative, an additional comparison was made between the post-tone reaction time and all the reaction times to go-trials in the task. The results were consistent. Within the random-sequence condition, the general reaction time was 335 ms (SD 60). Following a tone this increased to 353 ms (SD 109); $F(1, 29) = 11.15, p < .01$. For the fixed-sequence condition, the general reaction time was 210 ms (SD 85), while following a tone it increased by almost 40 ms to 248 ms (SD 109); $F(1, 29) = 11.15, p < .01$.

It was hypothesised that the degree of slowing provoked by the tone would be related to the entrained, automaticity of the responses during which it occurred and that, due to its predictable, repetitive sequence, the fixed condition would therefore show the greatest slowing. However, it would be expected that RTs in the highly predictable fixed-sequence condition would be generally faster (i.e., of smaller value) as responses can be prepared and

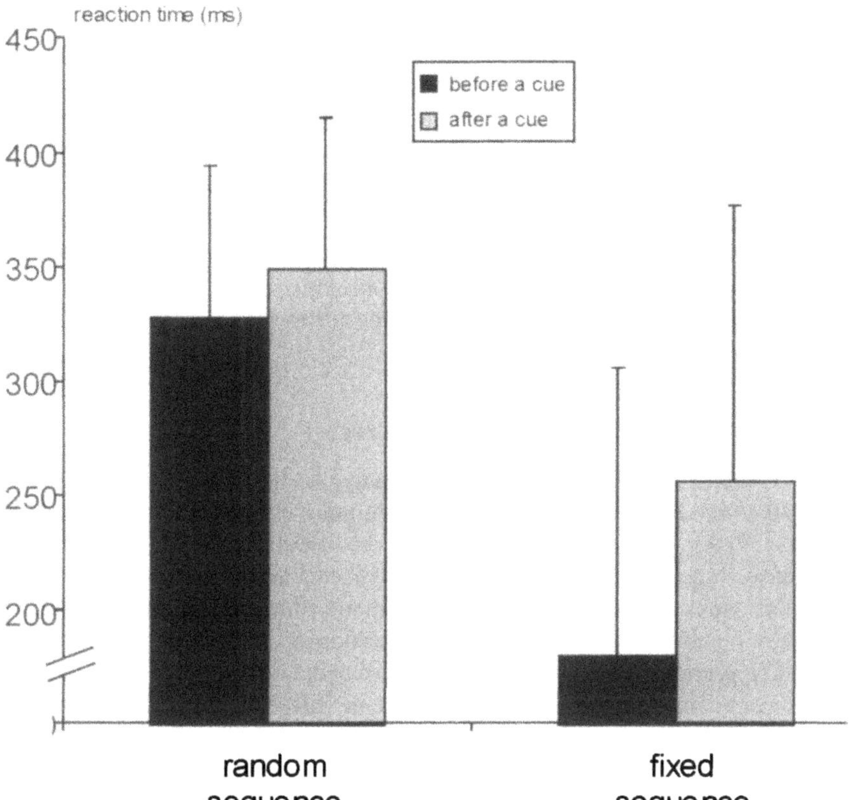

Figure 3. The effect of the cue on response production. Mean RT (ms) before and after the presentation of the tone (error bars = standard deviation).

executed without reference to the digit for much of the test. This was the case (mean fixed sequence RT = 206 ms: SD 81; mean random sequence RT = 330 ms: SD 76); $F(1, 29) = 35.38$, $p < .001$. As a consequence, expressing changes in RT as a *proportion* of pre-tone RT would therefore be unduly kind to our hypothesis (as a change of equal magnitude would represent a much larger proportion). The degree of slowing was therefore conservatively calculated by a simple subtraction of pre- from post-tone reaction times, which should be, if anything, predisposed towards showing greater change in the random-sequence condition.

For the random-sequence condition, the mean degree of slowing was 22 ms (SD 32), while for the fixed sequence condition the mean slowing was 75 ms (SD 81). The difference between the two conditions was statistically significant on repeated measures ANOVA, $F(1, 29) = 10.07$, $p < .01$.

A possible confound in this result is the variability in reaction times shown. For the fixed sequence this was considerable with participants ranging in mean response times from 68 ms (SD 58) to 452 ms (SD 314) (mean = 204 ms, SD 82.3). It is therefore possible that the increased size of the slowing observed in this condition may be attributable to the dramatic slowing of a few very fast responders. This was investigated by examining the correlation between the magnitude of the slowing observed and participants' mean reaction times over the task as a whole. There was, however, no such relationship, $r = -.162$, $p = .39$. It is therefore reasonable to conclude that the degree of slowing observed following a tone was significantly greater (both in absolute and proportionate terms) in the more "automatic" fixed sequence condition.

Effects of a cue on subsequent accuracy

The results from Experiments 1 and 2 suggest that the presentation of the cue is followed by a period of greater attentional control during which errors are less likely. The lack of clear carry-over effects from cued to un-cued conditions suggests this is rather short-lived, at least in the context of this particular task. In order to examine whether the cue acted to improve accuracy on subsequent no-go trial presentations in the random SART condition of Experiment 3, the data from all participants were pooled. No-go trials were sorted into two groups based on their "distance" in go-trials from a preceding tone. As the mean inter-no-go trial interval in the task is eight, no-go trials were defined as being "post-cue" if a tone had been presented within one of the preceding four trials. If no tone had been presented, they were defined as "un-cued". Exclusions from either category were made if another target trial or error of omission had occurred within the previous four trials.

Over the participant group as a whole, 119 targets fell into the "post-cue" bin and 118 into the "un-cued" bin. Errors of commission occurred on 30 of the post-cue trials and on 45 of the "un-cued" trials—a statistically significant difference, $\chi^2 = 4.58$, $p < .05$. The result suggests that cueing indeed increased the probability of successfully controlled responses—but again indicates that the results are rather short-lived in the context of the SART.

As might be expected given the highly predictable occurrence of the no-go trial, errors of commission were much lower in the fixed sequence version: mean = 1.13 (5%); SD 1.36, range 0–6. It is perhaps a notable indication of the extent to which control over responses could lapse, given the ease of the task, that they occurred at all. The relative rarity of errors, however, together with the more constrained presentation of the tone within trials 5, 6, 7, 8, or 9 precludes a useful analysis of error probability relative to cue presentation in this condition.

Discussion

In Experiment 2 the number of alerting tones presented to participants varied. In this study a fixed number of tones were used in an otherwise standard SART condition. The results replicated those of the previous experiment. The presentation of a tone caused a transient but significant slowing in reaction time and increased the probability of effective control over responses in the immediate post-cue period.

It was hypothesised that the effects of auditory cueing might be greater during periods of more automatic or "task driven" performance. In order to encourage such a stance to the task, a version was created in which the occurrence of the rare no-go trial was made entirely predictable—the argument being that delegation to a rather inattentive way of responding would have minimal consequences for accuracy.

The reaction time data support this hypothesis. Go trials in the fixed condition had significantly faster RTs than the random-sequence condition. This suggests that response preparation/initiation was occurring much earlier within, or even in anticipation of, the trial. Compared with the random-sequence condition, the fixed-sequence was associated with a significantly greater reaction time increase following a cue tone. The lack of a relationship to the general response speed in the task suggests that this does not stem purely from very fast responders but holds across the group.

GENERAL DISCUSSION

The results of these studies have shown:

1. On a simple go-no-go computerised measure designed to encourage "slips of action", patients who had suffered a right hemisphere stroke and who experienced problems in maintaining attention in everyday activities performed more poorly than age-matched controls. As with previous studies with traumatically brain injured people, the patients' response speed on go trials did not differ from that of the control group.
2. Presenting periodic auditory cues during task performance as a reminder to retain control over responding significantly reduced commission error rates in both patients and neurologically healthy volunteers. Errors of omission (failing to respond on go trials) were unaffected—strongly suggesting that the effect is not simply due to a generally reduced tendency to respond.
3. In experiment 1, however, the presentation of auditory cues was contingent upon "on-line" speeding in reaction times—previous research suggested this to be a useful, if approximate, marker of waning attention to task. As this link was explicit in the instructions, and as significant slowing was observed in the cued condition, it is possible that the accuracy gains

were simply related to generally slowed response production. Given the observed improvements in neurologically healthy participants as well as in patients in Experiment 1, this issue was explored further within the normal population in Experiment 2.

4. The results of Experiment 2 show that improvements in participants' control over their responses occurred even if the link between RT and cues was not made explicit and, indeed, even when the presentation of cues was unrelated to changes in response speed. The absence of any significant difference in overall response speed between cued and un-cued conditions suggests that a general slowing in response production cannot completely account for the accuracy improvements.

5. Finer grained analysis showed that the presentation of an auditory cue was associated with an immediate and temporary hiatus in the production of the subsequent response. This both serves as an indicator that the tones were detected by the participants and suggests that disruption to on-going responding may be an important stage in the re-assertion of more attentive control. The negative relationship between the magnitude of the immediate slowing effect and the number of tones presented suggests that the novelty or salience of the cue plays a role in this process.

6. Based on theoretical views on the relationship between automatic, routine responding and response to novelty, it was hypothesised that the disruption to on-going responding may be greatest if that behaviour had become increasingly "driven" by the repetitive task. In Experiment 3, this was assessed by contrasting two versions of the SART task. In the standard random digit sequence condition, the occurrence of the no-go trial was entirely unpredictable such that participants should ideally maintain a high level of control for each trial. In the fixed-sequence condition, the occurrence of the no-go trial was made completely predictable. Under these circumstances, allowing one's responses to be driven by the task over the 88% of trials where there would be no requirement to withhold an action was considered a more likely strategy. The significantly faster and apparently anticipatory RTs associated with the fixed condition were consistent with this view. In line with the hypothesis, the disruptive effect on subsequent RT was significantly higher within the fixed condition.

There are a number of candidate mechanisms that may underpin the observed improvements. It has been extensively demonstrated, for example, that immediate auditory or visual warnings can reduce RTs on reaction time tasks—helping participants to develop a "readiness to respond" that would otherwise wane during the interval between target presentations. Due to the increased number of false positive responses observed following such cues, this "alerting" is primarily viewed as lowering the *threshold* for responses, rather than as speeding processing (Posner & Snyder, 1975). The results from the SART are slightly at odds with this operational definition. First, the tone had no predictive value for the presentation of a no-go trial. Second, if there were an undifferentiated reduction in the threshold for *responding*, it would be expected that errors of commission would increase. Finally, it might be assumed that in the context of a go-no-go task, where withholding responses is as important as RT to go trials, alerting might *increase* the threshold for response production. The results of Experiment 2 show no such evidence—either in terms of a general increase in RT or an increased tendency not to respond to go trials.

A second related possibility is that the presentation of the tone acted to increase what might be termed "arousal". Beginning in the 1940s and 1950s, early research on attention often focused on the vigilance task (long and rather boring periods of monitoring a stream of information for the occurrence of a rare target (e.g., Mackworth, 1948). A number of studies examining the effects of environmental noise, adverse temperatures or even physical vibration of the participants found, rather paradoxically, that these distractions could actually *enhance* performance (Davies, Lang, & Shackleton, 1973; Kirk & Hecht, 1963; McGrath, 1963; Poulton, 1977; Warner, 1969; Warner & Heimstra, 1973; Woodhead, 1964)—findings that were generally interpreted in terms of increased arousal. Recently reported improvements in the allocation of spatial attention following the presentation of a (non-spatially predictive) tone among unilateral neglect patients has similarly been attributed to increases in phasic (short-term) arousal (Robertson, Mattingley, Rorden, & Driver, 1998).

The account we propose does not preclude the involvement of such "low level" processes but rather gives emphasis to the effect of the cue within a "supervisory" attentional/executive cognitive architecture. Although there is considerable terminological and conceptual blurring between "attentional", "working memory", and "central executive" processes (Baddeley, 1993), a common theme is that of limited capacity—if we are attending to one thing it is difficult to attend to another, if we are remembering one thing it is difficult to remember another, if we are thinking about one thing it is difficult to think about another, and so on. One consequence is that, if the executive system becomes engaged in one activity, it may be difficult without external intrusion or the obvious completion of that activity, for it to move on to another. In accounting for why we generally do not get "stuck in set", it has therefore been necessary to postulate a monitoring function within the executive system that uses some of the available capacity to keep "an eye out" for overall goals or other activities in which we might engage (e.g., Petrides, 1998; Shallice & Burgess, 1993; Stuss, Shallice, Alexander, & Picton, 1995). If this system is deficient, or overall capacity is restricted, the role of external intrusions that can disrupt current processing and allow potential other goals to compete for expression may be much more crucial. An ideal interruption in this respect would be sufficiently salient to intrude on current activity but have insufficient interest or content to itself divert the system for long from its intended goals. It is notable that a number of studies have shown that the beneficial effects of environmental noise or adverse temperature on vigilance performance were greatest when the stimulus was changing (intermittent noise or shifts in temperature) and therefore, presumably, more salient in briefly capturing attention but not forming a continual distraction (Davies et al., 1973; McGrath, 1963; Warner & Heimstra, 1973).

It seems quite possible that chance events serve this function for many of us for much of the time. To argue by example, let us assume that your mind had wandered from this article to the contemplation of a pleasant memory. If a door slammed nearby, once over your brief startle, would you be more likely to return to your intended goal than if it had not occurred? If you had planned to post a letter on your way home, is the expression of that plan more likely if other preoccupying issues are repeatedly disrupted during your walk? In other words, although distraction may have a deleterious effect on the performance on demanding activities, periodic interruption may serve a useful role in our overall "goal management".

The application of this basic idea to the observed effects in the SART are clear. Periodic and (relatively) unexpected tones could act to disrupt ongoing response production. Action is then resumed with a more controlled, "top-down" stance in which errors of commission are less likely—at least for a while before a subsequent lapse occurs. In addition to the observed improvements in accuracy, the reaction time, tone rarity and "automaticity" of preceding response are consistent with this view. This begs the question of whether the instructions to *"try and be aware of what you are doing in the task"* following the tone, were useful in facilitating this potentially rather automatic effect. While the relevant tests to examine this point have not yet been conducted, it is possible to argue that this instruction may produce benefits in two ways. First, it may act to reduce possibly distracting curiosity about why the tones are being presented, allowing participants to more quickly return to the task at hand. Second, it seems likely that repeated exposure to the tone over a long testing session could lead to habituation of more automatic orienting responses. By imbuing the tone with an additional, task-relevant meaning, such reductions may be attenuated—in much the same way as the ringing of a telephone remains "disruptive" to other activity because it has meaning.

One advantage of these studies, unrelated to any potential future rehabilitative intervention, is the information they provide about *why* participants are bad at the task. Performance on go-no-go tests, such as the SART, are often quite reasonably interpreted in terms of a "response inhibition capacity". Elegant approaches (using the somewhat different "stop-signal" paradigm) can be used to estimate this capacity based on RT to go trials and the accuracy on withhold trials (Logan, Schachar, & Tannock, 1997). In previous studies with the SART, however, as the name implies, poor performance has been interpreted mainly in terms of a poorly maintained attentional stance to the task (Manly et al., 1999, 2000, 2001; Robertson et al., 1997). The difficulty is that, in principle, deficiencies in either putative capacity could result in poor performance. Impaired response inhibition could lead to errors despite adequately maintained attention while poor sustained attention could undermine otherwise adequate response inhibition. The fact that tones cueing people to maintain attention (but which had no direct predictive value for no-go trials) lead to significant improvements in accuracy *without* significantly slowing go reaction times or leading to an *increase* in "false positive" withheld responses suggests some form of sustained attentional state is important in modulating response inhibition outcome. In future studies, using variants on the stop-signal paradigm, a more quantitative approach to separating these postulated components could be applied.

It is important to stress that these studies are not directly rehabilitative. Quite apart from improvements on the SART being unlikely to appear on many patients' lists of goals, it was notable that in Experiment 1, for example, the gains in accuracy in the cued condition were not even maintained over subsequent un-cued blocks. It is certainly difficult to conceive of many real-life situations where the goal is as simple and determined as that in the test and where the frequency of cueing used here would be practicable or even tolerable. Other studies, however, provide some optimism on the potential value of such techniques. Evans, Emslie, and Wilson (1998), for example, report the case of a woman who experienced predominantly frontal brain damage. Although her memory functions were generally well preserved, she had trouble in acting on her plans. She was given a pager that automatically cued her to perform key activities at the appropriate time (originally designed for densely amnesic patients—see Wilson et al., 1997a, 1997b). Her level of goal attainment significantly increased, often, it appeared, without her even needing to see the content of the messages. Either the sudden presentation of the salient alarm or the anticipated content of the message—or both—were acting in some way to facilitate links between her intentions and her actions.

Manly et al. (2002) examined the performance of TBI patients on a multitasking test designed to replicate at least some aspects of complex real-life situations. In the test, the patients were asked to attempt at least some of five different tasks over a 15-min period. As each task in isolation would take more than the total time available to complete, the test emphasised patients' ability to keep track of the overall goal and to flexibly switch between the tests at appropriate moments. In the standard version of the task, as with previous studies (Shallice & Burgess, 1991; Wilson et al., 1996), the patients had significant difficulties, showing a tendency to neglect the overall goal and get "caught up" in one of the activities. When, however, periodic and rather intrusive auditory tones were played at random intervals during the task, the patients performance was indistinguishable from that of an IQ-matched control group. As with the studies presented here, it seemed that the intrusion of the tone into current activity facilitated patients pausing to take an overview of the situation and to adjust their actions.

It should be noted that, in the current studies, the "training" component was cursory, amounting to a single instruction—"if you hear the tone, think about what you are doing". We would certainly argue that, if portable devices are to have a role in effectively cueing moments of "general" executive review (What am I doing? What are my goals?) then this should be conducted in the context of a broader, systematic rehabilitative approach. For example, combining automated cueing with Goal Management Training (Levine et al., 2000), Problem Solving Training (Von Cramon et al., 1991) or variants of these techniques, could have additive benefits. The association of the learned meta-cognitive routine with a distinctive tone, through imbuing it with meaning, could act against habituation to the tone or even make the cognitive strategy a rather automatic, habitual response to its occurrence. At the same time, we have discussed some of the potential barriers to dysexecutive patients actually making use of strategies that they have learned in the clinic when faced with complex, real-world situations. The use of portable devices to provide periodic cues to engage in these processes may serve a valuable role in fostering generalisation.

REFERENCES

Baddeley, A. D. (1993). Working memory or working attention. In A. D. Baddeley & L. Weiskrantz (Eds.), *Attention: Selection, awareness and control: A tribute to Donald Broadbent* (pp. 152–170). Oxford: Oxford University Press.

Broadbent, D. B., Cooper, P. F., FitzGerald, P., & Parkes, K. R. (1982). The Cognitive Failures Questionnaire (CFQ) and its correlates. *British Journal of Clinical Psychology*, *21*, 1–16.

Burgess, P. W. (1997). Theory and methodology in executive function research. In P. Rabbitt (Ed.), *Methodology of frontal and executive function* (pp. 81–111). Hove, UK: Psychology Press.

Burgess, P. W., & Shallice, T. (1996a). Bizarre responses, rule detection and frontal lobe lesions. *Cortex*, *32*(2), 241–259.

Burgess, P. W., & Shallice, T. (1996b). Response suppression, initiation and strategy use following frontal lobe lesions. *Neuropsychologia*, *34*, 263–273.

Cohen, J., MacWhinney, B., Flatt, M., & Jefferson, P. (1993). PsyScope: An interactive graphic system for designing and controlling experiments in the psychology laboratory using Macintosh Computers. *Behaviour Research Methods, Instruments and Computers*, *25*(2), 257–271.

Cohen, R. M., & Semple, W. E. (1988). Functional localization of sustained attention. *Neuropsychiatry, Neuropsychology and Behavioural Neurology*, *1*, 3–20.

Davies, D. R., Lang, L., & Shackleton, V. J. (1973). The effects of music and task difficulty on performance at a visual vigilance task. *British Journal of Psychology, 78*, 304–306.

Duncan, J. (1993). Selection of input and goal in the control of behaviour. In A. D. Baddeley & L. Weiskrantz (Eds.), *Attention: Selection, awareness and control: A tribute to Donald Broadbent* (pp. 53–71). Oxford: Oxford University Press.

Evans, J. J., Emslie, H., & Wilson, B. A. (1998). External cueing systems in the rehabilitation of executive impairments of action. *Journal of the International Neuropsychological Society, 4*, 399–408.

James, W. (1890). *The principles of psychology* (Vol. 2). New York: Dover (1950; reprint of original edition published by Henry Holt & Co.).

Kirk, R. E., & Hecht, E. (1963). Maintenance of vigilance by programmed noise. *Perceptual and Motor Skills, 16*, 553–560.

Levine, B., Robertson, I. H., Clare, L., Carter, G., Hong, J., Wilson, B. A., Duncan, J., & Stuss, D. T. (2000). Rehabilitation of executive functioning: An experimental-clinical validation of Goal Management Training. *Journal of the International Neuropsychological Society, 6*, 299–312.

Logan, G. D., Schachar, R. J., & Tannock, R. (1997). Impulsivity and inhibitory control. *Psychological Science, 8*(1), 60–64.

Mackworth, N. H. (1948). The breakdown of vigilance during prolonged visual search. *Quarterly Journal of Experimental Psychology, 1*(1), 6–21.

Manly, T., Davison, B., Heutink, J., Galloway, M., & Robertson, I. (2000). Not enough time or not enough attention? Speed, error and self-maintained control in the Sustained Attention to Response Test (SART). *Clinical Neuropsychological Assessment, 3*, 167–177.

Manly, T., Hawkins, K., Evans, J. J., Woldt, K., & Robertson, I. H. (2002). Rehabilitation of executive function: Facilitation of effective goal management on complex tasks using periodic auditory alerts. *Neuropsychologia, 40*(3), 271–281.

Manly, T., Lewis, G. H., Robertson, I. H., Watson, P. C., & Datta, A. K. (2001). Coffee in the cornflakes: Time-of-day, routine response control and subjective sleepiness. *Neuropsychologia, 40*(1), 747–758.

Manly, T., Robertson, I. H., Galloway, M., & Hawkins, K. (1999). The absent mind: Further investigations of sustained attention to response. *Neuropsychologia, 37*, 661–670.

McGrath, J. J. (1963). Irrelevant stimulation and vigilance performance. In D. N. Buckner & J. J. McGrath (Eds.), *Vigilance: A symposium*. New York: McGraw-Hill.

Norman, D. A., & Shallice, T. (1980). *Attention to action: Willed and automatic control of behaviour*. (Tech. Rep. No. 99). London: Centre for Human Information Processing.

Pardo, J. V., Fox, P. T., & Raichle, M. E. (1991). Localization of a human system for sustained attention by positron emission tomography. *Nature, 349*, 61–64.

Petrides, M. (1998). Specialized systems for the processing of mnemonic information within the primate frontal cortex. In A. C. Roberts, T. W. Robbins, & L. Weiskrantz (Eds.), *The prefrontal cortex: Executive and cognitive functions*. Oxford: Oxford University Press.

Posner, M. I., & Snyder, C. R. R. (1975). Facilitation and inhibition in the processing of signals. In P. M. A. Rabbitt & S. Dornic (Eds.), *Attention and performance, V* (pp. 669–682). London: Academic Press.

Poulton, E. C. (1977). Arousing stresses increase vigilance. In R. R. Mackie (Ed.), *Vigilance: Theory, operational performance and physiological correlates* (pp. 423–460). New York: Plenum Press.

Robertson, I. H., Manly, T., Andrade, J., Baddeley, B. T., & Yiend, J. (1997). "Oops!": Performance correlates of everyday attentional failures in traumatic brain injured and normal subjects. *Neuropsychologia, 35*(6), 747–758.

Robertson, I. H., Mattingley, J. M., Rorden, C., & Driver, J. (1998). Phasic alerting of neglect patients overcomes their spatial deficit in visual awareness. *Nature, 395*, 169–172.

Robertson, I. H., Ward, A., Ridgeway, V., & Nimmo-Smith, I. (1994). *Test of Everyday Attention*. Bury St Edmunds, UK: Thames Valley Test Company.

Robertson, I. H., Ward, A., Ridgeway, V., & Nimmo-Smith, I. (1996). The structure of normal human attention: The Test of Everyday Attention. *Journal of the International Neuropsychological Society, 2*, 523–534.

Rueckert, L., & Grafman, J. (1996). Sustained attention deficits in patients with right frontal lesions. *Neuropsychologia, 34*(10), 953–963.

Shallice, T. (1988). *From neuropsychology to mental structure*. Cambridge: Cambridge University Press.

Shallice, T., & Burgess, P. (1991). Deficit in strategy application following frontal lobe damage in man. *Brain, 114*, 727–741.

Shallice, T., & Burgess, P. W. (1993). Supervisory control of action and thought selection. In A. D. Baddeley & L. Weiskrantz (Eds.), *Attention: Selection, awareness and control: A tribute to Donald Broadbent* (pp. 171–187). Oxford: Oxford University Press.

Shallice, T., & Burgess, P. (1996). The domain of supervisory processes and temporal organisation of behaviour. *Philosophical Transactions of the Royal Society of London, 351*, 1405–1412.

Stuss, D. T., Shallice, T., Alexander, M. P., & Picton, T. W. (1995). A multidisciplinary approach to anterior attentional functions. *Annals of the New York Academy of Sciences, 769*, 191–209.

von Cramon, D. Y., & Matthes-von Cramon, G. (1992). Reflections on the treatment of brain-injured patients suffering from problem-solving disorders. *Neuropsychological Rehabilitation, 2*, 207–230.

von Cramon, D., Matthes-von Cramon, G., & Mai, N. (1991). Problem-solving deficits in brain-injured patients: A therapeutic approach. *Neuropsychological Rehabilitation, 1*, 45–64.

Warner, H. D. (1969). Effects of intermittent noise on human target detection. *Human Factors, 11*, 245–249.

Warner, H. D., & Heimstra, N. W. (1973). Target-detection performance as a function of noise intensity and task difficulty. *Perceptual and Motor Skills, 36*, 439–442.

Wilkins, A. J., Shallice, T., & McCarthy, R. (1987). Frontal lesions and sustained attention. *Neuropsychologia, 25*, 359–365.

Wilson, B. A., Alderman, N., Burgess, P. W., Emslie, H., & Evans, J. (1996). *Behavioural Assessment of the Dysexecutive Syndrome*. Bury St Edmunds, UK: Thames Valley Test Company.

Wilson, B., Emslie, H., Quirk, K., & Evans, J. (1997a). Reducing everyday memory and planning paging system: A randomised control crossover study. *Journal of Neurology, Neurosurgery and Psychiatry, 63*, 113–115.

Wilson, B. A., Emslie, H., Quirk, K., & Evans, J. (1999). George: Learning to live independently with Neuropage. *Rehabilitation Psychology, 44*(3), 284–296.

Wilson, B. A., Evans, J. J., Emslie, H., & Malinek, V. (1997b). Evaluation of NeuroPage: A new memory aid. *Journal of Neurology, Neurosurgery, and Psychiatry, 63*, 113–115.

Woodhead, M. M. (1964). Searching a visual display in intermittent noise. *Journal of Sound and Vibration, 1*, 157–161.

NEUROPSYCHOLOGICAL REHABILITATION, 2004, *14* (1/2), 117–134

A cognitive prosthesis and communication support for people with dementia

Norman Alm[1], Arlene Astell[2], Maggie Ellis[2], Richard Dye[1], Gary Gowans[3], and Jim Campbell[3]

[1] *Division of Applied Computing, University of Dundee, Dundee, Scotland*

[2] *School of Psychology, University of St Andrews, St Andrews, Scotland*

[3] *Department of Computer-Aided Design, Duncan of Jordanstone College of Art and Design, University of Dundee, Dundee, Scotland*

Computers may have the potential to augment human cognitive processes in ways that could be beneficial for people with dementia. This possibility is being investigated by a multidisciplinary team. Previous work on improving the performance of augmentative communication systems for non-speaking people has shown the value of conversation modelling and prompting in this setting. The impairment of short-term memory with dementia causes serious difficulties in communication. A conversation support and prompting system is being developed based on an interactive multimedia reminiscence presentation. Reminiscence has been chosen as a basis for the conversations because long-term memories can remain relatively intact with dementia, even where short-term memory is ineffective. Initial trials of the system involving people with dementia and their carers have shown that such a system can maintain the interest and active participation of a person with dementia, and increase carers' enjoyment of the interaction. Further work will focus on directing the impact of multimedia towards increasing the quantity and quality of the communication taking place.

Correspondence should be addressed to Norman Alm, Division of Applied Computing, University of Dundee, Dundee DD1 4HN, Scotland.

The first stages of this work were partially funded by the British Council in Japan and through a Lloyds TSB Foundation for Scotland/Royal Society of Edinburgh Research Fellowship. The current multimedia reminiscence project is funded by the Engineering and Physical Sciences Research Council, under the EQUAL programme. The advice, assistance and participation of Alzheimer Scotland Action on Dementia and Dundee City Council Social Work Department have been essential to this work.

http://www.tandf.co.uk/journals/pp/09602011.html DOI:10.1080/09602010343000147

THE POTENTIAL OF THE COMPUTER AS A COGNITIVE PROSTHESIS

The potential of computers to augment human intellect has long been noted (Engelbart, 1963). The term "cognitive prosthesis" has been applied to this relationship along with a useful description of how this might operate in practice (Kirsh, Levine, Fallon-Krueger, & Jarros, 1987). A cognitive prosthesis should provide a compensatory strategy for people with an impairment in cognitive processing which, when added to the user's environment, increases their ability to function effectively. Cole and his colleagues have devised such compensatory systems for people with acquired cognitive impairments, and they emphasise the need for highly personalisable systems (Cole, 1999). It has been speculated that advances in technology could eventually allow a cognitive prosthesis system to act as a "companion" for a person with cognitive impairments, helping them by monitoring their activities and offering appropriate prompts and advice (Vanderheiden, 1990).

One area in which the cognitive prosthesis approach has been taken is in assisting non-speaking people to communicate. It is necessary for the systems developed in this field to operate at the level of cognitive prostheses if realistic rates of communication are to be achieved (Alm, Waller, & Newell, 1996). Here the potential for computers to act as a kind of scaffolding to support communication and other cognitive tasks is beginning to be realised. Arnott points out that in this regard it will be important to draw clear boundaries between the person and the computer so that the person is ultimately in overall control, even if the computer is performing cognitive tasks on their behalf (Arnott, 1990).

Computers do therefore seem to have the potential to support cognitive tasks, taking over functions that have been affected by illness, accident, or ageing. Computers might also provide prompts for daily living, if they were able to track successfully the user's sequence of tasks and actions. One problem of growing prominence to which this could be usefully applied is in supplying support for elderly people with dementia and their carers. We have been working with this idea in a number of exploratory projects, building on our previous work in helping non-speaking people to communicate through computer-based systems.

SUPPORTING COMMUNICATION IN PHYSICALLY IMPAIRED NON-SPEAKING PEOPLE

People who are unable to speak due to physical impairment have benefited greatly from the development of computer-generated communication support, particularly in addressing the problem of rate of speech production. Current speech output technology limits severely physically impaired non-speaking people to speak at a much slower rate, typically 2–10 words per minute, compared with the 150–200 words per minute common in unimpaired speech. In an attempt to improve this, computers have been used to augment or even replace some of the cognitive aspects of communication. Based on theories generated to explain the cognitive processes underlying communication, one useful approach derives from the pragmatics of language use. Although the complexities of communication are incompletely understood, the functionality of communication systems for non-speaking people can be effectively improved. Focusing on the pragmatic use of language, that is, language as it is used in context, brings a "top-down" approach to communication, away from the more traditional "bottom-up" approach, which emphasises the word-by-word building blocks of utterances. This may well be a realistic simulation of the natural process, since the production of speech by an unimpaired speaker occurs at such a rate that conscious processing and controlling of the speech at a micro-level is not possible. In common with other learned skills, speech is produced to some extent automatically, with the speaker being aware of giving high-level instructions to the speech production system, but leaving the details of its implementation to the system (Higginbotham & Wilkins, 1999).

A number of projects have investigated the utility of focusing on pragmatics in increasing speech output rate. By using pre-stored conversational material, the communication rate can be substantially increased. For instance, the CHAT prototype (Alm, Arnott, & Newell, 1992) gave the user the ability to move easily through the more formulaic stages of daily interactions, such as openings, closings, and giving feedback to other speakers. Another system, TALK, experimented with modelling the way in which topic shifting occurs in a step-wise fashion during a casual conversation (Alm, Todman, Elder, & Newell, 1993). Work has also been carried out investigating the usefulness of providing "scripts" (Dye et al., 1998) and "frames" (Higginbotham et al., 2000) for use in common everyday situations.

What unites these projects is the provision of a partial model of communication to the user. This model basically comprises a structure within which reusable utterances are stored. Because the structure closely follows the way a natural conversation proceeds, utterances are made available to the user in a timely and appropriate way. Given such a structure in order to make it easier for users to have the right utterance at the right time, it is clear that the same structure could act as a "prompt" for communication, as well as being a passive store of useful utterances. The desirability of prompting conversational directions is the topic of hot debate, given that the overall intention of computer assistance is to improve the individual's control of conversation. Because the amount of conversational control possible at 2–10 words per minute is severely restricted, this argument seems to be a matter of judgement about trade-offs. It is relevant to note, however, that opportunism is a feature of a great deal of casual conversation in any case.

One attempt to examine the benefit and desirability of prompting looked at people with acquired aphasia (Waller et al., 1995). Here the participants' communication difficulties were compounded by problems in the cognitive processes that support communication, thus emphasising the cognitive prosthesis role of the computer. The system contained stored personal narratives, entered by the person with aphasia with the help of family members. Once entered, the narratives could be called up by the person and spoken out sentence by sentence, to facilitate interaction. These sessions were enjoyed both by the person using the system and their conversation partners. This provision of prompts for communication, using a model of communication as interaction, has potential application to the progressive cognitive and communication difficulties faced by people with dementia.

THE CHALLENGE OF DEMENTIA

As the proportion of the elderly population in many countries is increasing sharply, the number of older people who have dementia or other difficulties and are in need of support in their daily life will correspondingly increase. The numbers of people in the UK over the age of 65 are predicted to increase from 9.25 million in 1996 to 12 million in 2021. The number of people aged over 75 will have doubled and the number over 90 will have more than tripled. The USA Census Bureau states that the chances of having a disability increases with age, and shows that more than half of the population who are 65 or over have a disability (US Bureau of the Census, 1995). A significant proportion of these disabilities are cognitive in nature. Currently, it is estimated worldwide that after the age of 65 there is a steep increase in the incidence of dementia, rising to nearly one in four of those over 85 (Jorm, Korten, & Henderson, 1987). These rates of dementia have significant social and economic implications for the affected individuals themselves, their families and for the wider community. In addition, living with dementia poses a range of practical, physical and psychological problems that require support for both the person with dementia and their caregivers. Basic activities of daily living, as well as communication and a range of cognitive abilities can all be affected. Consequently, quality of life and well-being of both people with dementia and their carers are adversely affected. Creative solutions will be required to meet the significant challenge of coping with dementia.

Of all of the realms affected by dementia, arguably the most significant impact is on communication (Azuma & Bayles, 1997). Given the impairment of short-term memory common in dementia, holding and maintaining conversations becomes progressively difficult. Many social activities and interactions become increasingly difficult, as they depend on a working short-term memory for effective participation. As such, people with dementia can become socially isolated and deprived of the range and variety of social interactions that characterise everyday life for unimpaired people. Finding ways to promote communication in people with dementia is therefore vitally important for a number of reasons. First, communication is such a fundamental part of being human that when people are no longer able to communicate successfully they are treated as somehow less than human. This "dehumanisation" is, sadly, commonly seen in the treatment of people with dementia (Kitwood, 1990). Second, caring for someone with dementia can be frustrating and upsetting. When communication fails, carers are left to infer intention and meaning from behaviour and this can have negative consequences, such as believing incorrectly that someone is deliberately being difficult. Third, there is a progressive and uneven breakdown in communicative abilities in dementia. Thus the apparent loss of some abilities does not mean a person can no longer communicate altogether. Consequently, interventions must be targeted at the relatively intact functions (Astell & Harley, 1998, 2002; Azuma & Bayles, 1997; Rau, 1993).

REMINISCENCE AS A COMMUNICATION SUPPORT

Short-term memory impairments in dementia make various aspects of conversation very difficult and frustrating for the conversation partner. However, activities that do not require the person with dementia to keep a conversation topic active can provide a satisfying and interesting interaction for both parties. The provision of such positive interactions, at whatever level they are understood by people with dementia, can be considered as successful interventions (Woods, 1994). In addition, they can improve the relationship between carers and people with dementia, which is an appropriate aim in dementia care (Jackson, 1991). To do this successfully, two conditions must be met. First, it is important to discover ways of continuing to interact with the person with dementia that provide carers with a picture of the whole person and not just a set of needs. Second, methods of interaction must give the person with dementia a chance to experience satisfying communication.

One technique that has proved effective for both the person with dementia and caregivers is reminiscence work (Baines, Saxby, & Ehlert, 1987; Finnema, Dröes, Ribb, & Van Tilburg, 1999). Reminiscence takes advantage of the fact that long-term memory may be relatively intact, even where a person's short-term memory is severely affected. Reminiscence sessions are typically carried out by creating a scrapbook of photos and other memorabilia, and may incorporate audio and videotapes. These materials act not only as a memory aid, but also as a support to communication. They partly replace the person's own lost abilities to deal with immediate memories (such as what they said five minutes ago), while encouraging them to employ their still effective long-term memory (such as what happened 40 years ago).

Reminiscence is of course a natural and valuable form of interaction for older people in general. It can give them "dignity, a sense of purpose, in going back over their lives and passing on valuable information to a younger generation" (Thompson, 1978). In addition, "reminiscence [may serve] ... a variety of goals, including increased communication and socialisation, and providing pleasure and entertainment" (Woods, 1999). As well as being valuable to older people in general, reminiscence can act to empower older people who have dementia (Feil, 1993; Sheridan, 1992). Thus, reminiscence provides not only a tool to stimulate interaction, but also a contribution to improved quality of life for people with dementia and their families. Indeed the main impact of reminiscence may be the positive effect it has on general communication (Woods, 1994).

POSSIBILITIES FOR MULTIMEDIA

Recent work using videos to present life histories for people with dementia suggests that new technologies, where sensitively and appropriately applied, can add substantially to supportive and therapeutic activities (Cohen, 2000). Multimedia systems have the potential to provide a richness of interaction that is particularly appropriate for those elderly people with diminishing sensory and intellectual capabilities. There is potential for the communication of people with severely diminished short-term memory to benefit significantly through computer-aided reminiscence.

A reminiscence experience based on a computer, using multimedia techniques, may provide a livelier and more engaging activity for people who struggle with spontaneous interactions. This has the potential to enhance the communication support typically associated with reminiscence activities and build on them. Reminiscence sessions traditionally make use of a variety of separate media. It can be very time-consuming searching for a particular photograph, music, sound or film clip. Bringing all of these media together into a multimedia system could mean a more integrated framework for a reminiscence session and save valuable time. Multimedia technology affords the seamless inclusion of text, photographs, graphics, sound and film recordings, and also the ability to link the various items together in a dynamic and flexible way. "The key question is how can this technology be harnessed to facilitate learning and human endeavour?" (Preece, 1993). Effective design is the answer if the potential benefits of multimedia are to be reaped.

Valuable experience has been gained from the success of a "hypermedia" (information link) structure in establishing the popularity of the World Wide Web on the Internet. The user is invited to interact with the material presented in a more lively way than by just looking at text and pictures on a page. Interestingly, the highly flexible and multidimensional nature of hypermedia, which has been cited as a potential navigation problem for users, may in fact be of benefit for people with memory loss, in that it does not put any penalty on "losing the place" (Alm, Arnott, & Newell, 1990; Conklin, 1987; McKerlie & Preece, 1992; Peiris, Gregor, & Alm, 2000). Whatever place the user is in is the right place to be. Exploring and "getting lost" are actively encouraged as strategies to enjoy experiencing the material. The design challenge for a multimedia system that could act as a communication support is to make the interface engaging while at the same time prompting conversation away from the screen. The idea is for the user to be prompted into talking about something relevant to their own experience, and when they are finished, to help them quickly locate another topic which they would like to talk about. In this way, the multimedia display should act as far as possible as a kind of adjunct visual and auditory memory for the person with cognitive difficulties.

Pilot studies

Work has been carried out through a number of projects at Dundee University to test the feasibility and effectiveness of such a multimedia reminiscence system and communication support. It is essential that such a system is easy to operate by both carers and people with dementia. It is also important that the experience offered is one that can be enjoyed without relying on short-term memory.

Interactive games

A number of computer-based games have been developed to address a range of issues pertinent to the development of a computer-based reminiscence and conversation aid. First, is to investigate different ways of interacting with a computer system. Second, is to explore ways of engaging the attention of people with dementia. Third, is to examine ways of providing entertainment for people with dementia. These games have been developed in consultation with people with dementia and their carers, and were evaluated by them. The games took as their starting point a board game for people with dementia to enjoy with their families and friends. The game has no competitive element, nor finishing point, and does not rely on memory for successful play (Cohen, 2000). We developed two prototype computer-based games with similar features. They invited the user to press a button on the touch screen, which then activated an animation sequence and music. This sequence ended in the production of a graphic and some text, which was designed to elicit comments from the user. In use, these simple computer games demonstrated the effectiveness of touch screens with people who were not familiar with computers, including people with dementia. The games proved to be engaging, and were enjoyed by people with dementia.

Personal web pages

In order to explore ways of presenting and organising reminiscence material for a multimedia system, a project was carried out with a group of healthy older people at a community centre who were interested in learning about computers. The project had two aims. First, to evaluate the suitability of a specially developed tool for the purpose of constructing a personal reminiscence website. Second, to investigate the acceptability of this technology to a group of older people. The tool was designed for older people to use to create a personal reminiscence website, based on both their own and publicly available material. In order to elicit personal material easily, the system used a combination of pre-stored material and material supplied by the user, including newspaper cuttings, recipes, graphics and text.

The material was assembled with the help of a structured dialogue with the user that incorporated computer-interviewing techniques. These provided an interactive question and answer session that evoked memories while allowing users the freedom to answer in their own words. The person's own material was then combined with the prestored material, and automatically compiled for them into an attractive and easy to navigate website. We concluded that presenting a tool specifically designed for older people, and one that they have a good motivation for using, can help older people with few computing skills to learn to use the new technology. As well as participating in an enjoyable reminiscence session older people were learning about computers and the World Wide Web. Creating a personal page brought about a sense of achievement in coming to terms with new technology.

This project was helpful for two reasons. First, it explored ways to help older people to use technology easily, and in a way that they found rewarding and relevant. Second, it was also an investigation of the use of multimedia to present reminiscence material in an engaging and interesting way. A process of iterative design was used, with continuous feedback from users on a series of prototypes they were shown.

Reminiscence scrapbook

A pilot study was then undertaken to determine which aspects of multimedia would be most useful for a reminiscence experience specifically for people with dementia, and the best way to present this material. A number of prototype interfaces for a multimedia reminiscence experience were developed. These included text, photographs, videos and songs from the past life of Dundee. The materials were collected with the assistance of Dundee University and Dundee City archives and library, and the Dundee Heritage

Project. The prototypes were demonstrated for people with dementia and staff at a day centre run by Alzheimers Scotland Action on Dementia. The following questions were posed and conclusions drawn from these evaluation sessions:

Is it better for the display to use the metaphor of a real-life scrapbook or just provide very simple screen display? Staff members tended to prefer the simulated scrapbook presentation. However, the preference of the people who had dementia was for the simpler screen presentation. This could be due to reduced cognitive ability whereby the simulated book presentation may be giving the person with dementia more information to process than they are comfortable with. They would first have to see the book and recognise it as such before moving on to seeing the picture.

How should the scrapbook material best be organised—by subject or by medium? The majority of the staff evaluators preferred the arrangement by subject saying it was more logical, some were unsure, but no one showed a preference for the arrangement by media. The clients with dementia echoed these views. Despite preferring the arrangement being by subject the majority of evaluators could see benefits from having access to both arrangements. It was concluded that for basic reminiscence sessions the arrangement by subject is preferable. However, access to the arrangement by media should be an option, to make the software available for use in other ways.

How does each individual medium add to the reminiscence process, and what effects are produced by the various media—sounds, pictures, videos, music? It was found that with videos the clients were only able to strongly identify with them when they triggered off specific personal memories, whereas songs and photographs were more generally appreciated. Overall, most of the videos and photographs and all the songs were able to spur conversations however. Attention stayed longest with the songs, which were particularly enjoyed when played repeatedly with everyone singing along. The staff on the other hand felt that some individual clients enjoyed particular videos most. The topic of the video clip is clearly an important determinant of how much it is enjoyed but it is too early to say what topics should be focused on.

One general finding was that the multimedia presentation produced a great deal of interest and motivation from the people with dementia. Staff were also very keen to see the idea developed further. These preliminary studies highlighted the need for a more thorough exploration of ways in which this technology can act as an effective support for satisfying conversation for people with dementia. Our current project is taking a multidisciplinary approach to addressing this issue by developing a fully functioning multimedia reminiscence experience and communication support.

THE PROJECT

This multidisciplinary project aims to develop a reminiscence system as a cognitive and communication aid. We feel it is important to take a multidisciplinary approach in order to make the multimedia reminiscence system as engaging and effective as possible. From our previous work it is apparent that such a system will need to have sophisticated and reliable software, an engaging and well-designed presentation of the media, and be based on sound psychological and social principles that underlie interactions. The development of the architecture, navigational methods, and content of the reminiscence experience, along with the collation and digitalisation of an extensive audio/visual archive of material presents a demanding design and development challenge. The researchers in this project, from St Andrews University and Dundee University (Applied Computing and Duncan of Jordanstone College of Art and Design), are drawn from the fields of computer aided design, applied computing, and the psychology of dementia. A professional graphic designer using a multimedia design package is devising the interface and visual look of the system. A software developer with human-computer interaction expertise is carrying out the design and coding of the system structure and navigation methods, designing and building the multimedia database and developing the authoring system. A psychologist is responsible for providing design guidance throughout the development of the system, for creating and maintaining links with potential users and clinical professionals, for giving feedback on the system design as it progresses, and for carrying out the formal evaluations. Dundee Social Work Department and Alzheimer Scotland Action on Dementia also provide design and content advice.

We have carried out pilot work in day-care settings into current practice in reminiscence, looking at what works best and how such sessions might be improved by a multimedia system. The findings suggest that emphasis should be placed on failure-free reminiscence activities and that these should be as relevant as possible to the individual. Contacts with managers and other staff members of both Alzheimer Scotland and Dundee Social Work Department are being maintained and ‘link’ members of staff have been identified. A group of about 40 people with dementia have been contacted to take part in evaluating the material as it is produced. A further 25 carers and family members are also taking part as sources of ideas for the system and as evaluators of it. A number of sample themes and content items that the system might include have been developed and evaluated by this group.

The identification of appropriate software and hardware has been made: A professional multimedia presentation system accessing a multimedia database and outputting through the largest commercially available LCD touch-panel display. Photographic data, film footage (both archive and contemporary), local folk songs, sounds and music, are being identified and collected. A structure for the multimedia database has been devised. Flexible scripting in the programming will ensure that the process of involvement need not be repetitive—each use of the material will be a different experience if desired, while an index or search facility will allow for more predictable options.

The iterative design process has seen the creation of a prototype system, incorporating material from sound, video and photographic archives. This initial presentation package has been demonstrated to representatives of Alzheimer Scotland and Dundee Social Work Department. We have also carried out a pilot study into the acceptability of the system to people with dementia and their carers.

Pilot study of the acceptability and accessibility of the prototype multimedia system

The aim of this pilot study was to gauge immediate reaction to the system and identify any immediate problems in using it.

Participants

Three men and three women with dementia and six carers took part. Three of the people with dementia were seen at home with their family carer and the other three were seen in day care with a member of care staff. The mean age of the people with dementia was 74.3 (range 57–95) and severity of dementia, as measured by the Mini Mental State Examination (MMSE; Folstein, Folstein, & McHugh, 1975) was an average of 15.6 (range 10–25).

Materials

Assessment was made using a structured interview and, for carers, a self-report questionnaire with a Lickert scale for responding.

Results

In the interviews all participants said they enjoyed using the system and none identified anything they did not like. When asked what they found particularly good, care staff noted the choice of material available and the effectiveness of prompting clients to speak more than usual. Family carers particularly liked the video clips and the easiness of the system to use. They all found the touch screen easy to use but there were requests for greater on-screen contrasts. One carer suggested having the option to increase text and photograph size and there was some support for having supplementary text available to facilitate discussion. It was suggested that a pause button would be useful and also to have better control over volume. From the self-report questionnaires it was established that the colours were pleasant and the text size about right. The on-screen touch buttons were usable with practice and the system as a whole easy to operate. Useful feedback was gained about video and song clip length and picture size.

Prototype evaluation

Based on these findings, a more detailed evaluation study of the system in practice was carried out. The main aim was to make a close study of the system in use by people with dementia and carers. Their interactions were recorded and all participants were asked to evaluate the session at the end. The evaluation was to address the following considerations:

1. The effect on maintaining the interest and involvement of the person with dementia
2. The impact on carers' enjoyment in keeping company with the person with dementia

Participants

Nine people with dementia were recruited, four male and four female, with a mean age of 83 years (range 65–95). Severity of dementia was measured using the MMSE, giving a mean MMSE of 16 (range 8–22). Nine care staff at five day centres were also recruited. The care staff were paired with people with dementia to participate in the multimedia reminiscence sessions.

Materials

A prototype multimedia reminiscence package presented on a 20 inch LCD touch screen was used. The package contained three categories: entertainment, recreation and local Dundee life. Media for each category included photographs, video clips, songs and music. Navigation around the system was by touch screen menus. The MMSE was carried out with all participants with dementia. Two evaluation questionnaires were designed for the multimedia package, one for use with care staff and one for participants with dementia.

Procedure

Participants with dementia were paired with a member of care staff for each session. The MMSE was carried out with the participants with dementia at the start of each session. A demonstration screen provided instructions on how to use the multimedia package. Each pair spent 20 min using the computer. At the end of each 20-min session, each person with dementia completed the evaluation questionnaire. Following this, each member of care staff completed the evaluation questionnaire.

Results

Evaluation of the multimedia reminiscence system by people with dementia. All participants said that they enjoyed the multimedia reminiscence session. When asked to expand on what they liked best, a range of replies were elicited:

1. Picture of the bathing house.
2. Football.
3. Music.
4. Dundee life.
5. Judy Garland.
6. Pictures.
7. The fact that the items are "true to life".

Of these, the last comment reflected one participant's view that the photographs were not glamorised, but actually depicted the way things used to be, in this case in the jute mills of Dundee.

Participants were asked if there was anything that they did not like about the multimedia system. All but one said "no", but when questioned further the one dissenting individual was unable to supply any further information. However, a number of general comments were elicited of direct relevance for revising the system and making it more used. These included comments on the size of the typeface, the brightness of the visual images, the size of the screen and the selection of stimuli available.

When the participants with dementia were asked if there was anything else they would like to see in the system, there was a clear desire for items of personal relevance:

1. A picture of the participant's mother.
2. A picture of the participant.
3. A picture of the participant's local football team.
4. A picture of where the participant used to live.

All of the participants with dementia had no difficulty adapting to and using the touch screen. When encouraged by their care staff partner, all people with dementia used the touch screen. They all said that they would like to use the system again in the future with two people spontaneously commenting during sessions that they were enjoying using the system.

Evaluation of the multimedia reminiscence system by care staff. All of the care staff said that they enjoyed the multimedia session and that they believed the person with dementia did too. When asked to identify what they particularly liked and what they thought the person with dementia most enjoyed, a range of responses were elicited (Table 1). These relate to both the usability of the system and the response of the clients to the system.

All of the care staff felt that the session was worthwhile both for them as carers and for the people with dementia. When asked to explain why, the responses echoed those above, relating the success of the sessions to ease of use of the system and the reactions of the clients (Table 2).

For future development of the multimedia system, the care staff reported that they would like to see more variety available. One person also suggested that personal items be included. Overall, the feedback from the care staff about the sessions they participated in was very positive. One reported the belief that the multimedia system is beneficial both to people with dementia and carers, as it is a learning experience for both. Another suggested that the effect seems to be the same as normal reminiscence, just another way of doing it. Another reported not only enjoying using the multimedia system but also being glad to be part of the project.

TABLE 1
Parts of the multimedia system care staff liked best and thought that people with dementia liked

Carers	*People with dementia*
Photographs of Dundee	Singing
Old songs	Using touch screen
The fact that the system is easy to use	Talking about memories
Client's reaction	Music
Client's interest in using the system	All of it

TABLE 2
Reasons that care staff gave for finding the multimedia reminiscence session worthwhile

For carers	*For people with dementia*
Using technology and being able to use the system	Relating to things the client liked in the past
	Client remembering younger life—remembered a lot
Finding out about things that were previously unknown about the client's history	Looking at the different items
	Bringing back memories
Having more subjects to talk about	Focus of attention on the client
Seeing the client's reaction to the multimedia	Helps client to remember
	Gives clients a chance to talk about what they want
Interesting to find out more about the client	One-to-one time
Getting a chance to spend one-to-one time	Chance for clients to reminisce about their families

DISCUSSION

These findings make a case for the use of computers to promote and maintain conversation with people with dementia. The results of the evaluation show that people with dementia can happily adapt to the technology and quickly become comfortable using it. We have shown that a multimedia reminiscence system can assist people with dementia to talk about a wide range of topics. One positive benefit of the wide range of material available is that care staff can use the system with little or no background preparation. This is very important in care settings where staff time is constantly called on. Currently, preparing for a half hour chat with a person with moderate dementia can seem like a huge chore and often therefore does not happen. However, being able to sit down and interact with someone spontaneously would be a great boon to both staff and people with dementia. Additional benefit also accrues for both parties from spending one-to-one time. One consequence for staff is increased enjoyment not only in participating in the multimedia reminiscence sessions but in spending time with the person with dementia in general. The quality of the time spent together is clearly influenced by the perceived burden of maintaining conversation that falls on staff, and the multimedia system appears to alleviate this, allowing for a positive, shared interactive experience where both parties are more equal participants.

NEXT STEPS

We still have many questions to answer in the development of a multimedia reminiscence and conversation support for people with dementia. The next stage will be to compare the effectiveness of the prototype with traditional reminiscence. This will enable us first, to identify the critical features of reminiscence to supporting conversation and the aspects of the interaction that pertain purely from being in a one-to-one situation. Second, and more importantly, we aim to separate the features that make the multimedia system different and we hope better, than traditional reminiscence.

Subsequently we aim to address the following questions:

1. Determining what value will be added to a reminiscence experience by providing multi-media capabilities.
    - Its effectiveness in facilitating reminiscence experiences as a group activity.
    - Exploring its use both as an experience in which the session is guided by a participating carer or family member, and, potentially, as a standalone system to be enjoyed by people with dementia on their own.

2. Determining the optimum way to present the experience:
   - Configurable by carer, family member.
   - Random pathways through the material chosen by the system.
   - Using hypermedia links as opposed to sequential links.
3. A study of the effect of incorporating personal material into the general collection. Effects to be examined are:
   - Degree of interest shown by the person with dementia.
   - Degree of interest shown by the carer or family member.
   - Quality of the experience in terms of (i) Amount of personal reminiscences it triggers, and (ii) Views of the experience by the person with dementia and the carer or family member.

CONCLUSION

The realisation of computers as cognitive prostheses and communication supports for people with dementia will depend on good multidisciplinary co-operation, encompassing not only the software structures needed, but also good design, and a grounding in the psychological and social realities of the situation that people with dementia find themselves in. We feel a good starting point for communication support is to exploit intact long-term memories through providing prompts and stimulation for reminiscence conversations. The work we have done on this approach so far has demonstrated that computer-based multimedia systems do seem to have the ability to engage the attention and interest of people with dementia. They are usually able to make use of touch screens to control what happens with the interface. What now needs further exploration is just what features of such an experience will work well, and what features are to be avoided, where the aim is to provide a cognitive and communicational prosthesis that supports and stimulates conversation in a way that enriches the interaction between people with dementia and others who wish to maintain contact with them.

REFERENCES

Alm, N., Arnott, J., & Newell, A. (1990). Hypertext as a host for an augmentative communication system in *Proceedings of the European Conference on the Advancement of Rehabilitation Technology* (pp. 14.4a–14.4b). Maastricht, The Netherlands: ECART.

Alm, N., Arnott, J., & Newell, A. (1992). Prediction and conversational momentum in an augmentative communication system. *Communications of the ACM, 35*(5), 46–57.

Alm, N., Todman, J., Elder, L., & Newell, A. (1993). Computer aided conversation for severely physically impaired non-speaking people. *Proceedings of INTERCHI 1993, Amsterdam* (pp. 236–241). New York: ACM Press.

Alm, N., Waller, A., & Newell, A. F. (1996). Developing computer-based cognitive prostheses. *Communication ... Naturally–Proceedings of the Fourth ISAAC Research Symposium.* Västerås, Sweden: Mälardalen University Press, pp. 157–165.

Arnott, J. L. (1990). The communication prosthesis: A problem of human–computer integration. *Proceedings of European Conference on the Advancement of Rehabilitation Technology (ECART),* Maastricht, The Netherlands, 5–8 November 1990. Contribution 3.1.

Astell, A., & Harley, T. (1998). Naming problems in dementia: Semantic or lexical? *Aphasiology, 12,* 357–374.

Astell, A., & Harley, T. (2002). The structure of semantic memory in dementia: Evidence from a word definition task. *Brain and Language, 82,* 312–326.

Azuma, T., & Bayles, J. (1997). Memory impairments underlying language difficulties in dementia. *Topics in Language Disorders, 18,* 58–71.

Baines, S., Saxby, P., & Ehlert, K. (1987). Reality orientation and reminiscence therapy: A controlled cross over study of elderly confused people. *British Journal of Psychiatry, 151,* 222–231.

Cohen, G. (2000). Two new intergenerational interventions for Alzheimer's disease patients and families. *American Journal of Alzheimer's Disease, 15*(3), 137–142.

Cole, E. (1999). Cognitive prosthetics: An overview to a method of treatment. *NeuroRehabilitation, 12.* 39–51.

Conklin, J. (1987). Hypertext: An introduction and a survey. *IEEE Computer,* 17–41.

Dye, R., Alm, N., Arnott, J. L., Harper, G., & Morrison, A. (1998). A script-based AAC system for transactional interaction. *Natural Language Engineering, 4*(1), 57–71.

Engelbart, D. C. (1963). A conceptual framework for the augmentation of man's intellect. In P. Howerton & D. Weeks (Eds.), *Vistas in information handling* (pp. 1–13). Washington, DC: Spartan Books.

Feil, N. (1993). *The Validation Breakthrough.* Baltimore: Health Professions Press.

Finnema, E., Dröes, R.-M, Ribbe, M., & Van Tilburg, W. (1999). The effects of emotion-oriented approaches in the care for persons suffering from dementia: A review of the literature. *International Journal of Geriatric Psychiatry, 15,* 141–161.

Folstein, M. F., Folstein, S. E., & McHugh, P. R. (1975). "Mini-Mental State". A practical guide for grading the cognitive state of patients for the clinician. *Journal of Psychiatric Research, 12,* 189–198.

Higginbotham, D. J., Moulton, B. J., Lesher, G. W., Wilkins, D. P., & Cornish, J. (2000). Frametalker: Development of a frame-based communication system. *Proceedings of CSUN 2000,* California State University, Northridge, USA.

Higginbotham, D. J., & Wilkins, D. P. (1999). Slipping through the timestream: Time and timing issues in augmentative communication. In J. Duchan, D. Kovarsky, & M. Maxwell (Eds.), *The social construction of language (in)competence* (pp. 49–82). Mahwah, NJ: Lawrence Erlbaum Associates, Inc.

Jackson, A. (1991). To reminisce or not to reminisce. *Irish Journal of Psychological Medicine, 8,* 147–148.

Jorm, A. F., Korten, A. E., & Henderson, A. S. (1987). The prevalence of dementia: A quantitative integration of the literature. *Acta Psychiatrica Scandinavica, 76,* 465–479.

Kirsh, N., Levine, S., Fallon-Krueger, M., & Jaros, L. (1987). The microcomputer as an "orthotic" device for patients with cognitive deficits. *Journal of Head Trauma Rehabilitation,* 2(4), 77–86.

Kitwood, T. (1990). The dialectics of dementia: With particular reference to Alzheimer's disease. *Ageing and Society, 10,* 177–196.

McKerlie, D., & Preece, J. (1992). The hypermedia effect: More than just the sum of its parts. In *Proceedings of the St. Petersburg HCI Conference,* pp. 115–127.

Peiris, R., Gregor, P., & Alm, N. (2000). The effects of simulating human conversational style in a computer-based interview. *Interacting with Computers, 12*(6), 635–650.

Preece, J. (1993). Hypermedia, multimedia and human factors. In R. Phillips (Ed.), *Interactive multimedia.* London: Kogan Page.

Rau, M. T. (1993). *Coping with communication challenges in Alzheimer's disease*. San Diego, CA: Singular Publishing Group.
Sheridan, C. (1992). *Failure-free activities for the Alzheimer's patient*. London: Macmillan Press.
Thompson, P. (1978). *The voice of the past: Oral history*. Oxford: Oxford University Press.
US Bureau of the Census (1995). *Document No. IPC/95-2*. Washington, DC: Bureau of the Census, United States Department of Commerce.
Vanderheiden, G. (1990). Applications of artificial intelligence to the needs of persons with cognitive impairments: The Companion aid. *Proceedings of RESNA International 1992* (pp. 388–390). Arlington, VA: RESNA Press.
Waller, A., Dennis, F., Cairns, A. Y., Brodie, J. K., Newell, A. F., & Morrison, K. (1995). Evaluating the use of TalksBac with non-fluent dysphasic adults. *Proceedings of RESNA '95*. Vancouver, June 1995 (pp. 109–111) Arlington, VA: RESNA Press.
Woods, R. T. (1994). Management of memory impairment in older people with dementia. *International Review of Psychiatry*, *6*, 153–161.
Woods, R. T (1999). Psychological therapies in dementia. In R. T. Woods (Ed.), *Psychological problems of ageing*. Chichester, UK: Wiley.

NEUROPSYCHOLOGICAL REHABILITATION, 2004, *14* (1/2), 135–171

The efficacy of an intelligent cognitive orthosis to facilitate handwashing by persons with moderate to severe dementia

Alex Mihailidis,[1,3] Joseph C. Barbenel,[2] and Geoff Fernie[3]

[1]*Gerontology Research Centre and Engineering Sciences, Simon Fraser University, Vancouver, British Columbia, Canada*

[2]*Bioengineering Unit, University of Strathclyde, Wolfson Centre, Glasgow, UK*

[3]*Centre for Studies in Aging, Sunnybrook & Women's College HSC, Toronto, Ontario, Canada*

Dementia reduces a person's ability to perform activities of daily living (ADL) because of the difficulty of remembering the proper sequence of events that must occur and how to use the required tools. The current solution is to have a caregiver continually provide verbal prompts. Family caregivers find assisting their loved ones to be particularly upsetting and embarrassing as it necessitates invasion of privacy and role reversal. It has been suggested that dependence on a caregiver might be improved using a cognitive orthosis that provides needed reminders and monitors progress. This paper will report on the results obtained from an efficacy study conducted with such a device.

The COACH is a prototype of an intelligent computerised device that was developed to assist people with dementia complete ADLs with less dependence on a caregiver. The device was developed using a personal computer and a single video camera to unobtrusively track a user during an ADL and provided pre-recorded verbal prompts when necessary. It was tested with 10 subjects with moderate to severe dementia during handwashing in a study

Correspondence should be addressed to Alex Mihailidis, Department of Occupational Therapy, University of Toronto, 500 University Avenue, Toronto, Ontario M5G 1V7, Canada.

Funding for this research was provided by the Alzheimer Society of Canada, Lifeline Systems Canada, and the Ontario Rehabilitation Technology Consortium (ORTC).

http://www.tandf.co.uk/journals/pp/09602011.html DOI:10.1080/09602010343000156

lasting 60 days. These trials showed that the number of handwashing steps that the subjects were able to complete without assistance from the caregiver increased overall by approximately 25% when the device was present. Individual changes ranged from approximately 10–45%. These changes were proven to be statistically significant at a 99% confidence level.

INTRODUCTION

Dementia can be defined as a condition of acquired cognitive deficits, sufficient to interfere with social or occupational functioning in a person (Patterson, 1999). There are nearly 18 million people with dementia in the world today, and by 2025, this number is expected to reach 34 million people (United Kingdom, 2001).

The effects of dementia on a person's ability to perform activities of daily living (ADL) tasks have been well documented (Cockburn & Collin, 1988; Harrell, Parente, Bellingrath, & Lisicia, 1992; Mihailidis, Fernie, & Barbenel, 2001; Mihailidis, Fernie, & Cleghorn, 2000). The current solution is to have a caregiver continually provide verbal reminders. However, this dependence is difficult to accept and often contributes to anger or helplessness. Family caregivers find assisting with toilet-related activities to be particularly upsetting and embarrassing as it necessitates invasion of privacy and role reversal.

As described in previous papers by the authors, there have been many different types of interventions that have been used to ease the stress and difficulties of caring for a person with dementia, including implementing targeted interventions, task analysis, and using various verbal prompting techniques such as the system of least prompts and time-delayed procedures (Mihailidis et al., 2001). However, none of these techniques addressed privacy and dependency issues as a caregiver was still required to be present. It has been suggested that these issues might be addressed using a computerised device (a cognitive orthosis), that automatically provides needed reminders and monitors progress.

The authors have developed a prototype of such a device. The COACH—*C*ognitive *o*rthosis for *a*ssisting a*c*tivities in the *h*ome, is an intelligent computerised device that was developed to assist people with dementia complete ADL with less dependence on a caregiver. It used artificial intelligence algorithms and a single video camera to monitor progress and provide pre-recorded verbal prompts when necessary. The device was tested during an efficacy study with 10 subjects with moderate to severe dementia to determine whether the prototype could decrease the subjects' dependence on a caregiver as they washed their hands.

This paper describes the details of the efficacy study conducted with the device and discusses the results that were obtained. An overview of the device and its operation are provided in this paper, however, the reader is directed to Mihailidis et al. (2001) for a detailed description of the device and its algorithms.

BACKGROUND

Overview of previous work

Work in the area of cognitive orthotics has included the development of several research-based devices, and commercially available reminding devices and software programs. Researchers including Kirsch et al. (1988), Kirsch, Levine, Lajiness-O'Neill, and Schneider (1992), Chute and Bliss (1988, 1994), Steele, Weinrich, and Carlson (1989), Cavalier and Ferretti (1993), Napper and Narayan (1994), LoPresti, Friedman, and Hages (1997), and Bergman (1998), developed prototypes of computerised devices, and showed that subjects with brain injury and learning disabilities were able to complete various vocational and ADL tasks with more independence when the devices were used. There have also been several devices available that helped remind a person to complete basic ADL tasks such as taking his/her medication or attending doctor's appointments. Devices developed and tested include ISAAC by Cogent Systems Inc (1998), PEAT by Attention Control Systems Inc (Levinson, 1997), and Essential Step by MASTERY Rehabilitation Systems (Bergman, 1996). These devices and results from their efficacy studies have been described in more detail in other publications by the authors, Mihailidis et al. (2000, 2001), and in a paper by LoPresti, Mihailidis, and Kirsch (2004 this issue).

Previous computerised devices relied on input from the user for feedback (e.g., pushing "OK" after a task). This feedback and, for some devices, the expiration of a time limit were the only information used to determine whether corrective action or re-planning was required. Such an action may be achievable with persons who have less severe cognitive impairments, but is less likely to be completed by persons with moderate or severe levels of dementia because they lack the required planning and initiation skills. Persons with advanced dementia usually would not reliably remember what task they had just been asked to perform and the need to indicate that the task had been completed.

Researchers have concluded that for a cognitive device to be effective for a particular user, it must be developed as a "one-of-a-kind" device (Cole, 1999). To adapt to individual users, devices required manual re-programming by someone who was knowledgeable about the device and its software. Again, this cannot be expected from a person with dementia, or from his or her caregiver. A device is needed that can be automatically customised for a user through its own algorithms based on the user's performance. This can be achieved using artificial intelligence (AI). AI techniques are algorithms that can be used to make a computer program act more like a human when performing cognitive tasks such as decision making or planning (Russell & Norvig, 1995). A detailed summary of AI, and the techniques used in the development of the COACH can be found in a previous paper by the authors, Mihailidis et al. (2001).

Learning in dementia

There has been very little evidence in the literature showing that people with dementia are able to re-learn a task, especially an ADL. The conventional wisdom has been that once an ability to complete an ADL is lost, the affected person will not be able to re-learn the required skills. The best that can be done is to attempt to preserve as much of the person's remaining functioning as possible, and to slow down the deterioration of what remains (S. Black, personal communication, 2001).

The majority of non-pharmacological memory-oriented treatments for people with dementia have used two techniques: reality orientation and reminiscence therapy (DeVreese et al., 2001). The goals of these techniques are to maintain, or restore, temporal and spatial orientation and autobiographical memory through a continuous presentation of time, place, and person-related information. There has been some evidence that reality orientation has a positive effect on both the cognition and behaviour of a person with dementia, however, it has very little effect on the person's day-to-day functional abilities. In addition, it is unclear if a person is able to maintain any re-learned skills once the training programme has been discontinued (DeVreese et al., 2001). With respect to reminiscence therapy, there has been insufficient evidence to infer any conclusions about the efficacy of this re-training technique for people with dementia, although limited observations from clinical trials have suggested that there may be some beneficial effects (Bornat, 1994). De Vresse et al. (2001) suggested that these attempts at memory re-training have failed because these therapeutic interventions assume that all dementia patients suffer from similar cognitive disorders, and that, consequently, they may benefit to the same extent from the same rehabilitation programme. That is, rehabilitation techniques were not customised according to the abilities of each person (DeVreese et al., 2001).

DESCRIPTION OF THE DEVICE (THE COACH)

The operation of the device is illustrated in Figure 1. The device used image processing and artificial intelligence techniques to monitor and assist a user during an ADL. A detailed theoretical description of these techniques is provided in other publications by the authors, such as Mihailidis et al. (2001).

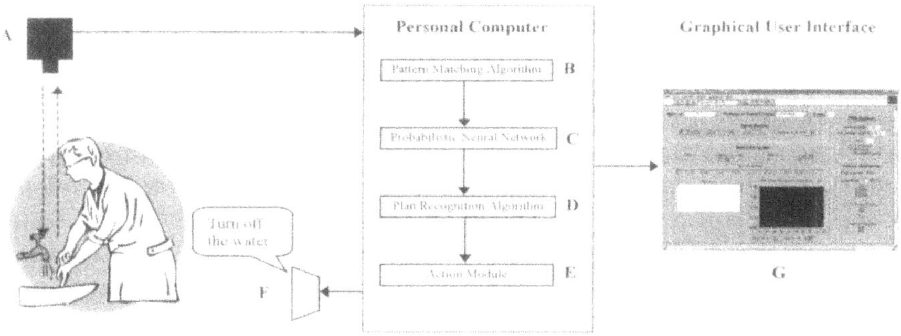

Figure 1. The operation of the device consisted of a video camera and associated software that tracked the position of a user's hand (A, B), and software that was used to determine the sequence of steps the user was completing, and deliver an appropriate verbal reminder over a set of stereo speakers (C, D, E, F). Information about the device operation and the user was displayed on a graphical interface (G).

A charge-couple device (CCD) digital video camera (A) was used to find the two-dimensional (x and y) coordinates of a user's hand using a tracking bracelet worn on his/her dominant hand. This monochrome video camera (Panasonic WV-BP330) was mounted above the sink and counter. The camera was connected to a National Instruments IMAQ-1408 frame grabber card (www.ni.com), which was installed inside the personal computer (Pentium III, 600 Mhz, 128 Mb RAM) that ran the device software. The bracelet was made from cotton material and used Velcro fasteners. It had a printed pattern of three black rings with an outer diameter of 4.45 cm and an inner diameter of 1.91 cm. The black rings provided high accuracy when tracked and allowed the highest sampling rate of all of the shapes tested. A sampling rate of approximately four points/second proved to be sufficient for tracking a user in real time. The pattern was repeated along the entire length of the bracelet to avoid occlusion when the user's hand was turned over (Mihailidis et al., 2001).

Determining which step the user was completing was accomplished using a pattern matching algorithm (B) and an artificial neural network (ANN) (C). An algorithm that uses pattern-matching techniques was developed to track the position of the user's bracelet. It was programmed using National Instrument's IMAQ Vision, which is a library of image-processing functions available in LabView. This algorithm was first trained by providing it with a sample image of the pattern on the bracelet. From this sample, a template of the pattern was stored in the memory of the device and was used to make matches of the same pattern in subsequent images provided by the camera. These matches were found using normalised cross-correlation techniques. Once a match was made within the new image, the x and y coordinates of the match were calculated (Mihailidis et al., 2001). These coordinates were used as input to the ANN, more specifically a probabilistic neural network (PNN), where they were analysed and classified into corresponding categories or step identification numbers—i.e., each step in the ADL was defined by a set of coordinates, or location of the user's hand. This type of ANN uses probability theory to learn which steps correspond with the various inputs from the environment (Mihailidis et al., 2001). The required algorithm was developed using a standard algorithm outlined by Masters (1993).

The next stage was the plan recognition algorithm (D). Using the output from the PNN, this algorithm determined which plan, or sequence of steps, the user was completing by conducting a search through a pre-existing plan library. If a match was found the device used it to guide the user through the remaining ADL steps. If the user changed the sequence of the steps required to be completed but could still reach the final goal, the program adapted itself to guide the user through the new sequence by re-searching the plan library and selecting a new acceptable sequence of steps (Mihailidis et al., 2001). If a match could not be found, the program attempted to predict which plan the user was trying to complete using all of the user's correct inputs up to that point, and hence which step he should be performing.

If the user made an error, such as completing a wrong step, or performed a step out of sequence, the action module (E) selected a pre-recorded verbal cue and played it over speakers inside the environment (F). These speakers were installed in the ceiling behind the user. Several different verbal cue details were available for a particular step before assistance from a caregiver was requested. The required cue detail was selected based on (1) the user's past performance of the step, and (2) how many errors the user had made while attempting the current step. The first option was used to select the starting level of cue detail (the device "remembered" the required starting point for each individual subject for each ADL step), and the latter was used to increase progressively the cue detail until the user successfully completed the step. If the user did not respond to any of the cues issued, the device stopped and called for a caregiver, via an audible and visual alarm on the graphical user interface, to give assistance (Mihailidis et al., 2001). Only verbal cues were used in this device. Plans for the addition of non-verbal/visual cues are being considered by the authors in the development of the next prototype, which should be ready for testing by August 2003.

For this device, an unfamiliar male voice was used to record the cues. The wording of the cues was based on prompts offered by caregivers in observed handwashing scenarios. From these observations, it was determined that many of the cues and the way they were worded were very similar from one subject to another. As a result, it was decided to record three different cue details for each step, where these detail levels were similar for each subject. The first level of detail was a general cue about the step to be completed. The second level provided more detail about the step to be completed, such as the location of the water tap. The third level was similar to the second, but included the name of the subject in order to gain his attention prior to provision of instructions (Mihailidis et al., 2001). A detailed study of the types of verbal and non-verbal prompts that caregivers use with dementia patients is currently being conducted by the authors.

Information about the user's progress, and actions taken by the device were displayed on a graphical user interface (GUI) located outside of the environment (G).

Further descriptions of the device operation and performance, including advantages and limitations of the technology, are provided in the Results and Discussion sections of this paper.

DEVICE EFFICACY STUDY

Assistive technology projects have been criticised for their insufficient evaluation of the device that was developed (Stevens & Edwards, 1996). The evaluation of a new assistive technology prototype is vital to ensure that the end product meets a user's needs, and does not have any adverse effects on the user's behaviour. Aspects such as the efficacy and effectiveness of the device need to be studied, where efficacy is a measurement of how well the device does what it is supposed to do, and effectiveness is a measurement of how well the device allows users to achieve the goals they wish to achieve (Salminen & Petrie, 1998).

A single-subject research design (SSRD) was completed with 10 subjects who had moderate to severe dementia while they performed the handwashing activity. These trials were used to determine the efficacy and effectiveness of the device: To determine whether the AI techniques, and other developed algorithms, were successful in designing a new, more adaptable cognitive orthotic device, and to determine the level of success of using the COACH to decrease the subjects' dependence on a caregiver during this ADL.

Hypotheses

1. Dependence on a caregiver during handwashing can be partially reduced using an intelligent computerised cognitive orthosis that can provide verbal reminders automatically.
2. AI can be used to develop a computerised cognitive orthosis that can automatically adapt to users' behaviours, and be easily set-up for an ADL.

Objectives

1. Determine if a subject can complete handwashing with less dependence on a caregiver when using the COACH.

2. Determine if using the COACH can decrease the number of interactions a caregiver needs to have with a subject during handwashing.
3. Determine how well the COACH and its algorithms—i.e., the AI techniques, execute the functions that they were designed to perform.

Subject selection

Ten subjects were selected from the residents of the long-term care and cognitive support units at Sunnybrook and Women's College Health Sciences Centre (SWCHSC) in Toronto, Canada. These 10 subjects, who were all male, were selected using the Mini-Mental State Examination (MMSE) and several inclusion and exclusion criteria. The MMSE is a standardised tool developed to assist in determining the current abilities and disabilities of an older adult. It can be used to assess the cognitive changes that a person may experience over time. The maximum score on the MMSE is 30. A score less than 20 is considered to be moderately impaired, and a score less than 10 is considered to be severely impaired (Agostinelli, Demers, Garrigan, & Waszynski, 1994; Folstein, Folstein, & McHugh, 1975).

Inclusion criteria. The following inclusion criteria were used to select subjects for this main study:

- Resident on the long-term or cognitive support units at SWCHSC.
- Clinical diagnosis of dementia.
- Requires assistance from a caregiver for one or more handwashing steps (based on interviews with primary caregiver and preliminary observations).
- Understands simple instructions and responds to verbal cueing (based on interviews with primary caregiver and preliminary observations).
- MMSE score of less than 20 (considered to be moderately impaired).
- Consent from the primary decision maker of each selected subject.

These inclusion criteria ensured that the subjects who participated in this study were residents who benefited the most from the use of the computerised device. These subjects were also residents whose results best indicated any problems with the device operation and its ability to assist them during the ADL.

Exclusion criteria. The following exclusion criteria were used to select subjects for this main study.

- Motor impairment that may interfere with a person's ability to complete an ADL independently, such as those resulting from a stroke or Parkinson's disease.

- Hearing impairment that may interfere with a person's ability to understand and follow verbal reminders.

Residents who were already independent during handwashing were not included since they never required prompts from the device.

Description of subjects. A description of the 10 subjects who were selected is presented in Table 1. These subjects provided a wide spectrum of functional abilities during handwashing. Some of the subjects (e.g., S29 and S32) were relatively independent during the ADL, however, they required an occasional verbal prompt from the caregiver. Other subjects (e.g., S15 and S39) were very dependent on a caregiver to complete the task. The caregiver was required to remain with them at all times and cue them for each required step. The remaining subjects fluctuated in the amount of assistance they required. This unpredictable behaviour is very common for people with dementia.

S29 was removed from the study after the first baseline phase because he often refused to participate, and when he did, he became very aggressive with the caregiver. Data were ultimately collected and analysed for nine subjects.

Apparatus and set-up

The efficacy study was conducted in a test washroom in the long-term care unit at SWCHSC. The test washroom was divided into two areas—an area where the sink and counter were located, and a concealed area where the equipment was located. The CCD video camera was installed directly above the sink and counter. Figure 2 is an illustration of the device set-up.

TABLE 1
Description of subjects who participated in the device efficacy study

Subject	*MMSE score*	*Level of cognition*	*Validation study observations*
S15	9 / 30	Severe	Required constant cueing
S19	11 / 30	Moderate	Required occasional cueing
S22	5 / 30	Severe	Required occasional cueing
S27	18 / 30	Moderate	Required cueing, but improved over the three trials
S29	18 / 30	Moderate	Required minimal cueing
S30	14 / 30	Moderate	Required occasional cueing
S32	10 / 30	Severe	Required minimal cueing
S34	13 / 30	Moderate	Required occasional cueing
S38	15 / 30	Moderate	Required occasional cueing
S39	11 / 30	Moderate	Required constant cueing and many non-verbal interactions

Figure 2. The device was installed in a test washroom located on the long-term care unit of SWCHSC. Photograph A shows the sink/counter area where each subject washed his hands during the trials. The only visible difference to the original set-up is the video camera installed on the ceiling. All other items, such as the towel and soap, were set up as identically as possible to the subject's own washroom. Photograph B shows the equipment that was used to run the device (personal computer, stereo amplifier, and monitor) and collect data (VCR and television monitor).

Method

Data collection and measurement scales. Data were collected for the subjects using various frequency measures and a new functional assessment score (FAS) that was based on the Functional Independence Measure (FIM) tool developed by Granger (C. Granger, personal communication, 2001). These scales are summarised in Table 2. These scales were validated during a preliminary study, the results of which will not be presented in this paper. The face and content validity of each scale was assessed using observations collected from the trials and interviews with "experts", such as caregivers and specialists in the field of assistive technology. It was found that the validity and inter-rater reliability of the scales were very good.

Data were ultimately collected for nine subjects. A score sheet was used to collect the data required to assess the target behaviour and device performance during handwashing. Checkboxes on the score sheet were used to keep a count of the various frequency measures, and the FAS scores for each handwashing step were entered in the appropriate column. The counter on the videotape of the subject's trial was used to record the time it took to complete the handwashing task. General comments and observations of the subject were also recorded on the score sheet for each handwashing step.

The subject performance measures, subject dependency measures, and the FAS were used to score the trials during each test phase (baseline and intervention). The device performance measures were used only during the intervention phases, for the purpose of determining whether the AI techniques and the adaptability of the device were effective.

TABLE 2
Summary of the assessment scales used in the efficacy study

Type of scale			
Subject performance	*Subject dependency*	*Device performance*	*Non-frequency*
Number of handwashing steps the subject completed without interacting with a human caregiver Total time to complete ADL	Number of *essential* interactions the subject had with a caregiver Number of *non-essential* interactions the subject had with a caregiver	Signal detection theory: ? Hits ? Misses ? False alarms ? Correct rejects Number of cues played by the device but ignored by the user Number of steps the subject completed with assistance from the device Number of failed assists by the device Responsiveness of the device to an error	Functional assessment score

The device itself collected the number of cues that were played for each handwashing step during both intervention phases.

Efficacy study design. A withdrawal type ABAB single subject research design was used for the efficacy study (Franklin, Allison, & Gorman, 1996; Harris & Brooks, 1992; Kratochwill, 1978; Portney & Watkins, 2000; Wolery & Harris, 1982). This type of design was chosen because flexibility was required as a result of the unpredictable behaviour and health of the subjects. In addition, an ABAB design was used to identify whether there were any carry over effects in subject performance during the second baseline phase to determine how the computerised device affected the behaviour and ability of a subject during handwashing, and to observe trends that may develop in a subject's ability to complete handwashing. It was also used to determine whether the computerised device's effects on the subject's target behaviour could be replicated during the second intervention phase. Finally, direct replication was used over nine subjects to strengthen the clinical relevance of the findings and to establish experimental reliability.

Four test phases were completed: two baseline phases (A_1 and A_2) and two intervention phases (B_1 and B_2). For each of these phases three primary target behaviours, or dependent variables, were observed: (1) the number of handwashing steps that a subject completed without any interaction with a human caregiver; (2) the number of interactions the caregiver had with the subject in order for the handwashing task to be successfully completed; and (3) the subject's functional assessment scores (FAS). During the baseline phases (A_1 and A_2), these target behaviours were observed and measured without the effects of the treatment, or independent variable, which was the use of the computerised device to monitor and assist the subjects instead of a human caregiver. The intervention phases (B_1 and B_2), measured the target behaviours in response to the treatment. These four phases were conducted for each subject.

Response-guided experimentation was used to determine the length of each test phase. The plan was to continue testing in each phase until stable target behaviour, or a trend that would have most likely continued with further trials, was achieved. However, after 21 days of testing it was determined that stability would not be achieved. It was assumed that if this test phase continued, the variability that was observed would have continued. The behaviour and health of the subjects was also taken into account in determining if a particular phase should continue, or whether the next one should be started. Using these criteria, a total of 60 days of testing was completed for each subject, with the exception of five subjects who missed a total of 10 days due to illness. Table 3 summarises the number of test days per phase.

It was attempted to achieve a stable baseline with the subjects.

Procedure. One trial per subject was conducted every day of the week, except for Saturday and Sundays. Testing did not occur on these days because the subjects normally had activities scheduled which took place outside of the hospital and with family members. The trials were conducted between 9:00 a.m. and 12:00 p.m. in order to test each subject before lunch and their regularly scheduled afternoon activities. A volunteer, who had previous experience in caring for people with dementia, acted as the caregiver for all of the subjects during these trials.

Each subject was brought to the test washroom from his room by the caregiver. A wheelchair was used to transport the subject if required. If the subject wished, or the caregiver thought it was necessary, he remained in the chair while he washed his hands. Before arriving at the test washroom, the caregiver placed the tracking bracelet on the dominant hand of the subject. All 10 subjects were right-handed. The subject was directed to the

TABLE 3
The number of days completed for each test phase per subject

	Baseline (A_1)	*Intervention (B_1)*	*Baseline (A_2)*	*Intervention (B_2)*
Length (days)	21	13	11	15

sink in the test washroom, or positioned in front of it if he remained in a wheelchair, and was given a simple prompt by the caregiver to wash his hands. The subject was required to complete six steps: (1) turn the cold water on; (2) perform initial rinsing of hands; (3) use the soap dispenser; (4) rinse the soap off the hands; (5) turn the water off; and (6) use a towel to dry the hands. These steps had been identified using task analysis and observations of several people with dementia completing handwashing.

During the baseline phases (A_1 and A_2), the caregiver was instructed to remain out of sight of the subject and only intervene when she saw that he required assistance. Once she intervened she was told to remain with the subject and assist him as much as she felt was necessary in order for him to complete the required step(s). During the intervention phases (B_1 and B_2), the caregiver was instructed to leave the subject alone while he washed his hands and remain in front of the device's graphical user interface (GUI), which was hidden in the other area of the test washroom. The caregiver only intervened and assisted the subject when she was told to do so by the device—i.e., a visual and quiet audible alarm on the GUI told the caregiver when to enter and which step to assist him through. Once she assisted him to the point that he was able to complete that particular step successfully, she returned to the GUI and re-started the device via a button on the screen. It took approximately 15 minutes to test each subject, which included escorting the subject to and from his own room.

The device was not turned on during the baseline trials. Prior to the start of the first intervention phase, the device was set up for each subject. This included recording all of the required cues, and initialising all the data files and matrices responsible for adjusting the various device parameters for each individual subject, such as the subject's performance history matrix, and the action taxonomy. The performance matrix for each subject was initialised with perfect scores for each step and the overall success rates. All of the acceptable handwashing plans were entered into the action taxonomy as row vectors. These initial sets of data were identical for all of the subjects. The device than automatically adjusted each one as the subject completed more trials. This set-up time, including the recording of the cues, took approximately 30 minutes per subject.

Analysis of subject data. Visual analysis was used to evaluate the data collected for subject performance and dependence. These techniques were used to look at changes in performance levels, determine trends, examine changes in slope, and to compare changes in variability in each phase.

Statistical analysis was used to corroborate the results from the visual analysis and to determine whether the overall findings were statistically significant. A three-factored repeated measures ANOVA (RANOVA) was used (Neter, Wasserman, & Kutner, 1985). The RANOVA was conducted using the combined data of the nine subjects who completed all four phases of testing. The number of steps the subjects completed without assistance from a caregiver, the total number of interactions required between the caregiver and subjects, and the FAS of the subjects were analysed. The three within-subject factors that were analysed were: (1) phase; (2) replication; and (3) block. A phase effect was determined by grouping the two baseline phases into one single phase and the two intervention phases into one phase. This determined if there were any effects on the subjects' target behaviours because of the device. A replication effect was determined by comparing the changes that occurred as a result of repeating the intervention and baseline phases using the withdrawal type SSRD. This determined if there were any differences in the target behaviours between the first baseline intervention phase and the second baseline intervention phase. A block effect was determined by sub-dividing the data in each test phase into three groups, or "blocks". These blocks of data represented the target behaviour for the subject group at the start, middle, and end of each phase. This is essentially the effect of time on the target behaviours. The first A phase was divided into block sizes of 7, 7, and 7; the first B phase was divided into block sizes of 5, 4, and 4; the second A phase was divided into block sizes of 4, 4, and 3; and the second B phase was divided into block sizes of 5, 5, and 5.

A sub-analysis was also completed in order to determine the changes and effects between the individual test phases—i.e., from the first A phase to the first B phase, from the first B phase to the second A phase, and from the second A phase to the second B phase. A two-factor approach was used for these sub-analyses, which included phase and block.

These analyses were run using the SAS software package.

Analysis of device and AI performance. The efficacy of the device was determined by calculating its error rate for two different scenarios: (1) detecting a wrong action by the subject; and (2) detecting a correct action by the subject. The total counts of hits, misses, false alarms (FA), and correct rejects (CR) for all of the subjects during each test day of the two intervention phases (B_1 and B_2) were used to calculate the device error using the following equations:

$$E_w = \frac{Misses}{Hits + Misses} * 100 \tag{1}$$

$$E_c = \frac{FA}{CR + FA} * 100 \tag{2}$$

Equation (1) calculated the error, E_w, associated with the device not properly detecting that the subject made an error, and therefore not playing a corrective cue. Equation (2) calculated the error, E_c, associated with the device not properly detecting that the subject had performed a correct action, therefore erroneously playing a cue to correct a mistake that did not exist. These two measures of error provided a good overall summary of the device efficacy—i.e., did the device and its algorithms detect errors by the subjects and play appropriate cues, and did they correctly determine that a step had been successfully completed by the subjects and start to monitor the next required step?

Autoregression was performed on the data obtained from the counts of the number of cues played by the device but ignored by the subjects, the number of steps the subject was able to complete because of assistance from the device, and the number of failed assists by the device, to determine whether a statistically significant trend occurred in each of these data. Autoregression is similar to simple linear regression with the addition of an error term ε_t, which consists of a fraction of the error that is produced from the previous data point, and a new disturbance term μ_t (Neter et al., 1985).

The responsiveness of the device was determined by measuring the average amount of time (in seconds) between the initiation of an error by a subject and the point when the device played a cue. This measurement was taken for 40 randomly selected error–response actions over all of the trials of the two intervention phases. It should be noted that measurements of responsiveness were made only for errors where the subjects completed a wrong step, and not for those errors that occurred because the subjects took too long to complete the required step. When this type of error occurred, the device waited a fixed amount of time (30 seconds) before playing the required cue. These values were compared with similar response time measurements made for the caregiver.

RESULTS

Data and observations were collected for nine subjects using the scales previously outlined in Table 2. The data showed that the subjects were able to complete the required handwashing steps with less dependence on a caregiver whenever the computerised device was used, and that the number of interactions required with the caregiver was reduced. The device operated with very little error. It assisted the subjects with approximately one-third of the required handwashing steps—i.e., two of the six steps described previously in the Procedure section, even though it was observed that the subjects ignored a relatively high percentage of the cues that were issued by the device.

Subject performance and dependency

All but one of the subjects' levels of dependence on the caregiver decreased when the device was introduced, and then increased when the device was removed. Individual improvements in the number of handwashing steps that were completed without assistance from a caregiver ranged from approximately 10% to 45%. This pattern was replicated in the data collected for the three target behaviours observed. S34 was the exception to these observations. This subject did not respond very well to the cues from the device, which resulted in many of them being ignored. It was often observed that this subject would speak back to the device stating that he had already completed the step that it was asking him to do, even though he had not, or he would become agitated. S34 was moved to the special behavioural unit at SWCHSC on day 55 of testing. This unit is for residents who have displayed behavioural problems and aggression. The subject refused to participate in the study on a few occasions.

Figure 3 illustrates S30's target behaviours. S30 required constant cueing during all of the test phases, especially during the steps of turning on the hot water and using the soap. The subject achieved a perfect score with respect to the number of steps that he completed without assistance from a caregiver, and with respect to his FAS only when the device was used. The device assisted him with 45% of the handwashing steps that he completed during the intervention phases. He responded well to the cues from the device, even though he had a few poor days for unknown reasons. Depending on the step that was being cued, the subject sometimes needed to hear all three levels of cue detail from the device before he was able to figure out which step to complete. This was most obvious when he was required to use the soap. He often had difficulties in using the soap bottle. He would place one hand on top of the bottle and start pressing down on the pump without placing his other hand underneath to catch the soap. Sometimes the third level of cue detail from the device was able to help him perform this step correctly, but often the caregiver was required to provide additional visual cueing. The subject did not miss any test days.

Visual analysis was performed on the data collected for each target behaviour. For each test phase (A_1 B_1 A_2 B_2) the levels, trends, and variability ranges were determined for the target behaviours. The results of the visual analysis for the data collected from S30 are summarized in Table 4.

Table 5 presents a summary of the overall data collected for the nine subjects. These data represent the overall means per test phase. It is clear that the use of the device had an overall positive effect on the various target behaviours measured. All three target behaviours improved when the device was introduced, and then reverted approximately back to their original values once the device was removed. The improvements were then evident once again during the second intervention phase.

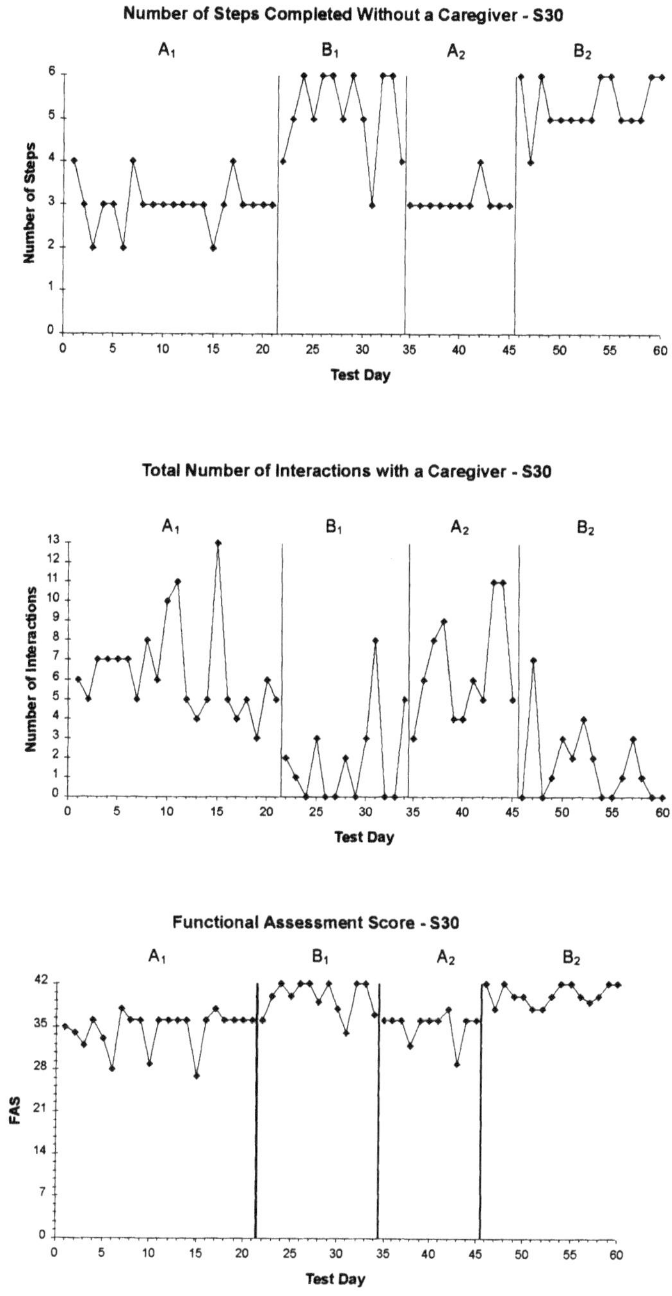

Figure 3. Target behaviours measured per day for S30: Number of steps completed without assistance from a caregiver, the number of interactions required with the caregiver, and FAS score.

TABLE 4
Summary of the results from the visual analysis conducted on the data collected for S30

Target behaviour	*Visual analysis*	A_1	B_1	A_2	B_2
Number of steps completed without a caregiver	Change in *levels* (means of each test phase)	3.0	5.2	3.1	5.3
Number of total interactions (essential + non-essential)	Change in *levels* (means of each test phase)	6.4	1.8	6.5	1.6
FAS	Change in *levels* (means of each test phase)	34.6	39.7	35.2	40.3
Number of steps completed without a caregiver	Change in *trend and slope* (a positive trend/slope was desired for this target behaviour)	0.00	–0.02	+0.02	+0.04
Number of total interactions (essential + non-essential)	Change in *trend and slope* (a negative trend/slope was desired for this target behaviour)	–0.08	+0.19	+0.30	–0.15
FAS	Change in *trend and slope* (a positive trend/slope was desired for this target behaviour)	+0.12	–0.05	–0.08	+0.08
Number of steps completed without a caregiver	Change in *magnitude of the variability range*	2	3	1	2
Number of total interactions (essential + non-essential)	Change in *magnitude of the variability range*	10	8	8	7
FAS	Change in *magnitude of the variability range*	11	8	9	4

TABLE 5
Mean scores per test phase

Measurement	A_1	B_1	A_2	B_2
Mean number of steps completed without a caregiver	3.89	5.41	3.92	5.49
Mean number of total interactions	5.48	1.07	4.12	1.21
Mean FAS per subject	36.51	40.21	36.82	40.59

These results from the RANOVA indicated that at a 99% confidence level there were significant effects between the overall test phases (combined A phases and combined B phases), and between each individual test phase (A_1 B_1 A_2 B_2) for all three target behaviours—i.e., the null hypothesis (Ho), which was that the phase means were equal, was rejected. It was also shown that the difference found between the phases with respect to the number of interactions between the subjects and the caregiver may have been because of effects from the time blocks. This effect occurred for the overall situation, and between phases A_1 and B_1.

Device and AI performance

The COACH assisted the subjects with approximately one-third of the steps that they were able to complete without assistance from a caregiver during the two intervention phases (Figure 4). The slope of the trend line in Figure 4 was found not to be statistically significance at a 95% confidence level. The number of misses and false alarms was relatively low over both phases, which resulted in relatively low error rates (Table 6). The device was able to monitor the actions of the subjects, determine which step was being completed, and decide whether corrective action was required. The AI algorithms used to adjust the various parameters seemed to have worked efficiently and properly. It was observed that the level of cue detail was

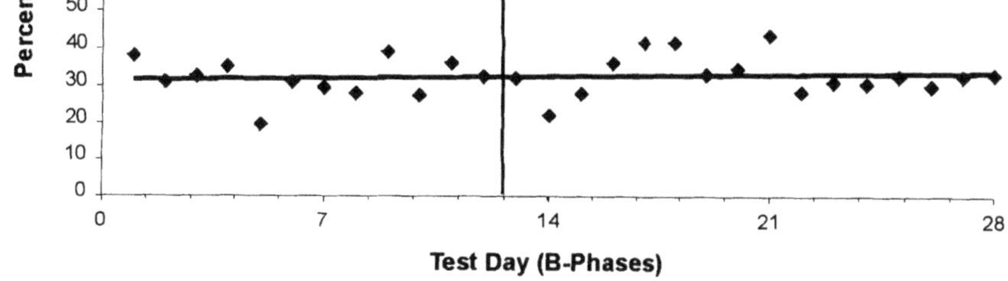

Figure 4. The percentage of steps that the subjects ($n = 9$) completed in response to the cues from the device per test day (i.e., the total number of steps completed in response to cues from the device divided by the total number of steps completed without a caregiver). These data were collected for each trial over the two intervention phases (B_1 and B_2). Autoregression was performed to obtain the trend line ($y = 0.078x + 31.525$).

TABLE 6
Number of hits, misses, false alarms and correct rejects per intervention phase, and the error rates E_w and E_c calculated using equations (8) and (9)

	Hits	*Misses*	*False alarms*	*Correct rejects*
First Intervention (B_1)	418	16	31	651
Second Intervention (B_2)	454	13	27	751
Total	872	29	58	1402
Error (%)	$E_w = 3.2$		$E_c = 3.9$	

properly adjusted according to each subject's own performance and past responses to the cues—i.e., those subjects who had more difficulties were played more detailed cues, while the more independent subjects were played less detailed cues. The progression through the cue details levels when the subjects did not respond to the first issued cue also worked properly and seemed to be effective in assisting the subjects through the required steps. However, the subjects ignored several cues from the device, and sometimes it was observed that they were not able to fully understand the directions they were being given (Figures 5 and 6). The latter was often the situation when the subjects were cued to use the soap. Many of them did not understand how

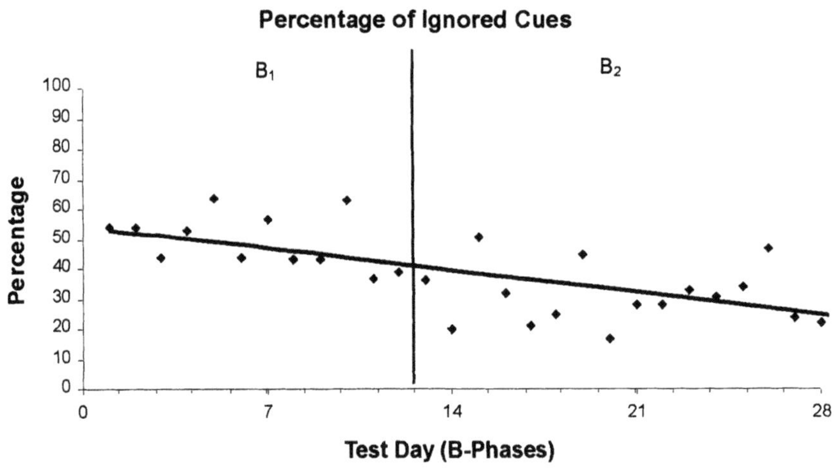

Figure 5. The percentage of cues played by the device but ignored by the subjects over all of the intervention test days (i.e., the total number of cues ignored by the subjects per test day divided by the total number of cues played by the device per test day). Autoregression was performed to obtain the trend line ($y = -1.043x + 54.14$).

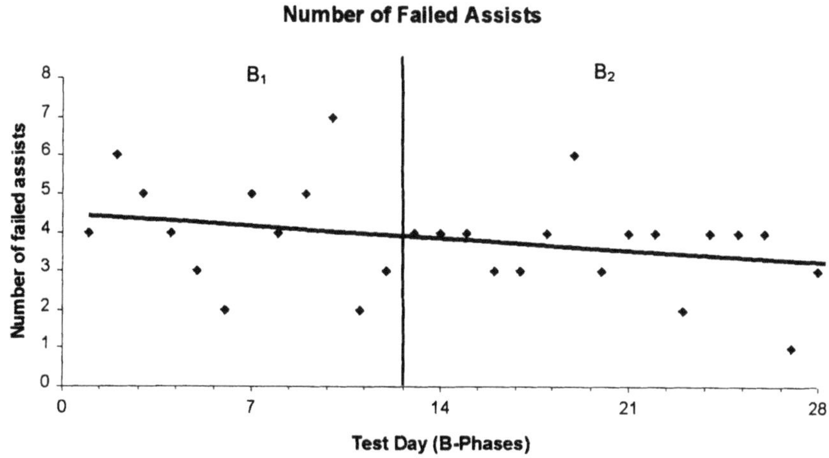

Figure 6. The number of times the device attempted to assist the subjects but failed to do so resulting in an interaction with the human caregiver. Autoregression was performed to obtain the trend line ($y = -0.0436x + 4.4648$).

TABLE 7
Responsiveness of the COACH compared with the responsiveness of the caregiver. Response times are in seconds, and based on 40 randomly selected samples from all four test phases (A_1 B_1 A_2 B_2)

	Device	*Caregiver*
Mean ($n = 40$)	1.67 seconds	3.17 seconds
Standard deviation	0.74 seconds	1.66 seconds

to use the soap, and how to complete the actions being described to them by the device. Some of the subjects were able to complete the step after hearing all three cue details, while others required an interaction with the caregiver. The slopes obtained in Figures 5 and 6 are statistically significant at 95% confidence, however, only the slope in Figure 5 is significant at 99% confidence. These confidence estimations were found using Autoregression techniques. The response time of the device was on average faster and more consistent than the caregiver (Table 7).

DISCUSSION

Subject performance

The results from the efficacy study showed that there was an increase in the average number of steps that the subjects were able to complete without assistance from a caregiver over both A–B phases. Overall, the subjects were able to complete approximately one and a half more handwashing steps and required approximately four less interactions with the caregiver during the intervention phases. As well, the average functional assessment scores for the subjects increased by approximately four points during the intervention phases. These results were statistically significant at a 99% confidence level. The stability of performance, or the variability in the data, was also improved during the intervention phases. The results from the visual analysis of each subject's data showed that the variability of the number of steps each subject completed without a caregiver was reduced on average by almost one step during the intervention phases. Similar changes were observed for the number of interactions required and the subjects' FAS.

Overall, the subjects were able to complete approximately 25% more steps without a caregiver when the COACH was used, however, more important is the number of steps each individual subject was able to complete. S30 was able to complete approximately 37% more handwashing steps during the intervention phases. Improvements for the other subjects ranged from approximately 10–45%. The device developed by Kirsch et al. (1992) helped increase the performance of its users during a janitorial task by approximately 17–22%, and improved the stability of the users' performances. The pilot efficacy study performed by the author also showed a 22% increase in the performance of handwashing for one subject with severe dementia. Cavalier and Ferretti (1993) observed substantial improvements in their subjects when their cognitive device was used—during the intervention phase no interactions with the teacher were required. Specific data for other researchers were not reported in the literature; however, the majority of them stated that improvements were observed. It should be noted however, that past studies did not include subjects with cognitive impairments as severe as the subjects who participated in this research, and since the specifics about the devices used were not reported, it is difficult to predict how these past results would have changed if subjects with moderate to severe dementia were included. Those subjects whose improvements were the least were observed to be more independent than the other subjects during handwashing, even though their MMSE scores may not have been higher. These subjects did not have as much room for improvement in their scores from the baseline to intervention phases. The same was true for their improvements in the number of interactions.

As previously described the overall number of interactions the subjects required with the caregiver was reduced whenever the device was introduced. This decrease was also visible for each individual subject and for each A–B phase. The trend of decreasing the number of interactions from the baseline phases to the intervention phases was consistent across all subjects, even those subjects who were fairly independent. For the more independent subjects the device acted more as a safety net in case the subject made an occasional error, whereas, the more dependent subjects, such as S30, required the device to be a constant presence.

The impact of decreasing the number of interactions with the caregiver can be viewed from two perspectives: (1) the caregiver; and (2) the subjects. The decrease in the number of interactions can be viewed as a positive result for the caregiver. There was an observed reduction in the amount of time that the caregiver had to spend with the residents as they washed their hands. This reduction in time resulted from the caregiver not having to assist the subjects through each step, and from the fact that when the caregiver was required to provide assistance, not as many interactions were required as during the baseline phases. The change in the amount of assistance the subjects required from the caregiver was reflected in the subjects' FAS. The FAS values increased during the intervention phases. This trend was evident in the overall data and for each individual subject. Beyond the efficacy study, this additional time could allow the caregiver to complete other tasks for the resident outside of the washroom, such as making his bed, or in her being able to tend to another resident. However, the effect of reducing the number of interactions with the caregiver from the perspective of the subjects is not as positive or as clear. Even though the subjects spent more time on their own during handwashing, they may not have perceived this as an increase in their privacy and autonomy. It was observed that the subjects did not always realise that a computerised device was assisting them; they thought that it was some person who was somewhere inside of the washroom. Therefore, even though the privacy of the subjects was improved, their perceived privacy most likely was not changed.

The results of the RANOVA showed that the observed changes in the number of steps that the subjects were able to complete without a caregiver, the total number of interactions required between the subjects and the caregiver, and the subjects' FAS were all statistically significant with 99% confidence between all phases—i.e., from A_1 to B_1, B_1 to A_2, and A_2 to B_2. These results confirmed the results obtained via visual analysis. These analyses also confirmed that there was no learning effect on the part of the subjects as a result of repeating the same task each day, and as a result of replicating the phases. This result supports the observations made of the subjects and the notion that people with dementia are unable to re-learn ADL tasks.

The introduction of a caregiver who was unfamiliar to the subjects did not seem to have any adverse effects on the performance of the subjects, however the caregiver's unfamiliarity with the subjects definitely had an effect on the way she provided assistance. It was observed that the number of interactions between the caregiver and subjects decreased over the course of the first baseline phase (A_1). This trend is also visible in the majority of the subject's individual data, however is more difficult to see as a result of the high variability that existed in the individual data. The caregiver may have been overzealous at first with respect to intervening and providing assistance to the subjects—i.e., she may have been premature in providing assistance for a particular step. Once the caregiver became more familiar and comfortable with the subjects, the level of interactions started to be more consistent during the second half of phase A_1. Approximately the same level of interactions was replicated during the entire second baseline phase (A_2). This initial trend in the overall number of interactions was shown to be statistically significant at a 99% confidence level. Results from the RANOVA showed that the changes observed in the number of interactions between test phase was influenced by time (i.e., a block effect existed), specifically between the first baseline and intervention phases (A_1 and B_1). This change in the caregiver's performance during these two phases over the three time blocks used in the RANOVA analysis is illustrated in Figure 7. This figure shows that during the first two time blocks of A_1 the number of interactions the caregiver had with the subject decreased, and then remained fairly constant during the final time block. The level of interaction remained relatively constant during B_1.

The FAS scores can be used to help determine whether the observed changes were clinically significant. As previously described, the FAS was based on the FIM? tool, which is widely used as a measure of caregiver burden and clinical significance of a rehabilitation programme. According to

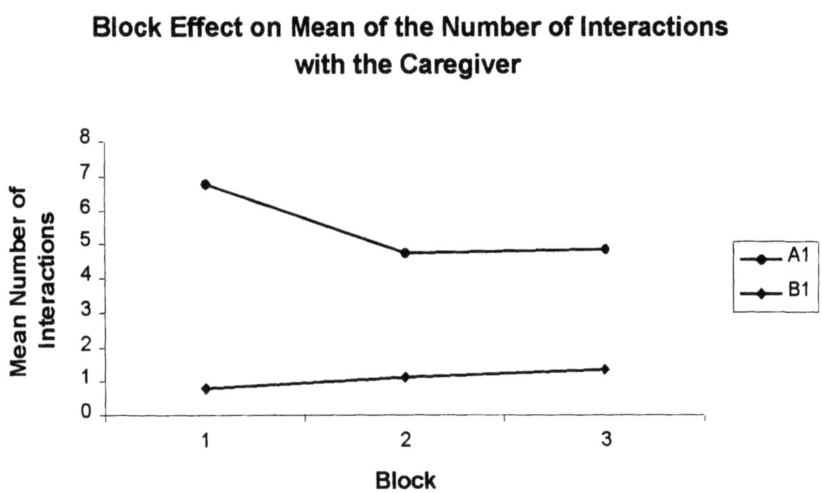

Figure 7. The block effect on the mean of the number of interactions between the caregiver and subjects. The upper line (A_1) shows that there was a decrease in the number of interactions during the first two phase blocks, while the lower line (B_1) shows that the number of interactions was relatively constant during all of the phase blocks.

Granger, the developer of the FIM? tool, this measure of clinical significance can be extended to the FAS. Clinical significance may be concluded if at least a 3–5 point increase on the FAS is seen in the results obtained from the efficacy study (C. Granger, personal communication, 2001). An approximate change of four points was observed for the overall FAS of the subjects. The changes in score for the individual subjects ranged from 0.7 to 6.6. Only three subjects (S32, S34, and S38) did not have changes above three points. These three subjects were more independent than the other subjects, and whenever they had an interaction with the caregiver, they usually required nothing more than a simple verbal prompt (unlike the other subjects who sometimes required visual prompting and physical interactions).

The changes observed in the subjects' abilities to complete the required handwashing steps during the intervention phases may not have been solely due to the device. It was noted that the subjects sometimes had the opportunity to complete more steps on their own because the caregiver was not present during the intervention trials and did not have the opportunity to instantly intervene. However, on some occasions the subjects had less of an opportunity to complete a step on their own, or to correct their own mistakes because the device provided assistance quicker than the caregiver would have. Using the data for S30 as an example, this subject was able to complete an average of 3.0 steps per trial without assistance from a caregiver during the first baseline phase. The number of steps he completed without assistance from a caregiver increased to an average of 5.2 steps per trial during the first intervention phase, where an average of 2.3 steps were in response to assistance provided by the device. Theoretically, if the device was not present during this phase, S30 would have only completed on average 2.9 steps, which is approximately equal to his performance during the baseline phase. In this scenario, it seems that the subject's increase in performance was solely as a result of the assistance provided by the device. Similar calculations on data collected for other subjects showed that in addition to this scenario, two others occurred: (1) the subject would have completed more steps on his own during the intervention phase than during the baseline phase if the device was not present (scenario two); and (2) the subject would have completed less steps on his own during the intervention phase than during the baseline phase if the device was not present (scenario three). Scenario three occurred in the overall data collected with respect to the average number of steps the subjects completed without a caregiver.

The occurrence of these three different scenarios was not consistent across subjects, nor across the test phases of each individual subject. For example, scenario one occurred for S30 from phase A_1 to B_1, however, scenario three then occurred for the same subject from phase A_2 to B_2.

The amount of time it took the subjects to complete all of the required steps was not considered in determining the effectiveness of the device. The goal of the device was not to reduce the amount of time it took the subject to complete the ADL. A reasonable amount of time to complete a step was determined by observing the subjects during the preliminary validation study and then using the average time it took them to complete the required steps. This value of 30 seconds was used to set the response time of the device.

Even though time was not considered in making the final conclusions on the device efficacy, it was measured for each subject. Using these recorded times, burst frequencies (count/minute) can be calculated for the number of steps the subjects completed without assistance from the caregiver. Using these frequencies it was observed that the level of performance of the majority of the subjects was relatively unchanged from phase to phase, and for those subjects where differences were observed, the changes were not as pronounced as in their daily frequencies. The amount of time it took a majority of the subjects to complete the activity either remained the same or increased during the intervention phases. This increase occurred because once the device responded to an error, it took more time than the caregiver to assist the subjects. When the caregiver provided assistance to the subjects she would give them one or two verbal prompts, and then either physically guide the subject through the step or complete it on her own. The latter was especially evident for those subjects who were more dependent on the caregiver, such as S30. The device, however, attempted to assist the subjects using all of the verbal prompts that were recorded for that particular step—i.e., up to three different verbal cues may have been issued before it called on a caregiver to assist the subjects because the pre-recorded cues failed. This process sometimes resulted in the amount of time it took the subjects to complete the activity to be longer than during the baseline phases.

The changes observed with respect to the trends and slopes for the target behaviours were not as expected for a majority of the subjects. For example, ideally the subjects should have had zero or negative trends during the baseline phases and zero or positive trends during the intervention phases for the number of steps that the subjects completed without assistance from the caregiver. However, a majority of the subjects had positive trends during the baseline phases and some negative trends during the intervention phases. Similar contrary results were also found for the other target behaviours (number of interactions and FAS). These results, however, are not significant because the slopes found for each subject and target behaviour were very small—there was not a single slope greater than 0.3 or less than –0.4. As well, one "bad day", or a device error that resulted in the caregiver having to interact with the subject, would change the sign of some of the slopes. For example, S30 experienced a bad day on day 31 of testing. If this point was removed, or moved to his mean for that phase, the slope would change from a negative trend to a positive one. This variability in the data was expected because of the effects of dementia.

Wolery and Harris (1982) stated that it can be concluded that a treatment is effective if three situations exist concurrently: (1) there must be either no change or very minor changes within experimental conditions; (2) the changes between experimental and environmental conditions must be replicated during additional phases of the experiment; and (3) a clear positive change in level, trend, or both must occur when the treatment is introduced (Wolery & Harris, 1982). With respect to the results found in this efficacy study, the environmental and experimental conditions remained constant during all test phases, and across all subjects, therefore satisfying the first two criteria. As well, a clear positive change in level was detected for the majority of the subjects and for the overall data over all of the measured target behaviours. Therefore, it can be concluded that the treatment—i.e., the cognitive device, was effective for these subjects.

Device and AI performance

The device was easy to set up for handwashing and for each individual subject. The most time-consuming part of the set up was recording the verbal cues for each subject. Once the device was set up for each subject, it was able to maintain a personalised memory of each subject's performances, settings, and preferences with respect to the starting detail level of each verbal cue, and the sequence of steps that the subject completed most often. If the subject did not respond to the first played cue, the device was able to increase the cue detail during subsequent attempts to assist him through the required step. The device was also able to effectively determine when the cue detail should be reduced because the subject's performance of the step was improving. The tracking hardware used to provide input to the software was effective and non-obtrusive, and except for the installation of the video camera, did not modify the sink area. Finally, the device's responsiveness was acceptable for the subjects tested.

The device was able to track the hand positions of the subjects and provide useful data to the software in order to determine which handwashing steps were being completed. The video camera and associated hardware were relatively inconspicuous and did not greatly modify the environment. In fact, it was often observed that if the video camera was not pointed out to people who entered the washroom (such as the patient care managers), differences were not noticed. The tracking system was also generalisable—i.e., it potentially could be set up for many different tasks.

Even though the tracking system used for this device was less obtrusive, it was not as reliable as using simple switches and sensors. The sampling rate of the CCD video camera and frame grabber card was 30 Hz. However, by the end of the image processing and pattern matching algorithms, the sampling rate, or matching rate, was at approximately 4 Hz. Volitional movements normally occur at approximately 3 Hz, and in order to avoid any errors in tracking these types of movements a tracking system should ideally be operating at approximately 2–3 times this frequency (Winter, 1990). The device's tracking system did not meet this criterion, which sometimes resulted in data points being missed.

The tracking system suffered from occlusion. Sometimes the tracking bracelet was obscured enough that the pattern-matching algorithm was not able to recognise one of the target shapes. This normally occurred when a subject leaned too far over the sink counter and blocked the view of the camera with his head. This resulted in some missed data points.

Finally, tracking hand movements in two dimensions was a source of error in the device because a subject may have his hand in a required position, but not necessarily complete the step that the hand position was associated with. For example, the subject could move his hand above the water tap but not turn it on. In this situation the device would still classify his hand position and think that the water had been turned on or off. This error resulted in the device missing potential mistakes and not playing required cues to the subject. This problem could be reduced in future devices by including the third dimension in the coordinates of the subject's hand, and by using more advanced tracking techniques such as hand gesture recognition.

In the development of a cognitive device, the most important criteria were that the device is inconspicuous and that it does not place additional cognitive requirements on its user. The use of a CCD video camera and the pattern-matching algorithms allowed these criteria to be met even though there was a trade-off with respect to accuracy.

The AI techniques that were used for the development of the COACH seemed to be effective with respect to training the device, and showed modest effects in improving the responses and performances of the subjects by automatically adjusting the cueing strategies and sequence of steps according to each subject's abilities.

Once a training set that was representative of all possible hand positions for handwashing was collected, the training of the device was instantaneous. After the addition of simple logic rules to account for ambiguities in the data, the neural network was robust enough to be able to classify new data with very good accuracy. In addition, these classifications were learned by the software using a relatively small training set. However, handwashing was a relatively simple activity making it easier to collect training data that was representative of all actions that a subject could complete. It is unknown if the device's neural network will be sufficient and robust enough for more complex activities such as tracking a subject while using the toilet. It can be speculated, however, that since similar neural networks have been used in the past for much more complex classification tasks, such as in the neural network house by Mozer (1998), the network used in the device will be sufficient for more difficult activities.

The planning algorithms and the action module were effective in determining the performance levels of each subject and then adjusting the cueing strategies of the device.

The plan recognition algorithm was effective in determining the sequence of steps a subject was completing and in selecting the appropriate plan from the action taxonomy. However, as a result of the observed unpredictable behaviour, the plan recognition algorithm was continually making calls to the action taxonomy to ensure that a subject was still completing the same plan. These continuous calls resulted in some inefficiency in the device performance since it was continually using memory to maintain and search the library. In addition, in order for the device to know which plan a subject felt the most comfortable in completing, and which one was successfully completed in the past, the action taxonomy was continually updated to reflect these changes. This resulted in the size of the taxonomy becoming relatively large for some of the subjects, and in the efficiency of the device to decrease. For those subjects whose action taxonomy was updated frequently, a manual "clean-up" of the library was required after the first intervention phase was completed. It was ensured that the library still reflected the most recent preferences of the subject. The situated planner algorithm worked very well with respect to determining which step required a cue and then inserting this cue into the current plan in order for the cue to be played to the subject.

The action module was able to determine starting levels of cue detail for each subject that were consistent with the levels used by the caregiver, and were consistent with observations of the subjects performing handwashing during the baseline phases—i.e., the subjects who were observed to require more assistance and detailed cueing from the caregiver, received more detailed cues from the device.

These automatic adjustments to the device's cueing strategies resulted in modest effects on the performance and response of the subjects; these effects were illustrated by the data collected with respect to device performance and by the data presented in Figures 5 and 6. The device's ability to automatically determine the best methods of assisting each subject, and adjust its cueing strategies accordingly, most likely had a part in the observed improvements in the device performance, especially in the decreases in the number of ignored cues and failed assists.

Features that have not been used before in the field of cognitive orthotics were incorporated in this device as a result of using AI, such as easily training the device for an ADL without the need to manually change several parameters and functions. It took approximately five minutes to train the device for handwashing, which only had to be completed once for all of the subjects. AI also made it easier to set up the device for multiple users. Even though some manual configuration was required, such as recording the verbal prompts and manually entering the corresponding step identification numbers for the data in the training set, the amount of set-up required was significantly reduced in comparison with past devices. With respect to assisting a subject, AI allowed this device to be able to adjust the types of cueing provided to each subject based on that person's own performance. The use of different cue detail levels instead of repeating the same cue to the user if he did not respond appropriately to the first one, proved to be very effective.

The number of steps that the handwashing task was divided into was sufficient for the subjects who participated in the efficacy study. Further division of the activity into smaller sub-steps most likely would not have significantly increased the subjects' performance for two reasons:

1. The majority of the subjects were already able to complete the required sub-steps in response to the cue played for the main step—i.e., it seemed that the primary cue triggered their memories with respect to which sub-steps were also required. If the sub-steps were not completed, it was often because the subjects became distracted in mid-step. This was normally corrected once a cue was played that reminded them to move on to the next required step—i.e., the subjects would first complete all of the required sub-steps for the current step.
2. The steps that would have benefited the most from further division were the more difficult steps for the subjects to complete, such as turning on the water or using the soap. Verbal cueing alone was not sufficient to assist some of the subjects during these more difficult steps, and they often would complete these steps only after visual prompting by the caregiver in addition to the verbal cues played by the device.

The three levels of verbal cues that were recorded and issued by the device were sufficient in assisting the majority of the subjects. When the subjects ignored a first cue, or did not understand the instructions, it was often observed that issuing a second, more detailed cue helped to gain their attention, and helped them to understand and complete the required step. These observations were validated by the data collected with respect to the number of ignored cues and the number of failed assists (Figures 5 and 6). These data showed that as the device adjusted the starting level of the cue details for each subject, the number of cues that the subjects ignored, or did not understand, decreased.

It was found that the number of ignored cues was dependent on the step that was being completed and the subject who was being assisted. The cues played for the more difficult steps, such as turning the cold water on (step one) and using the soap (step three), were ignored most often by the subjects.

The number of ignored cues may have increased for these steps for three reasons:

1. The number of cues required to complete these steps was greater than the other steps, therefore, there was an increased opportunity for the cues to be ignored.
2. The cues were not descriptive enough, or clear enough to help the subjects complete these steps and therefore were ignored by the subjects.
3. The subjects did not feel that it was necessary to complete these steps and refused to respond to any of the cues.

The steps of turning on the cold water and using the soap required the most cues from the device. Even after the cues were issued it was sometimes observed that the subjects refused to complete the steps because they appeared to feel that it was not necessary. This was especially true when they were told to turn on the cold water. Many of the subjects would only turn on the hot water, and did not see it necessary to turn on the cold water as well. This also sometimes occurred when they were told to use the soap. Some of the subjects would reply that they did not need to use the soap, or that they had already used the soap when in fact they had not. When this occurred all of the cues that were played by the device were normally ignored, and the caregiver was required to enter the washroom and convince the subjects to complete the required step. In addition, some of the cues did not provide proper assistance to the subjects, such as those used to help use the soap dispenser. It was observed that the less detailed cue—"Use the soap in the pink bottle" was not descriptive enough to assist some of the subjects, while the most descriptive cue—"[Name], put one hand on top of the pink bottle [pause]. Push down to use the soap." confused the subjects because they would only remember the second half of the cue. In these situations, some of the subjects sometimes became agitated and would ignore subsequent cues from the device for that particular step. This scenario did not occur very often, but did play a role in the increase in the number of ignored cues. The cues for more complex and difficult steps should have been further customised to each individual in order to include certain characteristics that would have been more helpful to each subject. This may have included addressing the subjects by name earlier in the cues, or having more than three levels of cue detail.

The optimal characteristics of the cues with respect to wording, tempo, volume, and gender required further study. The wording of the cues was kept as simple as possible, and similar terminology to that used by the caregiver was incorporated in the cues. It was also found that adjusting the volume of the cues to the preferences of each subject was also very effective.

Subjects S15 and S29 stated that the male voice reminded them of being in the army, and because of this they did not "like" the voice. This was one of the main reasons why S29 was removed from the study; he became very agitated by the voice. Even though S15 did not "like" the male voice, he still responded to a majority of the cues that were played by the device. Using a female voice for these two subjects may have improved their performances and decreased the number of cues they ignored. However, a female voice may also have been more difficult for the subjects to hear and understand because it has a higher frequency.

Overall the subjects seemed to be very comfortable with the recorded voice. They were often observed replying back whenever a cue was given, and many of the subjects often commented on the "person" in the washroom who was helping them. Interestingly, S32 always commented about the "person on the radio" who was assisting him while he washed his hands.

The following are some recommendations for future cueing strategies for devices that may be used by people with dementia.

1. Different levels of cue detail should be used. The cues should be played at appropriate times based on the performance of each individual user.
2. These cues should include as much detail as needed by a subject to be able to complete the required step. Depending on the subject's level of cognitive impairment, as much detail as required should be included in the first level of cue detail—i.e., the first level of cue detail should not be a generic cue, such as "Dry your hands".
3. The cues should only describe one action at a time.
4. The wording of the cues should be as simple as possible and attempt to incorporate terminology that is familiar to the subject, such as using the word "tap" instead of "faucet" if that is what the subject is familiar with.
5. The volume of the cues should be adjusted according to each subject's preferences and hearing abilities.

The device operated with relatively little error, and was able to detect a variety of mistakes made by the subjects and provide assistance in response. The device averaged approximately one miss and two false alarms per day over all nine subjects—i.e., on average once per day the device missed an error by the subjects and did not play a cue, and twice per day played an unnecessary cue. Performance errors for cognitive devices have not been reported in the literature, so a comparison of the performance of this device with those from other researchers is not possible. However, the clinical impact of the device errors on the performance of the subjects can be used to determine if the device error was acceptable. Misses by the device normally occurred because the device thought a step had been completed because the neural network misclassified the subject's hand position. False alarms normally resulted because the device missed data points that were associated with a particular step being completed. These missed data points were primarily as a result of the low sampling/matching rate of the device's tracking system. It was observed that a false alarm was more detrimental to a subject's performance than a miss because the unnecessary cues from the device sometimes agitated the subjects. They would often reply that they had already completed the step that was being cued by the device, and sometimes would tell the device to "shut-up". When a miss occurred, the caregiver was required to enter the test washroom and assist the subject through the step, therefore increasing the number of interactions between the caregiver and subject, and decreasing the number of steps the subject completed on his own. In determining whether these errors are acceptable, it is important to look at which steps the errors normally occurred. If the device continually missed a critical step such as the subject not turning on the water, this is an unacceptable error. However, if the error normally occurred for a less critical step such as the subject not initially rinsing his hands, then this may be more acceptable. With respect to false alarms, the amount of agitation that the unnecessary cues caused the subjects must be looked at, and it must be determined whether their levels of agitation negatively affected their performances of the ADL. Neither of these situations occurred as a result of the device errors. Misses by the device did occur for some critical steps, but not enough to adversely affect the subjects' performance and results. As well, the false alarms by the device did not cause the subjects' performance to suffer because they were agitated. Improving the sampling rate and the target acquisition accuracy of the tracking system should reduce these errors.

Figures 5 and 6 illustrated that the number of cues played by the device but ignored by the subjects, and the number of times that the device attempted to assist the subjects and failed decreased over the 28 days the device was used. These decreases were statistically significant with 95% confidence. The number of cues that were ignored by the subjects may have decreased for two reasons:

1. The device's AI algorithms adjusted the cue details so that the most effective cue for each individual subject was eventually used.
2. The subjects became more familiar and comfortable with the voice used to record the cues.

A majority of the subjects did not remember that they had been going to wash their hands each day in the test washroom, and many of them often commented after each trial about the "person telling them what to do" and that they have "never met the person before". These observations were indicative that the majority of the subjects did not remember that the same "person" was providing them with assistance, and therefore it was very unlikely that they became familiar with the recorded voice. This leads to the possible conclusion that the decrease in the number of ignored cues was as a direct result of the AI algorithm's ability to adapt the device's cueing strategies for each subject. This includes adapting the sequence of steps that the device used to guide the subjects.

The responsiveness of the device was faster than the responsiveness of the caregiver. The responsiveness of other cognitive devices has not been reported, so it is not possible to make comparisons between this device and those developed by other researchers. The device response time was appropriate for the majority of the subjects, however, it was sometimes too slow for those subjects who were able to complete the required steps at a faster rate. For example, sometimes S30 would not use the soap but instead used the towel right after he initially wet his hands. He would complete this incorrect sequence so quickly that by the time the device detected the error and played the cue for him to use the soap, he had already turned the water off and started to walk away from the sink. When this occurred he ignored all of the subsequent cues from the device, and the caregiver was required to assist him. In addition, the consistency of the device's response times to errors was better than the caregiver's response times (standard deviation of 0.74 s compared with a standard deviation of 1.66 s). The measured difference in standard deviation was shown to be statistically significant with 95% confidence. The caregiver was very inconsistent in her responsiveness to an error committed by the subjects. On some occasions she would respond immediately, sometimes even before the subject had the chance to commit an error, while other times it took her more than 5 s to respond. The device was fairly consistent in its response times during each trial, and for each subject. This provided the subjects with a more consistent level of care.

The results from the efficacy study showed that the device performed the majority of the functions that it was supposed to with relatively little error. The results also showed that it decreased the dependence of the subjects during the intervention phases. These results lend some support to the hypothesis that AI can be a useful tool in the field of cognitive orthotics, even though the changes that were observed in this study as a result of the AI algorithms were modest. With the development of more advanced algorithms, the techniques used in this device might be able to be applied to more complex tasks. Perhaps AI techniques can be used to develop devices that can automatically set themselves up for various situations and users.

Limitations

In addition to the previously described limitations of the device, such as the sampling/matching rate being too slow, and classification errors which resulted in false alarms and misses, there were also limitations in the efficacy study and analysis tools. Some limitations were:

1. The subjects who participated in the efficacy study were all male and war veterans. The latter may have affected how some of the subjects responded to the cues from the device.
2. The measurement scales did not give a good indication of the effects of the AI techniques on the performance of the device and its ability to assist each individual subject. Direct observations and limited data had to be used to make conclusions on the efficacy of the AI algorithms. The scales also did not take into account the amount of time that the caregivers spent assisting the subjects, which may have been useful in determining the clinical significance of the device.
3. Visual analysis was sometimes difficult to complete properly because of the unequal and relatively short phase lengths. The unequal phase lengths made it difficult to make comparisons from phase to phase, especially during the statistical analysis. However, the frail health of the majority of the subjects would have made it difficult to extend the test phases.
4. In order to conduct parametric statistics on the data, several assumptions about the data had to be made, such as the data were normally distributed and there was very little autocorrelation. Even though these assumptions did apply to the device, some researchers in SSRD may disagree that the use of these statistics was valid.

CONCLUSIONS

A cognitive orthosis (the COACH) was developed using artificial intelligence (AI) techniques to assist subjects with moderate to severe dementia while they washed their hands. The device was successful in the fact that it helped the subjects perform more handwashing steps without the caregiver.

The COACH is one of the first cognitive devices to successfully use AI techniques, and one of the first devices that had the ability to automatically adjust its parameters with respect to the cueing strategies used when assisting a subject. These, and other parameters, were automatically adapted according to each subject's individual performance of the required steps. In addition, the COACH was one of the first devices to successfully use a non-obtrusive tracking system to provide automatic feedback to the device. The subject was not required to interact with the device in any way as typically was required in the past.

An efficacy study showed that the COACH was effective in assisting the majority of the subjects who participated. The number of handwashing steps that each subject was able to complete without a caregiver improved whenever the device was used, and the number of interactions required with the caregiver decreased.

REFERENCES

Agostinelli, B., Demers, K., Garrigan, D., & Waszynski, C. (1994). Targeted interventions: Use of the Mini-Mental State Exam. *Journal of Gerontological Nursing* (*August*), 15–23.

Bergman, M. (1996). Computer orthotics: Fostering self-sufficiency in people with cognitive challenges. *Disability Today, Fall*, 54–55.

Bergman, M. M. (1998). A proposed resolution of the remediation–compensation controversy in brain injury rehabilitation. *Cognitive Technology, 3*(1), 45–51.

Bornat, J. (1994). *Reminiscence reviewed. Perspectives, evaluations, achievements.* Buckingham, UK: Open University Press.

Cavalier, A. R., & Ferretti, R. P. (1993). *The use of an intelligent cognitive aid to facilitate the self-management of vocational skills by high school students with severe learning disabilities.* Paper presented at the RESNA '93 Annual Conference, Arlington, VA.

Chute, D. L., & Bliss, M. E. (1988). *Prosthesis ware: Personal computer support for independent living* [Website]. http://www.homemods.org/library/life-span/prosthesis.html

Chute, D. L., & Bliss, M. E. (1994). Prothesisware. *Experimental Aging Research, 20*, 229–238.

Cockburn, J., & Collin, C. (1988). Measuring everyday memory in elderly people: A preliminary study. *Age and Ageing, 17*(4), 265–269.

Cole, E. (1999). Cognitive prosthetics: An overview to a method of treatment. *NeuroRehabilitation, 12*, 39–51.

DeVreese, L. P., Neri, M., Fioravanti, M., Belloi, L., & Zanetti, O. (2001). Memory rehabilitation in Alzheimer's disease: A review of progress. *International Journal of Geriatric Psychiatry, 16*, 794–809.

Folstein, M., Folstein, S., & McHugh, P. (1975). Mini-Mental State: A practical method for grading the cognitive state of patients for the clinician. *Journal of Psychiatric Research, 12*, 189–198.

Franklin, R. D., Allison, D. B., & Gorman, B. S. (1996). *Design and analysis of single-case research.* Hillsdale, NJ: Lawrence Erlbaum Associates, Inc.

Harrell, M., Parente, F., Bellingrath, E. G., & Lisicia, K. A. (Eds.). (1992). *Cognitive rehabilitation of memory: A practical guide.* Gaithersburg, MD: Aspen Publishers.

Harris, S., & Brooks, D. (1992). N of one: Single case research design for the practising clinician. *CPA Research Division Newsletter*, 10–13.

Kirsch, N. L., Levine, S. P., Lajiness, R., Mossaro, M., Schneider, M., & Donders, J. (1988). *Improving functional performance with computerized task guidance systems.* Paper presented at the ICAART 1988 Annual Conference, Arlington, VA.

Kirsch, N. L., Levine, S. P., Lajiness-O'Neill, R., & Schneider, M. (1992). Computer-assisted interactive task guidance: Facilitating the performance of a simulated vocational task. *Journal of Head Trauma Rehabilitation, 7*(3), 13–25.

Kratochwill, T. R. (1978). *Single subject research: Strategies for evaluating change.* New York: Academic Press.

Levinson, R. (1997). PEAT: The Planning and Execution Assistant and Training System. *Journal of Head Trauma Rehabilitation, 12*, 85–91.

LoPresti, E. F., Friedman, M. B., & Hages, D. (1997). *Electronic vocational aid for people with cognitive disabilities.* Paper presented at the RESNA 1997 Annual Conference, Arlington, VA.

LoPresti, E. F., Mihailidis, A., & Kirsch, N. (2004). Assistive technology for cognitive rehabilitation: State of the art. *Neuropsychological Rehabilitation, 14*(1/2), 5–39.

Masters, T. (1993). Probabilistic neural networks. In *Practical neural network recipes in C++* (Vol 1, pp. 202–222). New York: Academic Press.

Mihailidis, A., Fernie, G. R., & Barbenel, J. C. (2001). The use of artificial intelligence in the design of an intelligent cognitive orthosis for people with dementia. *Assistive Technology, 13*, 23–39.

Mihailidis, A., Fernie, G. R., & Cleghorn, W. L. (2000). The development of a computerized cueing device to help people with dementia to be more independent. *Technology & Disability, 13*(1), 23–40.

Mozer, M. (1998). The neural network house: An environment that adapts to its inhabitants. In *Proceedings of the AAAI Spring Symposium on Intelligent Environments*. (Tech. Rep. No. SS-98-02, pp. 110–114). Menlo Park, CA: AAAI Press.

Napper, S. A., & Narayan, S. (1994). *Cognitive orthotic shell.* Paper presented at the RESNA 1994 Annual Conference, Arlington, VA.

Neter, J., Wasserman, W., & Kutner, M. H. (1985). *Applied linear statistical models* (2nd ed.). Homewood, IL: Richard D. Irwin Inc.

Patterson, C. (1999). Focusing on Alzheimer's disease. *The Canadian Journal of Diagnosis, (December)*, 62–74.

Portney, L. G., & Watkins, M. P. (2000). Single-subject designs. In *Foundations of clinical research: Applications to practice* (pp. 223–264). Upper Saddle River, NJ: Prentice Hall Health.

Russell, S., & Norvig, P. (1995). *Artificial intelligence: A modern approach.* Englewood Cliffs, NJ: Prentice Hall.

Salminen, A.-L., & Petrie, H. (1998). *Evaluating assistive technology prototypes: Laboratory or real life contexts.* www.dinf.org/tide98/70/salminen_petri.html

Steele, R. D., Weinrich, M., & Carlson, G. S. (1989). *Recipe preparation by a severely impaired aphasic using the VIC 2.0 interface.* Paper presented at the RESNA 1989 Annual Conference, Arlington, VA.

Stevens, R. D., & Edwards, A. D. N. (1996). *An approach to the evaluation of assistive technology.* Paper presented at the ASSETS, Vancouver, BC, Canada.

United Kingdom (2001). *Prevalence and incidence of dementia* [Website]. Alzheimer Society (UK). http://www.alzheimers.org.uk/society/p_demography.html

Winter, D. A. (1990). *Biomechanics and motor control of human movement* (2nd ed.). Toronto: Wiley-Interscience.

Wolery, M., & Harris, S. R. (1982). Interpreting results of single-subject research designs. *Physical Therapy, 62*(4), 445–452.

NEUROPSYCHOLOGICAL REHABILITATION, 2004, *14* (1/2), 173–206

Aphasia rehabilitation and the strange neglect of speed

M. Alison Crerar

School of Computing, Napier University, Edinburgh, Scotland

Timing data is infrequently reported in aphasiological literature and time taken is only a minor factor, where it is considered at all, in existing aphasia assessments. This is not surprising because reaction times are difficult to obtain manually, but it is a pity, because speed data should be indispensable in assessing the severity of language processing disorders and in evaluating the effects of treatment. This paper argues that reporting accuracy data without discussing speed of performance gives an incomplete and potentially misleading picture of any cognitive function. Moreover, in deciding how to treat, when to continue treatment and when to cease therapy, clinicians should have regard to both parameters: Speed and accuracy of performance. Crerar, Ellis and Dean (1996) reported a study in which the written sentence comprehension of 14 long-term agrammatic subjects was assessed and treated using a computer-based microworld. Some statistically significant and durable treatment effects were obtained after a short amount of focused therapy. Only accuracy data were reported in that (already long) paper, and interestingly, although it has been a widely read study, neither referees nor subsequent readers seemed to miss "the other side of the coin": How these participants compared with controls for their speed of processing and what effect treatment had on speed. This paper considers both aspects of the data and presents a tentative way of combining treatment effects on both accuracy and speed of performance in a single indicator. Looking at rehabilitation this way gives us a rather different perspective on which individuals benefited most from the intervention. It also demonstrates that while some subjects are capable of utilising metalinguistic skills to achieve normal accuracy scores even many years post-stroke, there is little prospect of reducing the time taken to within the normal

Correspondence should be addressed to Alison Crerar, Room C58, Napier University, School of Computing, Merchiston Campus, 10 Colinton Road, Edinburgh EH10 5DT, Scotland. Tel: 0131 455 2710, Fax: 0131 455 2727, E-mail: a.crerar@napier.ac.uk.

http://www.tandf.co.uk/journals/pp/09602011.html DOI:10.1080/09602010343000174

range. Without considering speed of processing, the extent of this residual functional impairment can be overlooked.

INTRODUCTION

This paper is a sequel to Crerar et al. (1996). While it has been written to stand alone as far as possible, readers are referred to the previous paper for more detail since its length and complexity forbid more than a brief recapitulation here. Both that paper and the present one are based on Crerar (1991).

By way of introduction and orientation, part of the abstract of Crerar et al. (1996) is reproduced here:

> . . . fourteen aphasic patients were selected for having problems with sentence–picture matching involving reversible verb and preposition sentences. These problems were shown to be stable across three pre-intervention assessments. All assessments were computer-based and involved the matching of written sentences to pictures. A small vocabulary was used in assessment and therapy which involved a "microworld" of three characters (ball, box, and star) which could engage in a limited number of actions and could occupy a limited set of spatial relationships. Before therapy began, all the patients were given an assessment battery which included a 40-item Verb Test and a 40-item Preposition Test. The patients were then divided into two groups, A and B. Group A received two one-hour sessions of therapy per week for three weeks aimed at improving the comprehension of verb sentences, then a second full assessment, followed by the same amount of therapy aimed at improving the comprehension of preposition sentences, and finally a third assessment. Group B received the preposition therapy first, followed by the verb therapy. The therapy involved the patient and therapist interacting with the computer, either assembling pictures to match written sentences ("picture-building mode") or assembling sentences to match pictures ("sentence-building mode").
>
> Group A showed a classical "cross-over" treatment outcome. Performance on treated verb sentences improved during verb therapy and was retained when therapy switched to preposition sentences. Performance on treated preposition sentences was unaffected by verb therapy but improved when therapy switched to the processing of prepositions. Performance on untreated verb and preposition sentences showed a similar pattern, though the improvements observed were not as great. Improvement was also shown on a paper-based "Real World Test" which involved a wider range of more naturalistic sentences. Performance on a third aspect of sentence comprehension which the patients also had difficulty with, namely the comprehension of morphology, remained unchanged throughout, providing further evidence that the effects obtained were treatment-specific. The results of Group B were less clear-cut. Comprehension of both verb and preposition sentences improved during the period that prepositions were being treated then remained static during verb treatment. Comprehension of morphology remained unchanged throughout.

> At the level of the individual patient, the majority of patients obtained higher scores on both the Verb Test and the Preposition Test after therapy, but only three patients showed improvements on both verbs and prepositions that were statistically significant. Six patients showed significant improvements on verbs but not prepositions while one showed the opposite pattern. Only three patients failed to show so much as a borderline improvement on either verbs or prepositions. Finally, seven of the patients returned for an additional assessment five months after completing the therapy. These patients, who had demonstrated significant improvements during the therapy, were shown to have maintained their improved comprehension skills.

"Reversible sentences" are those in which the subject and object of the sentence can be interchanged equi-plausibly, so, for example, *the girl chased the boy* is a reversible sentence (because *the boy chased the girl* is equally feasible), whereas *the girl ate the carrot* is not (because carrots cannot eat girls). Reversible sentences are routinely used in the diagnosis and treatment of agrammatism because their meaning can only be gleaned if grammatical processing is intact. The meaning of non-reversible sentences, on the other hand, can be worked out using a variety of pragmatic means such as knowledge that inanimate objects, such as carrots, cannot eat anything. The computer-based microworld created for this study was inspired by Schwartz, Saffran, and Marin (1980). By creating a restricted linguistic environment in which to test and treat clients, one in which resulting sentences such as *the ball paints the box* or *the star is behind the ball* are equi-plausible when reversed, we had a diagnostic environment which avoided many of the problems of trying to devise truly reversible sentences in natural English (and of the single word recognition problems agrammatic subjects might have even in recognising a range of nouns).

The general term for acquired disorders of language is aphasia (Berndt, 2001). The subset of aphasia which concerns us is known as *agrammatism* (see Kean, 1995; Schwartz, Fink, & Saffran, 1995; Schwartz et al., 1994, for overviews of the nature and treatment of agrammatism). Agrammatism may be expressive (agrammatic speech) or receptive (often known as asyntactic comprehension). It is asyntactic comprehension of written English sentences with which this study is concerned. So the participants recruited for this work had good single word recognition for the vocabulary of the Microworld, but when those words were combined into reversible sentences, they were unsure, for example, of who was doing what to whom.

The purpose of this paper is to present complementary data, to show how one-sided so much of the aphasia therapy literature is (including our own work), in reporting only accuracy data, or scores. Reaction times are a staple measure in experimental psychology, but due perhaps to the difficulty of capturing these without a computer, they have largely been neglected in reporting the effects of speech and language therapy. In particular, speed data is virtually unknown in reporting remediation of sentence-level deficits. Where reaction times are reported, they are most often associated with eliciting the nature of impairments rather than attempting treatment. Examples of (sentence-level) diagnostic studies including reaction time data are: the study of plausibility judgements to auditory sentences reported by Saffran and colleagues (Saffran, Schwartz, & Linebarger, 1998); verb preference effects in auditory sentence comprehension reported by Russo and colleagues (Russo, Peach, & Shapiro, 1998); results of auditory grammatical judgement tasks given by Devescovi and colleagues (Devescovi et al., 1997) and the auditory picture-naming study of McCall, Cox, Shelton, and Weinrich (1997). Speed of processing has been a major consideration in other avenues of research, for example, the affect of temporal disorders on lexical access (e.g., Prather, Zurif, Love, & Brownell, 1997), theoretical studies of real-time language processing (e.g., Balogh et al., 1998), and a growing body of work on resource-based accounts of aphasic symptomatology (e.g., Miyake, Carpenter, & Just, 1994, 1995; Haarmann, Just, & Carpenter, 1997). However, from a pragmatic point of view, a clinician wishing to know how long an aphasic patient is likely to take to complete a battery of sentence comprehension tasks, how many sentence processing tasks it is feasible to give such a patient, or what the prospects of recovering useful functional speed are, will find a paucity of literature for guidance.

Ways of predicting recovery have been explored by a number of researchers. Code (2001) provides a review of the three main approaches that have been taken. Searching *post hoc* in large group studies for the effect of factors such as age, handedness, presence of dysarthria, site and extent of lesion, etc., has produced little reliable evidence, since, as Code points out, the studies have considered together patients with vastly different ages and aetiologies. However, out of this work, there is evidence that psychosocial adjustment and emotional state are important factors in recovery (Hemsley & Code, 1996). A second approach was based on classification by the now largely discredited construct of "aphasia types", which likewise seemed to produce equivocal results. The third method is to use mathematical techniques to predict scores on standardised aphasia batteries from initial early post-onset measures, to expected scores at specified times (typically 3, 6 and 9 months post-onset). This has been done using multiple regression analysis on the Porch Index of Communicative Abilities (PICA; Porch, 1967) by Porch, Collins, Wertz, and Friden. (1980) and using a neural network trained on the Western Aphasia Battery (WAB; Kertesz, 1982) by Code, Rowley, and Kertesz (1994).

However, the emphasis in these latter studies is on measuring propensity for spontaneous recovery, by taking measurements early post-onset and then later at a chronic post-morbid stage, typically not more than12 months post-onset. The result is prediction of an overall score or quotient. On the other hand, the work reported here tackles recovery prospects in long-term aphasic individuals, specifically asking about whether such individuals can respond to tightly focused therapy for the most impaired aspects of their asyntactic comprehension, and if so, whether we can account for why some individuals improved and others did not. We are interested to understand the quality of the improvement, by looking both at scores, and also at effects on time taken.

Rather than presenting and justifying the experimental method and describing the contents of the novel computer-based assessments used (which is done elsewhere), this paper concentrates on exploring the relationship between the already published accuracy data (Crerar et al., 1996), and the speed data which have not been seen before.

To get a feel for the severity of impairment of the aphasic participants compared with controls, baseline screening tests were administered prior to the efficacy study reported in Crerar et al. (1996). The results of these exploratory assessments are discussed in the next section.

COMPARING APHASICS AND CONTROLS

The 14 aphasic participants (known as P1–P14) recruited for this study were 12 males and 2 females. Their mean age was 52.4 years (range 27–74), and mean interval post-onset was 4 years 4 months (range 0/7–11/2). In order to establish baseline data for the aphasic participants to discover which grammatical elements were preserved and which impaired, and to compare their performance, both for speed and accuracy, with 45 controls matched for age and educational attainment, a Syntax Screening Test (SST) was developed. It used the same computer-based microworld as was described above and contained 42 sentences: seven sentences in each of six grammatical categories. The sentences within each category varied in grammatical complexity. The six grammatical categories (in italics) and one example sentence selected from each is shown below.

- *Verbs*: e.g., The box gives a star to the ball.
- *Adjectives*: e.g., The small red ball and the big yellow box.
- *Scope and quantification*: e.g., None of the balls is red.
- *Pronouns*: e.g., She thinks of him.
- *Prepositions*: e.g., The star is behind the box.
- *Morphology*: e.g., The ball is bigger than the box.

A detailed analysis of the SST can be found in Crerar (1991) and a simpler account in Crerar and Ellis (1995).

The interface design for this test and all subsequent assessments reported here was the same. Four rectangular windows (dimensions 96 cm by 57 cm), one for each of the candidate pictures, were displayed against a black background, with the target sentence displayed boldly beneath them in yellow. Figure 1 illustrates the layout with a schematic diagram of a typical SST screen.

The relative accuracy of the two groups (aphasics and controls), overall, across the six grammatical categories tested, is shown in Figure 2. The aphasics took the test on three occasions and the controls just once. Thus 45 control trials and 42 aphasic trials (14 aphasic participants × 3 trials) are summarised below. The difference in performance between the two groups was marked, especially in the processing of verbs, prepositions and morphology: Expressed as a percentage of normal performance, taking the SST modules shown in Figure 2 in left to right order, the aphasic group achieved 39%, 66%, 70%, 72%, 51%, and 57%, respectively. Overall accuracy on this test was 56% for the aphasics and 93% for the control group (best performance among the control subjects was achieved by those educated to degree level: 97%; worst performance was from the subgroup comprising those with no formal education post-school, and from the subgroup comprising those aged 55 and over: both of these subgroups scored 90%).

Turning to timing data, Figure 3 charts cumulative response latencies accurate to the nearest minute (vertical axis), against the number of participants returning that performance (horizontal axis). The aphasic participants and control subjects were even more widely separated on timing than they were on accuracy. P10 was an exceptional individual, who was well below normal on accuracy but operated at normal speed (his three values in Figure 3 are clearly seen, hatched, at the right of the 5, 6 and 7 minute bars). P10 aside, the maximum and minimum values were 3 minutes and 10 minutes for the control subjects, and 17 minutes and 47 minutes for the

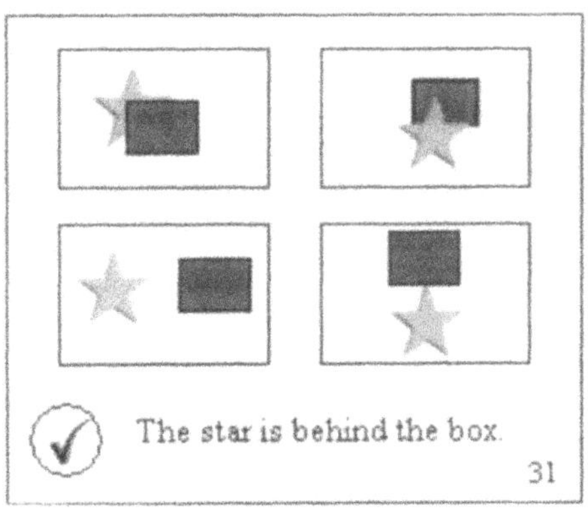

Figure 1. Diagram showing the layout of a typical Microworld assessment screen (This example is from the Syntax Screening Test).

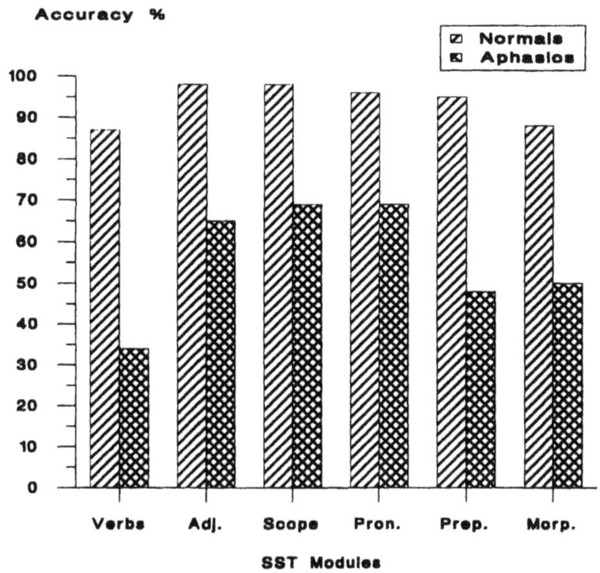

Figure 2. Aphasic and control performances on the six grammatical categories of the Microworld Syntax Screening Test. The aphasics' values are averaged over their three exposures to this test.

aphasic participants. Thus, a very large difference between the two groups was found in their overall speed of processing.

Table 1 shows the results of comparisons of time taken by the aphasic participants and the control subjects on the different grammatical categories contained in the SST.

From this preliminary consideration of the speed and accuracy of the aphasic participants compared with the controls on sentence comprehension tasks exercising six grammatical functions, we have obtained a much richer picture of the nature and severity of their impairments than by the usual accuracy scores alone. It is apparent that the aphasic participants will typically take between 20 and 35 min, with some taking much longer, to complete a 42-sentence test which most controls will complete in 3 to 6 min[1]. This very marked contrast gives us a deeper insight into the severity of the functional impairment the aphasics suffer, and of the very considerable challenge it poses the clinician.

[1] As expected, the time taken increased, and the accuracy of the control subjects decreased, as a function of age and educational attainment, with older and less well-educated subjects tending to perform less well than younger graduates.

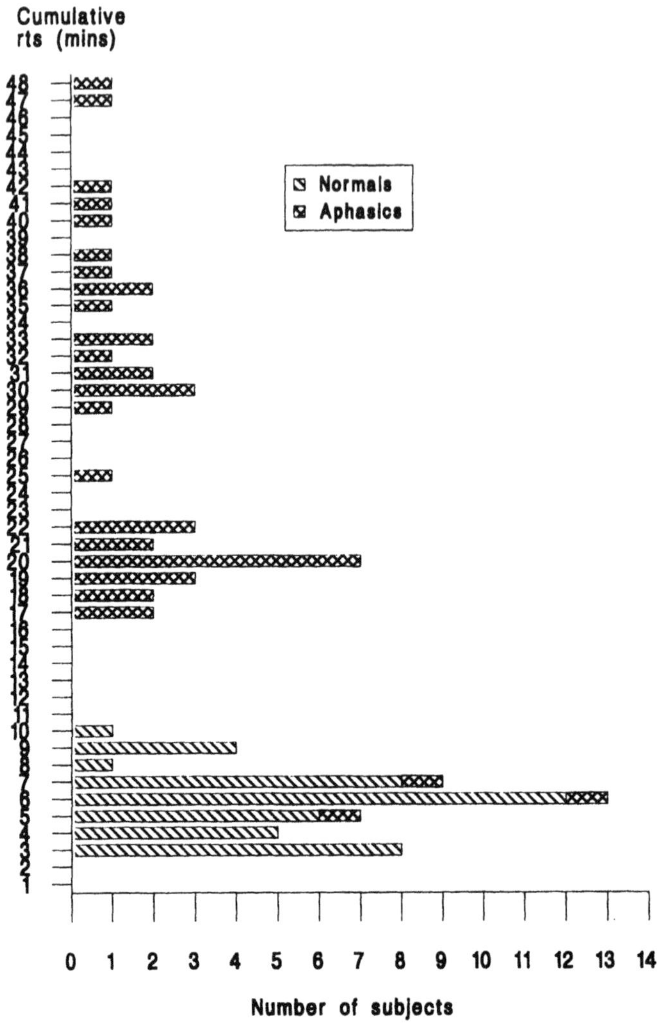

Figure 3. Cumulative response latencies for all participants on the 42-item Syntax Screening Test. 45 control subjects took the test once; 14 aphasic subjects took it three times.

Readers may be curious to know how much of the time taken to respond to these sentence-level tasks was "think time" and how much was "selection time", that is the process of using the computer mouse to make a choice. Repeated baseline measurements were taken prior to the start of this treatment study to establish stability and as part of these tests, ability to use the computer interface was tested. To do this, the same interface as shown in Figure 1 was employed, but presenting 20 trials of a non-linguistic task. Each

TABLE 1
Mean reactions times (sec) of the control subjects and the aphasic participants to the grammatical categories tested by the Microworld Syntax Screening Test. The aphasics' values are averaged over their three exposures to this test.

Group	*Verbs* (*n* = 7)	*Adjectives* (*n* = 7)	*Scope and quantification* (*n* = 7)	*Pronouns* (*n* = 7)	*Prepositions* (*n* = 7)	*Morphology* (*n* = 7)
Controls (n = 45)	11.61	6.48	7.54	7.26	6.78	8.62
Aphasics (n = 14)	50.64	29.95	37.50	32.30	38.04	36.18

screen comprised four windows, three empty ones and a red rectangle (2.5 cm by 2 cm) displayed in the centre of the fourth. The window position of the rectangle was randomly generated for each screen. Participants were required to use the mouse to move the cursor anywhere inside the window containing the red rectangle and to indicate their choice by clicking the mouse button. The program recorded each participant's score out of 20 and mean response latency[2]. The Interface Test was given as a preliminary warming up exercise on each of the three occasions that the SST was administered, thus it was possible to monitor the durability or improvement in mouse skills over a period of months when there was no opportunity to practice between sessions. The mean response times for the 14 aphasic participants on their three exposures to the 20-item Interface Test were 10.20 seconds, 6.14 seconds and 3.88 seconds respectively (overall accuracy was 839/840). The inter-test gaps ranged from 4 weeks to 16 weeks. Only one of the aphasic individuals had previously used a mouse.

The 45 control subjects, who were matched with the aphasics for age and educational attainment, took the Interface Test on one occasion only. Four of these non-aphasic participants had used a mouse before. The control subjects were asked to use their non-dominant hand for all the tests reported here, as 10 of the aphasic group were forced to do this through hemiplegia. The overall accuracy rate for the control group was 899/900 and the mean response latency was 2.25 second with a standard deviation of 0.97 second. (Mean response latencies by ascending order of age class were 1.66, 2.21 and 2.91 seconds).

[2] Measured as the elapsed time from onset of task to selection of a window (including changes of mind) but not including the extra time required to select the confirm button (the tick button in Figure 1), which invoked the next task.

From this comparison, we see that the aphasic participants quickly mastered the mouse, that their accuracy in selecting the desired target was virtually 100% and that the mean time taken to identify and select a (non-linguistic) target was under 4 s prior to the start of the treatment phase.

TREATMENT EFFECTS ON SPEED AND ACCURACY

For the treatment phase of this study, the aphasic participants were randomly allocated to one of two treatment groups, known as Group A and Group B. Both groups were treated and assessed over the same 12 week period. During weeks 1 and 2 they took assessment tests including the 40-item Microworld Verb and Preposition assessment tests reported below. In weeks 3, 4 and 5 each participant received two one-hour treatment sessions (6 hours in total). Group A received verb therapy during these weeks and Group B received preposition therapy. During weeks 6 and 7 the assessment tests were repeated. In weeks 8, 9 and 10 Group A received 2 hours per week of preposition therapy and Group B received the same amount of verb therapy. Finally, during weeks 11 and 12 the assessment tests were administered for a final time.

Given the very long test completion times for the SST (which contained some parts of language relatively well preserved in the aphasics: namely adjectives, scope and quantification, and pronouns), it was anticipated that, confronted subsequently with tests comprising 40 "verb only" sentences or 40 "preposition only" sentences, many of the aphasic participants would be even slower. Thus it was considered that accuracy apart, most of the aphasic individuals were seriously functionally impaired by virtue of not being able to operate at anything approaching normal speed. Where the total time taken for an assessment test exceeded about 40 minutes[3] it was considered particularly important to try to reduce it, and large increases in time taken (even accompanying increases in accuracy) after therapy were regarded as detrimental to the overall treatment outcome. Indeed, the purpose of this paper is to highlight this very issue and to find a way of expressing treatment outcome in a way that takes account of effects on speed as well as on accuracy.

In this section an overview is presented first of the changes in total time taken by the two aphasic groups (Group A who received verb therapy followed by preposition therapy and Group B who received the treatments in the opposite order) for both functions treated (verbs and prepositions), between assessment sessions 1 and 2 (pre-therapy to post-first function

[3] That is, participants were averaging more than 1 minute to complete each of the 40 sentence/picture-matching tasks.

treated) and assessment sessions 2 and 3 (post-first function treated to post-second function treated). This is followed by an examination of individual participant's performances, comparing changes in accuracy with total time taken for the tests.

Total time taken was chosen as the performance measure for this comparison for several reasons. While the software collected mean reaction time (RT) for every task presented, and these values were used in other parts of our analysis, we found that total time taken was a more useful figure for describing overall treatment effects. Total time taken gives much more of a feel for the severity of impairment than a mean RT, it is a measure understandable by all parties and; it gives a meaningful measure that can be used to schedule clinical appointments. These tests consisted of a range of sentence structures, some taking much longer to complete than others: in this context a mean RT might not represent typical performance on any of the items. Finally, total time taken captures elapsed time due to attention span and stamina. This we felt was important in gaining a richer understanding of the effort involved for these individuals in completing these demanding assessments and in discovering how treatment might affect it. In practice, we found that the pause facility in the software (which could only be invoked by the clinician) was rarely ever needed, and that these subjects were generally able to concentrate for the duration of the test and to self-administer the tests discussed here with barely any assistance from the observing researchers.

An ANOVA was carried out on the total test completion times (in minutes) for the Verb Test and Preposition Test of Group A, Group B and both aphasic groups combined. The group analyses were performed with two within-subjects factors: Sessions (3 levels: session 1, session 2 and session 3) and Function type (2 levels: verbs and prepositions), and no between-groups factors. The combined analysis used the same within-subjects factors and one between-groups factor: Groups (2 levels: Group A and Group B).

No significant main effects were found. Group A: Sessions $F(2, 12) = 1.48$, $MSe = 156.02$, n.s., Function type $F(1, 6) = 0.32$, $MSe = 17.36$, n.s. Group B: Sessions $F(2, 12) = 0.22$, $MSe = 19.45$, n.s., Function type $F(1, 6) = 0.54$, $MSe = 126.88$, n.s. Combined: Groups $F(1, 12) = 1.25$, $MSe = 960.19$, n.s., Sessions $F(2, 24) = 1.08$, $MSe = 104.57$, n.s., Function type $F(1, 12) = 0.83$, $MSe = 119.05$, n.s. The mean test completion times for Group A collapsed across Function type were 30.36, 23.86 and 28.43 minutes for sessions 1, 2 and 3, respectively, and for Group B the corresponding values were 35.50, 34.28 and 33.14 minutes. None of the interactions approached significance with the exception of Group B's first order interaction between Sessions and Function type, $F(2, 12) = 3.20$, $MSe = 27.60$, $p = .08$.

The ANOVA showed that considering the data overall, or separately by treatment group, therapy had not had a significant effect on the speed of processing of the Microworld items (although significant effects were found for real world items[4]). This outcome was not unexpected in view of the very large variability in test completion times and in speed/accuracy relationships at initial assessment. For example, the baseline Verb Test produced a maximum test completion time of 84 minutes (P2) and a minimum test completion time of 6 minutes (P10). P10 functioned at normal speed but was inaccurate, while P12 was accurate on prepositions but slow (39 minutes), and less accurate on verbs and even slower (73 minutes), P14 was very inaccurate (20/40 verbs, 10/40 prepositions) but fairly fast by aphasic standards (26 minutes verbs; 21 minutes prepositions). With such a range of starting positions, it was predictable that the patients should exhibit different treatment effects with respect to time taken. Moreover, it was necessary in any event to scrutinise their data on an individual basis to determine how far therapeutic goals (which for the slower patients specifically targeted speed) had been met. Similarly, in considering individuals who had maintained improvements in accuracy on the first-treated function throughout therapy in the second function, it was important to examine corresponding changes to speed for a better understanding of the quality of the treatment effects.

In view of the very large range of values in the timing data, and wishing therefore to avoid the calculation of means, the timing data for Groups A and B (both Verb Test and Preposition Test) was examined to determine the changes that had taken place in total time taken for test completions between assessment sessions 1 and 2 and assessment sessions 2 and 3. The method used was (for each test taken) to sum the total time taken by each member of a group for each test session and then to subtract the session 2 total from the session 1 total to obtain a measure of change after the first function treated, and to subtract the session 3 total from the session 2 total to do the same for the second function treated. This yielded the nett change in minutes for the group as a whole. The results for Group A are shown in Figure 4b (with the accuracy results for comparison at Figure 4a) and the corresponding results for Group B are given in Figure 5b (with their accuracy results shown in Figure 5a). The pre-therapy status of each function treated is plotted with an origin of zero in Figures 4b and 5b, so positive slopes indicate increases in time taken and negative slopes indicate decreases in time taken. Hence in these graphs and the individual ones that follow, negative slopes are desirable. Additionally, throughout this section the graphs are annotated with a plus sign where the associated accuracy increased, if accuracy remained constant this is indicated by a zero and if accuracy declined this is indicated by a minus sign. Thus the optimum combination is a negative slope with a

[4] This result refers to time taken to complete the paper-based Real World Test mentioned in the abstract quoted above.

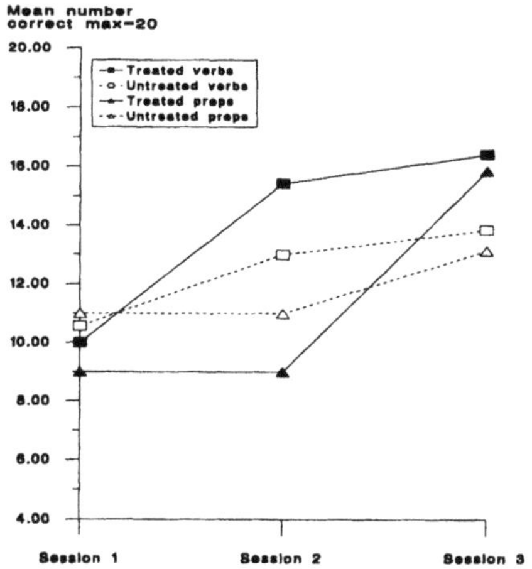

Figure 4a. Treatment effects on accuracy for Group A (verbs treated first). (See Note.)

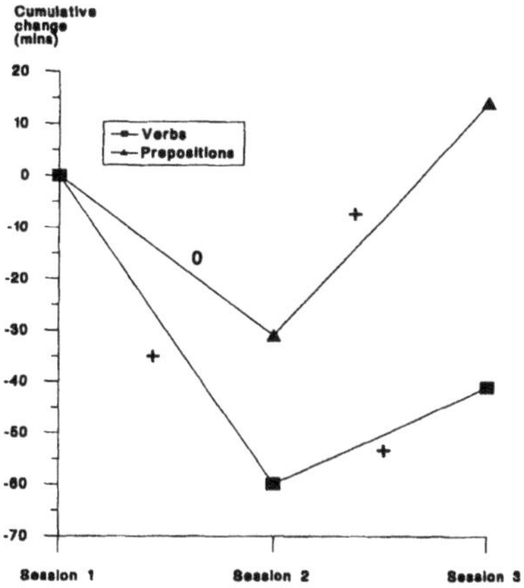

Figure 4b. Treatment effects on total time taken for Group A.

Test session 1 was done pre-therapy. Test session 2 was done after verb therapy. Test session 3 was done after preposition therapy.

Note: In Figure 4a, the verb and preposition test each comprised 40 sentences: 20 of these had been treated in therapy and 20 had not. The tests were constructed in such a way as to probe different sentence structures, but we will not be concerned with that detail here.

plus sign beside it, as in the Verb Test results between sessions 1 and 2 plotted in Figure 4b.

Figure 4b highlights the interesting result that therapy was conspicuously more successful in reducing Group A's overall time for completing the Verb Test (where the nett change for the group between sessions 1 and 3 was 41 minutes)[5] than for completing the Preposition Test (where an overall increase of 14 minutes between sessions 1 and 3 was observed). Another noteworthy feature of this data is the extra information it furnishes about the effects of verb therapy on the Preposition Test (i.e., that there was an overall reduction of about 30 minutes in Group A's cumulative time taken to complete this test). The annotation (zero) on the preposition line-segment between sessions 1 and 2 in Figure 4b is a reminder that accuracy on preposition items remained unchanged following verb therapy. This is an interesting finding that modifies the impression gained from accuracy data alone, i.e., that there had been no change in Group A's Preposition Test performances as a result of verb therapy. Figure 4b also shows that verb items took slightly

[5] However, from the individual graphs (Figure 6a) it will be seen that P2 was responsible for 41 minutes of the Group's overall improvement of 60 minutes between sessions 1 and 2.

longer after preposition therapy than directly after verb therapy, so while accuracy continued to increase there is evidence of the tasks being a little more effortful after a lapse of five weeks (this may have been due to their not having been practised recently, or to some interference from preposition therapy). Finally, it is clear from Figure 4b that Group A's excellent preposition results were not obtained without some loss of speed. Interestingly, following verb therapy the group saved 31 minutes on prepositions without loss of accuracy, but following preposition therapy lost 45 minutes on their improved speeds in attaining the results summarised in Figure 4a. This observation gives some insight into the effort expended, even by the better group, in achieving the results reported in Crerar et al. (1996).

The corresponding results for Group B are shown in Figures 5a and 5b. Their pattern of performance is quite different. Overall, in marked contrast to Group A, there was barely any change at all in the time taken to complete preposition items (although individuals, of course, contradict this). While their overall performance was disappointing compared with Group A, it was good to see that the significant improvement in performance on prepositions and verbs *combined* between sessions 1 and 2, was achieved without a time penalty. The decline in preposition performance between sessions 2 and 3 was disappointing, but at least it was not accompanied by an overall decrease in speed (there were exceptions e.g., P11, see Figure 7b). However, the heaviest losses to preposition accuracy after verb treatment were suffered by

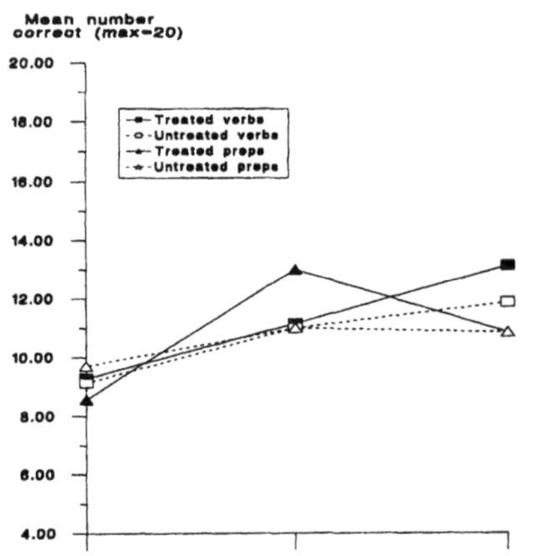

Figure 5a. Treatment effects on accuracy for Group B (prepositions treated first).

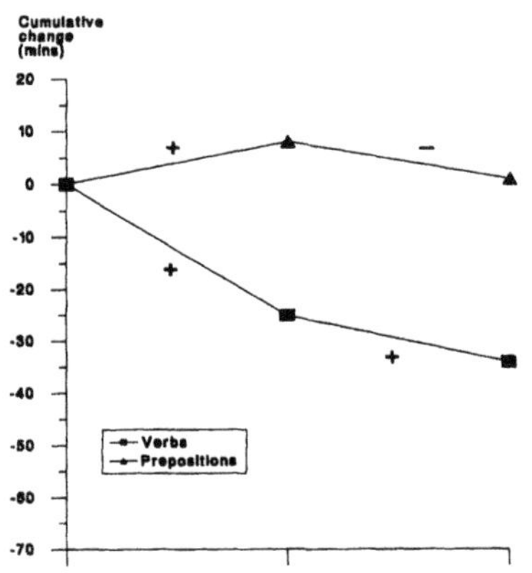

Figure 5b. Treatment effects on total time taken for Group B.

Test session 1 was done pre-therapy. Test session 2 was done after preposition therapy. Test session 3 was done after verb therapy.

P9 and P14—their graphs in Figures 7a and 7b tend to suggest that if verb therapy had undermined their grasp of prepositions, it certainly had done so at a level which caused them no conscious dilemma.

Group B's results show that the increases in performance on verb items after preposition therapy and after verb therapy were both accompanied by decreases in overall time taken, with the larger gains, oddly, being apparent after preposition therapy. The differential between changes to verb processing time and preposition processing time between sessions 1 and 3 was not as great as for Group A, but nevertheless the two groups showed the same trend with Verb Test times much reduced compared with Preposition Test times.

The presentation of individual results which follows has also been based on the total time taken for completion of the Verb Test and Preposition Test recorded at sessions 1, 2 and 3 (rather than mean response latencies). This was found to be a useful global measure for practical purposes (e.g., for communicating a tangible measure of progress to patients and their relatives and for planning appointments and transportation) as it yields one readily assimilable value for each test, allowing patients to be easily compared and the changes both over sessions and between the two treated functions to be easily appreciated. The test completion times for members of Group A are summarised in the graphs comprising Figures 6a and 6b and similar data for Group B is shown in Figures 7a and 7b. As in Figures 5a and 5b, the line segments of the single-case graphs are annotated with either "+", "0" or "–" to indicate whether the accuracy score associated with that particular test increased, remained static, or declined. It was not possible to use the same vertical axis scaling for all graphs because of the very large ranges involved. The graphs of P2, P10 and P12 are different from the others in this respect, so care should be taken when making comparisons.

The individual performance graphs were very informative in a number of ways, facilitating a speed-related overview of the whole data set, a comparison of intra-group results and detailed observations on single cases. Figures 6a, 6b, 7a and 7b show that the majority of participants took longer to complete the Verb Test at session 1 than to complete the Preposition Test (eight participants took longer on the Verb Test, four participants took longer on the Preposition Test and two participants took equal times for both). Interestingly, three of these individuals (P2, P11 and P14) who initially took longer to complete the Verb Test than the Preposition Test returned quite noticeably longer preposition times at session 3. The opposite change (prepositions taking longer at session 1 but being faster than verbs at session 3) did not occur. Thus in this set of participants, if prepositions were slower than verbs at session 1 (P3, P4, P5, P7), therapy never reversed that pattern.

A pictorial representation of relative timings is useful in identifying subjects with, for example, an unusually large discrepancy between the time

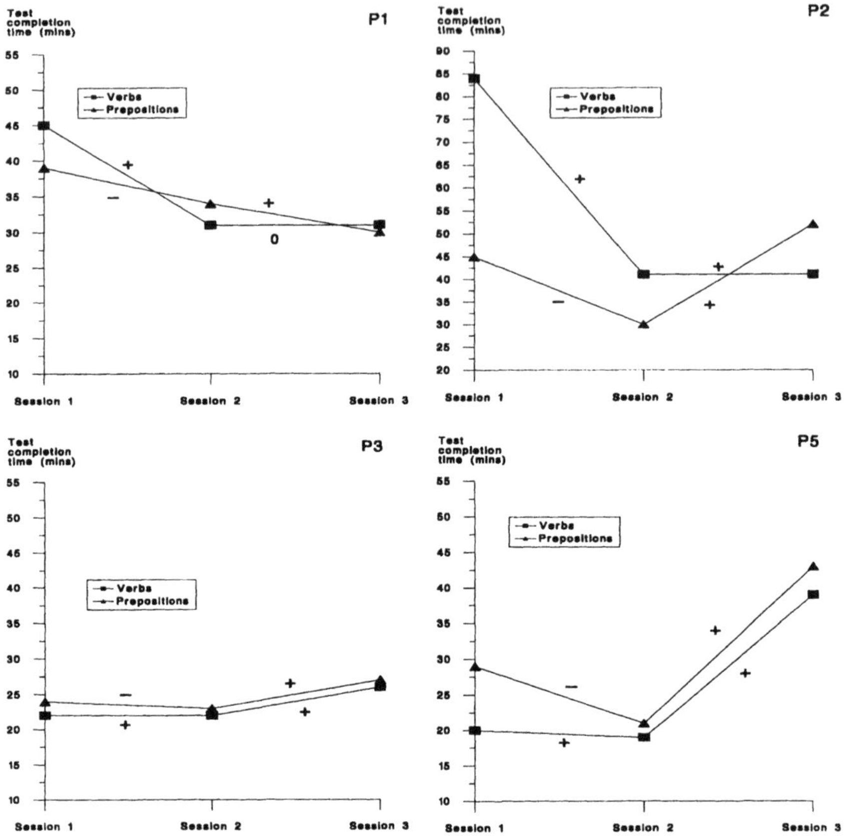

Figure 6a. Group A treatment effects (speed). Verbs were treated between test sessions 1 and 2 and prepositions were treated between test sessions 2 and 3.

taken for one test and the other. P2 and P12 stood apart from the other participants at session 1 in displaying very large differences between their completion times for the Verb Test and the Preposition Test (both taking of the order of twice as long to complete the verb items as to complete the preposition items). One can see from their graphs that the outcome of therapy was different in each case. The initial pattern was reversed in the case of P2 who responded well (time-wise) to verb therapy, but showed an increase in the time taken to complete preposition items after preposition therapy. P12, on the other hand, managed to decrease the time taken for both treated functions, more so in verbs than in prepositions, but at session 3 still showed a striking difference in the time taken to complete the two tests (verbs 55 minutes; prepositions 31 minutes). (Interestingly, P4's graph

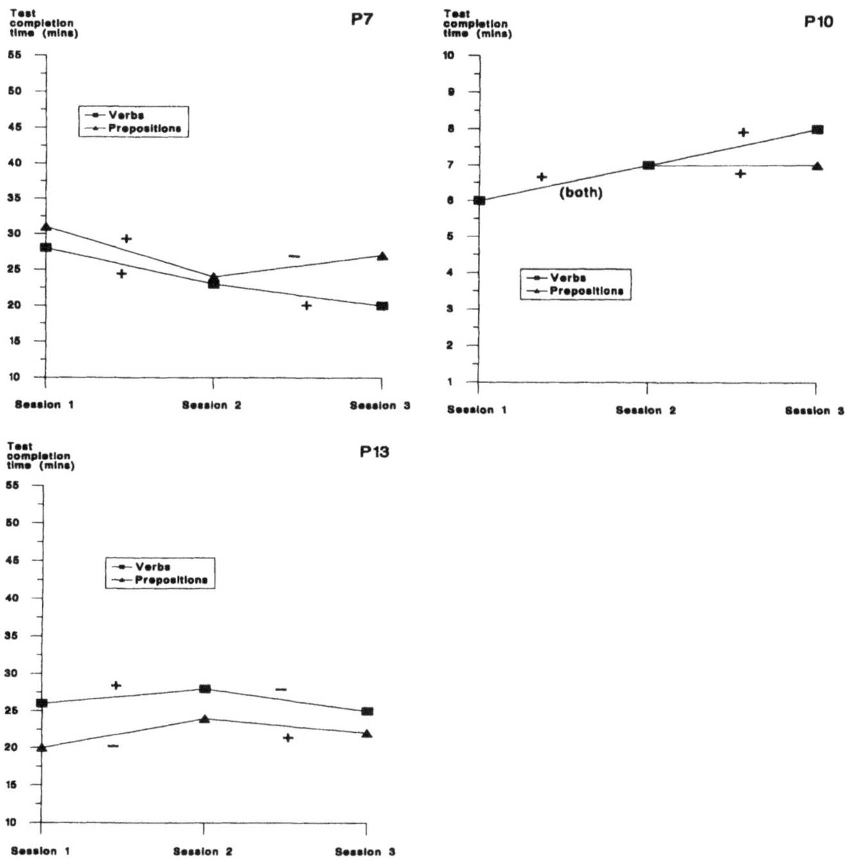

Figure 6b. Group A treatment effects (speed) (cont.). Verbs were treated between test sessions 1 and 2 and prepositions were treated between test sessions 2 and 3.

shows the opposite pattern of performance, i.e., a consistent and large difference in time between the two tests, with prepositions taking longer). From this single example it is obvious that accuracy data alone furnish a very incomplete picture of cognitive performance. Indeed, the contrast between the timing data of P4 and P12 indicates that it may prove worthwhile to detect and explore dissociations of speed as routinely as those of accuracy in analysing pathological performances. A profile such as P12's in Figure 7b is suggestive of a residual disorder for some aspect particular to the verb processing tasks, despite a reduction in time taken from 73 minutes to 55 minutes and an increase in accuracy from 25/40 to 30/40. In fact P12's difficulty was found to be one of visual interpretation. P12 was worse in the Microworld, where he often found the salient aspects of the Verb Test

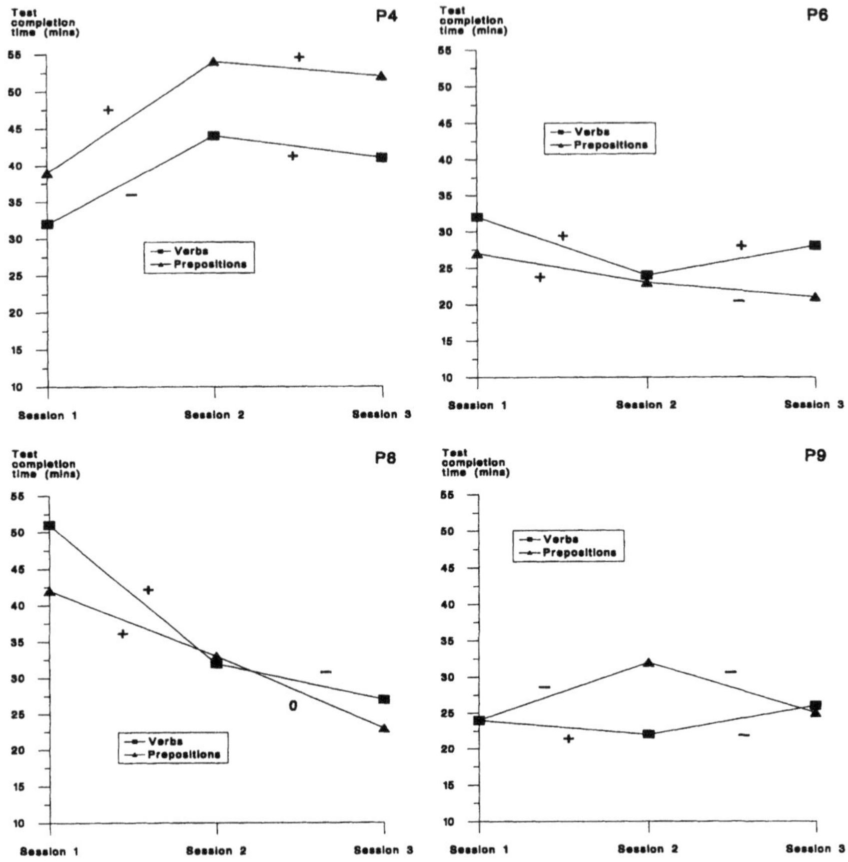

Figure 7a. Group B treatment effects (speed). Prepositions were treated between test sessions 1 and 2 and verbs were treated between test sessions 2 and 3.

pictures hard to identify (this was discovered during remediation sessions), but his Real World Test[6] performance also showed a smaller but still constant difference between the time taken to process verb items and to process preposition items.

With respect to the overall timing results and the extent to which therapy was successful in improving processing speeds, inspection of the individual

[6] This was a paper-based sentence/picture-matching test, presented in the same format as shown in Figure 1. There were 20 verb and 20 preposition sentences, maintaining the same contrasts of treated and untreated verbs, prepositions and sentence structures as presented in the computer-based Microworld, but the Real World Test had a much wider vocabulary describing more naturalistic scenarios. It was used to test generalisation to "real world" reading tasks.

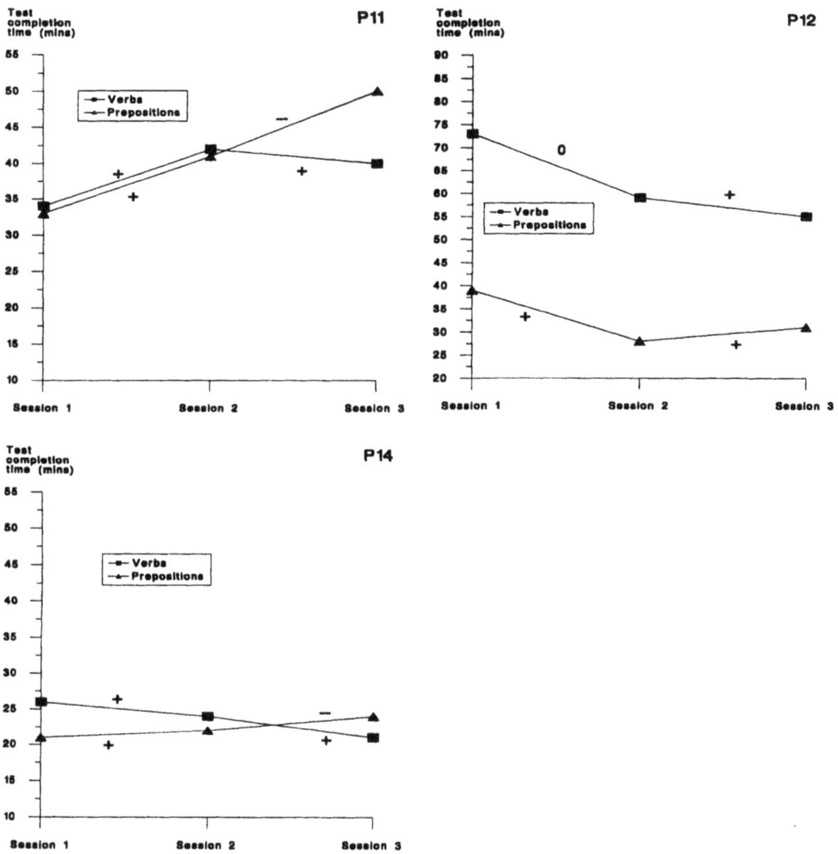

Figure 7b. Group B treatment effects (speed) (cont.). Prepositions were treated between test sessions 1 and 2 and verbs were treated between test sessions 2 and 3.

graphs shows that the most dramatic improvements were made in cases where the pre-therapy speeds were very slow (i.e., 40 minutes or longer). Particularly successful instances included P1 (verbs: 45 minutes at session 1; 31 minutes at sessions 2 and 3), P2 (verbs: 84 minutes at session 1; 41 minutes at sessions 2 and 3) and P8 (verbs: 51 minutes at session 1; 27 minutes at session 3; prepositions: 42 minutes at session 1; 23 minutes at session 3). Where times taken initially were between 20 and 40 minutes, large improvements seemed much more difficult to make. The largest improvement recorded in this band was made by P1 (prepositions: 39 minutes at session 1; 30 minutes at session 3) and many patients in this middle range became considerably slower after therapy (e.g., P4, P5, P11). *In no case was therapy successful in reducing the time taken for either of the assessment tests below*

20 minutes. P10 continued to be an exception (as he had been on the Syntax Screening Test reported above) taking between 6 and 8 minutes to complete his verb and preposition tests. He showed distinct improvements in accuracy between sessions 1 and 3, achieving final scores of 33/40 (Verb Test) and 31/40 (Preposition Test). These results could not have been obtained by chance, hence we can be confident that P10 was completing the sentence processing tasks and doing so well within a normal time span.

An analysis was also done of timing data relating to the aphasics' performances on treated versus untreated verb and preposition sentences in the computer-based Microworld environment, to different sentence structures used in the Microworld assessments and also on their performance on the Real World Test. Interested readers are referred to Crerar (1991).

OVERALL TREATMENT OUTCOME

A commonly recurring theme in the aphasia literature relates to the difficulty of proving the efficacy of speech and language therapy, and relatedly, about issues of accountability. In response to the case made by Petheram and Parr (1998) for the value of qualitative dimensions of treatment outcome, Cappa (1998, p. 455) wrote,

> I am afraid that health care providers (or health care buyers as the story seems to go nowadays) are not in general ready to accept qualitative methods for outcome evaluation.

Hence, in attempting a summary of the results of this efficacy study three related issues emerged which are at the forefront of current clinical debate. The first, and central one, is the notion of overall *treatment outcome*; finding some global measure of treatment[7] effect by which an individual's progress can be gauged and by which the outcomes of different subjects can be compared. The other two issues depend on amassing a database of treatment outcomes together with a method of analysing them. One concerns the ability to formalise, study, rationalise and debate the bases for decisions regarding ongoing patient management, the other is the complementary process of selecting the most appropriate candidates for therapy programmes in the first place, based on previous treatment histories (they both hinge on being able to derive useful prognoses). As a first step towards doing this we offer a tentative measure of overall treatment outcome for each patient in this study, an indication of whether any factor or combination of factors could be identified that would have predicted treatment outcome, and finally, based on the

[7] By this we mean a measure specific to the deficit treated and not some more general global measure such as one of the standardised language batteries like PICA or WAB.

experience of this clinical trial, what the recommendations for P1–P14 would have been were therapy to have continued, and why.

Table 2 summarises the changes to accuracy and speed of P1–P14 in verbs and prepositions and for both functions combined. The participants are presented in descending order of overall treatment outcome according to a formula outlined below. Negative results do not necessarily imply that patients got worse, but show that when speed *as well as* accuracy was taken into account these outcomes were judged to be, on balance, negative. Negative treatment outcomes are not synonymous with unsuccessful treatment (the accuracy of the four participants at the bottom of Table 2, on verbs and prepositions, had improved in seven out of eight cases), on inspection they may indicate a strong case for further treatment, possibly of revised complexity. All the data in Table 2 are based on changes in performance between sessions 1 and 3 (i.e., the difference between pre-therapy status and performance after completion of the second treatment block). The accuracy entries in Table 2 have been calculated by subtracting the score at session 1 (expressed as a percentage of 40) from the score at session 3 (expressed as a percentage of 40: The maximum score achievable). Thus for every improvement of 1 point on an assessment test a patient was deemed to have improved by 2.5%, irrespective of his or her baseline score. The speed entries were calculated slightly differently, there not being a fixed target. For these, the changes were based on the participant's test completion time at session 1. For

TABLE 2
Indicators of treatment outcome P1–P14

	Verb Test			*Preposition Test*			*Overall treatment outcome*
Patient	*Accuracy*	*Speed*	*PI*	*Accuracy*	*Speed*	*PI*	
P1	+45.00	−31.11	+38.06	+57.50	−23.08	+40.29	+39.18
P8	+7.50	−47.06	+27.28	+20.00	−45.24	+32.62	+29.95
P2	+37.50	−51.19	+44.35	+25.00	+15.56	+4.72	+24.54
P6	+22.50	−12.50	+17.50	+12.50	−22.22	+17.36	+17.43
P12	+12.50	−24.66	+18.58	+5.00	−20.51	+12.76	+15.67
P7	+17.50	−28.57	+23.04	−5.00	−12.90	+3.95	+13.50
P10	+25.00	+33.33	+12.50	+25.00	+16.67	+12.50	+12.50
P14	+15.00	−19.23	+17.12	+7.50	+14.29	+3.75	+10.44
P3	+20.00	+18.18	+10.00	+10.00	+12.50	+5.00	+7.50
P13	−2.50	−3.85	+0.68	+27.50	+10.00	+13.75	+7.22
P9	+25.00	+8.33	+12.50	−22.50	+4.17	−13.34	−0.42
P4	+7.50	+28.13	−10.32	+32.50	+33.33	−0.42	−5.37
P11	+25.00	+17.65	+3.68	+5.00	+51.52	−23.26	−9.79
P5	+27.50	+45.00	−8.75	+17.50	+44.83	−13.67	−11.21

PI: performance indicator

example, P1 took 45 minutes to complete the Verb Test pre-therapy and 31 minutes at session 3, so his speed datum is –31.11%, (45–31/45) × 100, an improvement of just under one third. Where a patient's pre-therapy time was less than 30 minutes (a threshold explained below) and his session 3 time exceeded 30 minutes, only the increase beyond 30 minutes was considered in calculating the speed component (P5 was the only patient to whom this rule applied).

In calculating the overall outcome for each treated function (the columns headed PI, an abbreviation for performance indicator) the signs preceding the speed data were reversed (because a negative change to speed constitutes an improvement). Increases in time taken were ignored (scored as zero in the calculation of the PI) where the test completion time at session 3 was under 30 minutes[8] *and* there had been an increase in accuracy (e.g., P3 Verb Test), in all other cases the speed and accuracy changes were summed and divided by two[9]. Similarly the final column, marked "overall treatment outcome", was obtained by summing the two performance indicators and dividing the result by two.

Thirty minutes was chosen as the functional speed threshold for the calculations in Table 2 based on the performance characteristics of P1–P14. The rationale for this was as follows: It was felt that the patients fell into three categories; first, P10 was a singleton, being the only subject to operate in the normal speed range. Second, there was a set of participants such as P3, P7, P13 and P14 who operated in the 20–30 minute range in both functions before and after therapy. Third, there was a set of individuals with excessively long response times, e.g., P1, P2, P4 and P12, and/or who declined in speed following treatment to overly long times, e.g., P5 and P11. In no case was therapy successful in reducing total time taken below 20 minutes and on the whole the patients in the 20–30 minute band remained fairly static. Thus on the basis of this small sample of subjects and this small input of therapy (6 hours in each of the two functions treated), there is little cause for optimism in seeking to substantially reduce the processing speed of patients

[8] This was to avoid small increases in time taken negating or diminishing increases in accuracy, where the final operating speed was still very acceptable (P3, P9, P10, P13 and P14 were involved). P4 and P10 provide data to clarify this principle. Both subjects showed increases of 33.33% in time taken to complete assessments (P4 prepositions; P10 verbs) however P4's time taken increased from 39 minutes to 52 minutes whereas P10's increased from 6 to just 8 minutes. These are extreme examples, but show that when considering the implications of increased response times, it is necessary also to bear in mind the absolute time taken and whether the increase represents a functional handicap.

[9] Notice, for example, that a large improvement in speed without an improvement in accuracy would result in a halving of the impact of the speed increase, because in that case the accuracy component would be zero. The same is true of an accuracy increase without a speed increase (subject to the "30 minute rule").

into the vast gulf between P10's speeds of 6–8 minutes and P7's next best time of 20 minutes. On the other hand, there was considerable success in reducing the very long processing speeds down towards the 30 minute mark, e.g., P1. Thus 30 minutes was selected as a functional cut-off point; a realistic target speed for slower aphasic subjects, and for faster individuals, a speed below which increases in accuracy were considered to outweigh increases in time taken.

It must be stressed that Table 2 *is a guide only* as to how the quantitative results of treatment may be used to calculate and rank outcomes. This analysis is presented as an example of a mathematical approach: There can be much debate about how the calculations are done and whether weightings should be applied[10]. The point is that having produced such a preliminary model, it becomes much easier to formulate relevant questions as to appropriate weightings and whether, for example the introduction of functional thresholds (or performance bands) would be better than applying the same rules no matter what the pre-therapy/post-therapy level of impairment. For example, it may be felt that the method used above places too high a weighting on speed compared with accuracy and that a patient such as P5, who improved on both functions (verbs 21/40 → 32/40; prepositions 22/40 → 29/40) although showing large increases in time taken (verbs 20 minutes → 39 minutes; prepositions 29 minutes → 43 minutes) still merits a positive overall treatment outcome. As explained above, an effort has been made to ameliorate the effect of a speed increase where the patient was still operating at a good (aphasic) functional level (30 minutes or less). On the other hand, P12's performance indicator for the Preposition Test is possibly lower than his achievement merits because he was at ceiling on accuracy and his increase in speed had been diluted by a very small positive change in accuracy. In most cases, of course, objectives will be to improve both speed and accuracy, but this example highlights the need for flexibility in building evaluative systems so that exceptional objectives can be accommodated. Appropriate threshold levels are clearly a matter for debate and much more work needs to be done on treating sentence processing deficits to establish recovery patterns and thus be able to set realistic therapeutic goals and make informed judgements as to efficacy.

Given the range of performances evident in this small cohort, it is unlikely that the development of any evaluative algorithm, no matter how sophisticated, would satisfy all aphasic cases equally well. It is certainly not

[10] There is no reason why other important qualitative factors should not be added to such a model. For example, this study found anecdotal evidence of other benefits of this style of therapy in these long-term aphasic individuals. For example, if effects on self-confidence are being observed, or reported by carers, and these are important and measurable in some way, then they can be included and weighted appropriately.

suggested that automation should supplant human clinical judgement, but that it provides the basis for objective decision-making (the premises of which are open to scrutiny) and for shareable clinical databases. What is clear from this study is that speed must be an important parameter in the evaluation of sentence-level therapy, because of the very long response latencies that typically arise and the potentially serious functional consequences of unduly prolonging them. Moreover, in assessing treatment outcome it is important to be able to distinguish cases where increases in time taken constitute increases in handicap (irrespective of accuracy, e.g., P4), and conversely, for instance, to be able to credit improvements in speed independent of changes in accuracy (e.g., to P12 who was near ceiling on prepositions prior to therapy, but was slow).

There is no such thing as a definitive formula and certainly a realistic clinical model would want to take a number of variables into account, perhaps favouring one version over another for different purposes. However, Table 2 does produce a principled ranking of P1–P14 suitable as the core of an equation that could be fine-tuned for increased sensitivity and to which additional factors could quite easily be added. It was pleasing to see that even by this rather stringent measure of treatment outcome, only four patients gave concern that the overall treatment effects had been other than resoundingly positive. An examination of the two accuracy columns shows that between sessions 1 and 3, all patients except P13 made progress on verbs and all patients with the exception of P7 and P9 made progress on prepositions. Therefore, of the 14 participants treated, 11 showed improvements in accuracy on both verbs and prepositions, the remaining three improved on one function and declined on the other (only one of these latter patients, P9, failed to respond to therapy on the function that was weaker at session 3 than at baseline; P7 and P13 both improved after treatment and then regressed). However, it is also clear from Table 2 that response time suffered in many cases; 6 patients took longer to complete the Verb Test at session 3 than at the baseline test and 9 of the 14 patients took longer to complete the Preposition Test. Hence, response time was adversely affected in many cases, a few of which resulted in serious degradations of "performance" as shown by the performance indicators (Table 2). Since the amount of therapy given was very short (six hours in each function), it is possible that extending the treatment period might have shown greater benefits to time taken, and perhaps even larger improvements to accuracy.

The method used to calculate the overall treatment outcomes in Table 2 produces a very different impression of the patients' performances than would have been obtained by considering only changes in accuracy. To explore the degree of difference between the method used above and the more usual score-based evaluations, the two accuracy entries in Table 2 were summed for each patient and the rank ordering, shown in Table 3, was

TABLE 3
Ranking of P1–P14 by overall improvement in verb and preposition accuracy only

Rank	*1*	*2*	*3*	*4*	*5*	*6*	*7*	*8*	*9*	*10*	*11*	*12*	*13*	*14*
Participant	P1	P2	P10	P5	P4	P6	P3	P11	P8	P13	P14	P12	P7	P9

compared with the ordering given in Table 2. The correlation between the two was found to be low ($r = 0.2$).

Finally, considering the participants as individuals, we wondered whether it was possible to identify a factor or factors that might have been predictive of treatment outcome. In fact, Table 2 indicates that treatment was beneficial to some degree in all patients, and that it certainly changed the behaviours of all of them, so in looking for predictive factors we were seeking indicators of particular receptivity, and not of response versus non-response. In looking for prognostic factors, three domains were considered: The Microworld, the additional pre-therapy assessments, and factors external to the assessments that may have been salient. Within the Microworld the SST results were examined; the session 1 Verb Test and Preposition Test results (accuracy and timing) were also examined. The additional assessments conducted with these participants were the Western Aphasia Battery (WAB; Kertesz, 1982), the Test for Reception of Grammar (TROG; Bishop, 1982) and a computer-based test of digit–span recall (DSR) created by the author. The "external factors" considered were age, sex, interval post-onset, nature of neurological damage, motivation, previous occupation/intellectual level, domiciliary situation, density of hemiparesis and any relevant medical or social factors affecting the treatment period. All mentions of treatment outcome below refer to outcome as shown in Table 2 unless otherwise stated.

The "external factors" were unenlightening. There was no relationship between age and treatment outcome rank order ($r = -.23$) or number of months post-onset and treatment outcome rank order ($r = .26$). There were only two female patients in the cohort and they were not distinguished from the males in outcome. Premorbid intellectual level or occupation does not seem to have been a factor (e.g., P11 and P4 would have been well-matched with P1 in this respect yet their outcomes were very different, whereas P8, P2 and P6 had much poorer educational backgrounds and occupations, but all responded well to treatment). All the participants were motivated enough to take part in this voluntary and exacting research programme and therefore deserve to be rated "highly motivated", yet knowing them well it was possible to make subtle distinctions. However, there was no evident relationship between strength of desire to succeed and treatment outcome. Likewise domiciliary situation proved irrelevant; participants alone in long-term care or sheltered accommodation (P6, P8, P9) were not distinguished from the others who were in family environments. By the same token, patients who suffered minor incidents such as falls (P6, P7) or fits (P8, P14) or underwent surgery (P3) during the period of study performed at least as well as patients who did not. P1's wife and P4's family both mentioned independently and spontaneously that a change of anti-convulsive medication just prior to the treatment phase of the research had stabilised both men greatly, increasing confidence; yet their overall outcomes were quite different. P6 suffered a deep emotional upset coinciding with the onset of the treatment phase, yet still managed to make progress. So none of these factors appears to have been significant.

The only two "external factors" that could not confidently be rejected as at least partial predictors of outcome were the related ones of nature of neurological damage and density of hemiparesis. Unfortunately the superficial details of the neurological damage sustained by P1–14 available from their speech therapy cases notes and supplied by referring therapists were inadequate to be able to undertake a detailed comparison of site and extent of brain damage with treatment effects. A question mark must therefore hang over whether such a study would have been fruitful. There is *perhaps* a suggestion in the ranking of patients in Table 2 that degree of paralysis may be negatively correlated with size of treatment outcome. P4, P6, P11 and P14 were the most severely affected in this respect and three of these appear in the bottom half of the table[11]. (P4 and P14 were known to have had particularly massive cerebro-vascular accidents.) However, one can find counter-evidence: P3 (who had no hemiparesis) and P9 who was mildly affected are also both in the bottom half of Table 2.

Comparison of the patients' pre-therapy WAB, TROG and DSR performances with their treatment outcomes also yielded little of predictive value. Patients were not sufficiently well differentiated by the DSR for it to be very useful. However, it was noticeable that P1 and P2 had respectively the best and worst digit-span recalls and P11 and P12 had identical ones, so clearly digit-span had not been critical to treatment outcome. The treatment outcome rank order of P1–P14 was compared with their pre-therapy aphasia quotients ($r = .24$) and with their pre-therapy TROG scores ($r = 0$) and the degree of correlation was found to be low in the first case and zero in the second[12].

Finally, P1–P14's pre-therapy performances on Microworld assessments were examined to see whether there was any indication of future responsiveness to treatment. The rank ordering of the patients by score over the three Syntax Screening Tests (SST1–SST3) was compared with that in Table 2

[11] Though P4 performed much better by accuracy alone (see Table 2).

[12] Similar correlations were obtained using the participants' accuracy-alone rankings and comparing them with their ranking on the pre-therapy WAB ($r = .02$) and with pre-therapy TROG scores ($r = .13$).

and the correlation between the two was found to be zero[13]. The patients' session 1 scores out of 40 and total times taken for test completion (Verb Test and Preposition Test separately) were compared to see whether there was any relationship on initial assessment between accuracy and time taken (as had been found in aphasics and normals in the SST results reported above). The correlation approached zero in both cases, indicating no correspondence (Verb Test $r = .04$; Preposition Test $r = .16$).

The participants' speeds for test completion at session 1 and their speed outcomes as shown in Table 2 were then compared for both tests. There was only a very low negative correlation for prepositions ($r = -.25$) but the result for verbs ($r = -.73$) confirmed that there was an inverse relationship between length of time taken initially to complete the Verb Test and the size of the reduction recorded at session 3. Essentially, the slower patients had been initially, the larger their speed increases had been. The inconsistent pattern for prepositions reflects the greater difficulty patients seemed to experience with locatives; long completion times were almost as likely to increase (P4) as to decrease (P8).

A further comparison was done to explore the predictive value of accuracy results obtained at session 1. The initial accuracy scores out of 40 were compared with the accuracy outcomes shown in Table 2 for each test separately. The results for verbs and prepositions were once again different, tending to reinforce the results reported in the previous paragraph. No relationship was found between initial accuracy in prepositions and the overall change to accuracy shown in Table 2 ($r = -.04$), but a moderate degree of negative correspondence was present in the verb results ($r = -.5$). The latter shows some tendency for patients with the weakest initial scores to have made the largest improvements in accuracy.

In view of there being a correlation of zero between participants' initial accuracy in prepositions and the change in preposition accuracy recorded at session 3, P1's result was particularly striking. His Preposition Test results were the most successful in the entire study and the improvement was maintained on re-testing five months after cessation of treatment. The reason for this was that it was possible to discover *the reason* for his very consistent role reversal errors[14] and therefore help where a number of previous

---

[13] This was almost the same as comparing rank by SST1–SST3 with rank by accuracy gains only ($r = .05$).

[14] The software recorded the choices made, and the distractors were devised in such a way, that printouts of an individual's performance provided a great deal of diagnostically useful information. Much head-scratching still went on to figure out *why* the choices had been made, but in the case of P1, if 8/8 times to simple locative constructions (e.g., The ball is under the box), the reverse role distractor is chosen from four options, then we are certain that a strategy is being employed, this cannot happen by chance.

therapies had failed. The point to be made here is that increased diagnostic precision enables better targeted therapy, which in turn has better chances of success. We attribute much of the success of this treatment study to the diagnostic edge afforded by both assessment and remediation software coupled with the scientific approach taken in their use. If the nature of the problem is consistent and conscious application of an inappropriate rule and this rule can be discerned, the prospects of remediation are extremely good. In other words, if metalinguistic knowledge is being used by the individual in a conscious way, we can tap into that preserved ability to replace an incorrect strategy with a successful one. Notice that no claims are being made that the aphasic individual is now doing the tasks in the same way as an unimpaired individual. We have no evidence from this work that anything approaching normal automaticity can be restored.

To summarise: The search for factors predictive of individuals' outcomes to treatment yielded nothing compelling. There was insufficient consistency in the data set to be able to establish anything other than a good prospect of substantially increasing accuracy and reducing time taken in patients impaired in verb processing, presenting with slow initial speeds and poor initial accuracy. However, this is perhaps hardly surprising. The number of patients studied was small and they exhibited a very broad spread of abilities both in speed and accuracy at session 1. In spite of this, therapy was successful in improving aspects of the performance of all of them. Had treatment been unequivocally beneficial in some cases and totally ineffective in others the chances of identifying predictive factors might have been higher. In fact, this short amount of treatment changed the behaviours of the patients in different ways, some improving in speed and accuracy, others in speed at the expense of accuracy and so forth, producing a complex data set that cannot be satisfactorily reduced to one or more simple input/output relationships.

However, the lack of a prognostic indicator that would account for the degree of benefit observed in P1–P14 is not seen as a major disadvantage. The value of prognostic information obviously increases with the cost of the treatment, (in resources, wasted effort in administering inappropriate treatment, lack of opportunity for treatment of suitable patients or delay in treatment of patients who would benefit, by misselection of others, etc.). If the improvements reported had been obtained after hundreds or even tens of hours of therapy, extending over many months, it would have been more important to be able to say who improved most and why. In fact they were obtained in only six hours per function administered in twice weekly sessions. Moreover the assessment used to select the patients for treatment (SST) took only one session to administer. The results of this study support offering similar treatment to any patient who qualifies on initial assessment. Only by experience with much larger numbers of patients and with longer periods of treatment will it be possible to discover for whom and in what circumstances the benefits are greatest and most enduring, and what the limits are to the recoveries that can be made.

Three issues were raised at the beginning of this section; the formulation of a global measure of treatment outcome, the feasibility of predicting the outcome of future cases on the basis of the performances of P1–P14 and the implications of the performances of P1–P14 for ongoing treatment recommendations. We have discussed the formulation of a global measure of treatment outcome and used it and its components in the subsequent search for a prognostic indicator. The last issue to address is how one might proceed with P1–P14 if treatment were to continue.

Clinical decision-making is both hard to do and difficult to justify. Increasingly, practitioners are becoming aware of the benefits of collating and codifying expertise which is at present unavailable as a unified body of knowledge, and of subjecting their intuitions to more formal appraisal. It was therefore of interest to find some way of rationalising a set of ongoing treatment recommendations for P1–P14 and then to explore the suitability of these by offering a second phase of treatment to a small number of participants and studying the outcomes.

As with the generation of a global measure of treatment outcome, any algorithm to assist in making clinical recommendations will be found to throw up anomalous cases, or cases who have only just failed to reach some designated threshold. However, having such a formula at all provides an objective framework whereby such individuals can be identified and discussed, and can lead, as with all adaptive systems, to the refinement and improvement of the formula itself over time. On the basis of the performances of P1–P14 and the insights gained into, for example, average test completion times and what one might consider to be reasonable accuracy levels compared with accuracy levels that would indicate the need to simplify treatment materials, a computer program was written to generate tentative recommendations for ongoing management. The object of the exercise was to begin to identify the factors that might guide decision-making and to see whether subsequent therapy sessions would confirm or deny these intuitions.

The program was based on summarising the potential speed/accuracy combinations between sessions 1 and 3 as four mutually exclusive outcome conditions shown in Table 4.

These were considered in conjunction with just four constants which were compared with session 3 outcomes. These constants were: "Functional speed" (which was set at 30 minutes and denoted the speed at or below which response time was not considered to warrant treatment); "acceptable speed" (which was set at 40 minutes, this was used as an indicator that complexity of treatment items should be reduced, or in combination with

TABLE 4
Treatment outcome combinations

Condition	*Accuracy improved*	*Speed improved or was static*
1	Yes	Yes
2	Yes	No
3	No	Yes
4	No	No

unacceptable accuracy (defined below), was an indicator that therapy should be discontinued as unsuccessful); "functional accuracy" (set at 32/40, the level of attainment at or above which further therapy for accuracy was not warranted) and "acceptable accuracy" (which was set at 20/40—below this, complexity should be reduced, or if speed was also unacceptable, then therapy should be abandoned). It would be premature to include the detail of the algorithm since the utility of any such decision aid can only be established through verification with a large number of cases. To give a single example; setting functional speed at 30 minutes caused P1 to be recommended for further verb treatment for speed and P12 to be recommended for further preposition treatment for speed (they both took 31 minutes). If future experience of longer duration therapy shows that the chances of improving speed below 30 minutes is very small, then clearly the algorithm should be modified accordingly, for re-treating P1 and P12 would not be a cost-effective or even useful recommendation.

Out of interest, the treatment recommendations generated for P1–P14 are reproduced in Table 5. Fulfilling the objectives of this efficacy study precluded inviting P1–P14 to continue with treatment as recommended in Table 5, since it was important to ascertain whether the benefits of therapy they had shown thus far would endure after treatment had ceased. The cross-over design had permitted re-assessment of the first functions treated after an interval of five weeks, but there had been no such durability measure for the second functions treated. It was decided to re-test some of the more successful participants (P1, P2, P3, P5, P8, P10, and P13) after an interval (with no further treatment) of five months; the results obtained are reported in Crerar et al. (1996)[15].

However, three patients whose responses to therapy had been disappointing in contrasting ways were invited to undertake a second phase of

[15] The treatment effects (significant improvement in verbs and prepositions, collapsed, between session 1 and session 3) were found to have persisted after 5 months with no further treatment. There was no significant change to time taken.

TABLE 5
Suggested ongoing treatment recommendations for P1–P14

Patient	*Verbs*	*Prepositions*
P1	Re-treat (speed)	Discharge successful
P2	Re-treat (speed)	Reduce complexity and re-treat
P3	Re-treat (accuracy)	Re-treat (accuracy)
P4	Reduce complexity and re-treat	Reduce complexity and re-treat
P5	Re-treat (speed)	Reduce complexity and re-treat
P6	Re-treat (accuracy)	Re-treat (accuracy)
P7	Re-treat (accuracy)	Reduce complexity and re-treat
P8	Re-treat (accuracy)	Discharge successful
P9	Re-treat (accuracy)	Re-treat (accuracy)
P10	Discharge successful	Re-treat (accuracy)
P11	Re-treat (speed) (accuracy)	Reduce complexity and re-treat
P12	Re-treat (speed) (accuracy)	Re-treat (speed)
P13	Re-treat (accuracy)	Discharge successful
P14	Re-treat (accuracy)	Re-treat (accuracy)

treatment. They were P4, P7 and P9. P4 had suffered serious degradations in speed and the recommendation for him was to simplify the treatment material, both for verbs and for prepositions. If he did not improve in speed after a second phase of treatment exactly like the first, this recommendation for simplification would have been supported, however, if a second treatment period improved his speed, it would be an indication that the initial treatment was not too complex, but too short. P9 had plummeted catastrophically in his final preposition assessment. His session 3 preposition responses were reminiscent of P1's at session 1 in the preponderance of reversal errors, it was therefore possible that his difficulty was similar and might respond to more therapy. P7 was chosen as a contrasting case. She was not of great concern speed-wise, but had failed to maintain her progress in prepositions and had considerable room for improvement both in verbs and prepositions. The recommendation in Table 5 had been to reduce the complexity of her preposition treatment. Again, we wanted to test this, as with P4, by offering her "more of the same".

The effects of this extended phase of therapy are summarised in Table 6. Comparing this Table with Table 2, it can be seen that P4 was the only one of the three to benefit overall from this addition intervention. More details can be found in Crerar (1991).

CONCLUSION

This paper has presented data to illustrate the importance of considering speed as well as accuracy in reporting the results of cognitive neuropsychological intervention. It has been argued that assessing the functional impair-

TABLE 6
Treatment outcomes for three patients after extended therapy based on changes in performance between sessions 1 (pre-therapy) and session 5 (post-second function treated in second treatment phase)

	Verb Test			*Preposition Test*			*Overall treatment outcome*
Patient	*Accuracy*	*Speed*	*PI*	*Accuracy*	*Speed*	*PI*	
P4	+22.50	+15.63	+3.44	+37.50	+7.69	+14.91	+9.18
P7	+15.00	−25.00	+20.00	−10.00	−22.58	+6.29	+13.15
P9	+27.50	+16.67	+13.75	0.00	+75.00	−37.50	−11.88

ment of an individual in a meaningful way, necessitates understanding, not just their accuracy scores, but also their speed of processing. In this study, which involved 14 asyntactic comprehenders, it was found that their response to treatment as measured by accuracy scores alone, correlated very weakly ($r = .2$) with a composite measure of treatment effect that also took into account effects on the time taken to complete a battery of 40 sentence–picture matching tasks. Furthermore, it was evident that statistically significant and durable treatment effects in some patients, which alone would create the impression of near cure (e.g., P1) told only part of the story. Consideration of response times revealed that slow processing speeds were much more resistant to change. Indeed, in this short treatment study, we were singularly unsuccessful in restoring the speed of processing of these long-term aphasic participants, to anything approaching normality (as measured against control subjects). In spite of some impressive and durable improvements in accuracy for many of these subjects, functional impairment in all of them remained considerable.

The insights this study afforded would not have been possible without the use of a computer to automate the data collection and analysis. There are many benefits of using a computer to assist both in diagnosis and therapy, not least the objectivity of the test results (these assessments were entirely automated—presentation and scoring—and self-administered by patients with minimal clinician involvement). By taking multiple baseline measures using the Microworld SST, pre-intervention stability was established, and we also confirmed durability of treatment effects five months after cessation of therapy. Thus this work goes some way towards furnishing a methodology that answers the concerns of reliability and validity. It also contributes to the dearth of negative findings in the literature (the tendency not to publish negative results), by setting the record straight regarding speed, when accuracy scores painted an altogether rosier picture. Robertson (1994) called for all these things, and drew attention also to the need for cost-justification of rehabilitation strategies. The quantitative approach taken here to calculating overall treatment outcomes is a contribution towards more explicit grounds for clinical decision-making.

REFERENCES

Balogh, J., Zurif, E. B., Prather, P., Swinney, D., & Finkel, L. (1998). Gap-filling and end-of-sentence effects in real-time language processing: Implications for modeling sentence comprehension in aphasia. *Brain and Language*, *61*, 169–182.

Berndt, R. S. (Ed.) (2001). *Handbook of neuropsychology: Language and aphasia*. (2nd ed.). New York: Elsevier Science Ltd.

Bishop, D. (1982). *T.R.O.G. Test for Reception of Grammar*. (Printed for the Medical Research Council.) Abingdon, UK: Thomas Leach.

Cappa, S. F. (1998). Do we really need non-quantitative approaches in aphasiology. *Aphasiology*, *12*(6), 453–455.

Code, C. (2001). Multifactorial processes in recovery from aphasia: Developing the foundations for a multileveled framework. *Brain and Language*, *77*, 25–44.

Code, C., Rowley, D., & Kertesz, A. (1994). Predicting recovery from aphasia with connectionist networks: Preliminary comparisons with multiple regression. *Cortex*, *30*, 572–532.

Crerar, M. A. (1991). *A computer-based microworld for the assessment and remediation of sentence processing deficits in aphasia*. Unpublished PhD dissertation. Napier University, Edinburgh.

Crerar, M. A., & Ellis, A. W. (1995). Computer-based therapy: Towards second generation clinical tools. In C. Code & D. Muller (Eds.), *Aphasia therapy* (2nd ed.). London: Cole & Whurr.

Crerar, M. A., Ellis, A. W., & Dean, E. C. (1996). Remediation of sentence processing deficits in aphasia using a computer-based microworld. *Brain and Language*, *52*/1, 229–275.

Devescovi, A., Bates, E., D'Amico, S., Hernandez, A., Marangolo, P., Pizzamiglio, L., & Razzano, C. (1997). An on-line study of grammaticality judgments in normal and aphasic speakers of Italian. *Aphasiology*, *11*(6), 543–579.

Haarmann, H. J., Just M. A., & Carpenter P. A. (1997). Aphasic sentence comprehension as a resource deficit: A computational approach. *Brain and Language*, *59*, 76–120.

Hemsley, G., & Code, C. (1996). Interactions between recovery in aphasia, emotional and psychosocial factors in subjects with aphasia, their significant others and speech pathologists. *Disability and Rehabilitation*, *18*, 567–584.

Kean, M-L. (1995). The elusive character of agrammatism. *Brain and Language*, *50*, 369–384.

Kertesz, A. (1982). *Western Aphasia Battery test booklet*. London: Harcourt, Brace, Jovanovich.

McCall, D., Cox, D. M., Shelton, J. R., & Weinrich, M. (1997). The influence of syntactic and semantic information on picture-naming performance in aphasic patients. *Aphasiology*, *11*(6), 581–600.

Miyake, A., Carpenter P. A., & Just M. A. (1994). A capacity approach to syntactic comprehension disorders: Making normal adults perform like aphasic patients. *Cognitive Neuropsychology*, *11*(6), 671–717.

Miyake, A., Carpenter P. A., & Just M. A. (1995). Reduced resources and specific impairments in normal and aphasic sentence comprehension. *Cognitive Neuropsychology*, *12*(6), 651–679.

Petheram, B., & Parr, S. (1998). Diversity in aphasiology: Crisis or increasing competence? *Aphasiology*, *12*(6), 435–447.

Porch, B. E. (1967). *The Porch Index of Communicative Ability*. Palo Alto, CA: Consulting Psychologists Press.

Porch, B. E., Collins, M., Wertz, R. T., & Friden, T. P. (1980). Statistical prediction of change in aphasia. *Journal of Speech & Hearing Research*, *23*, 312–321.

Prather, P.A., Zurif, E., Love, T., & Brownell, H. (1997). Speed of lexical activation in nonfluent Broca's aphasia and fluent Wernicke's aphasia. *Brain and Language*, *59*(3), 391–411.

Robertson, I. H. (1994). Editorial: Methodology in neuropsychological rehabilitation research. *Neuropsychological Rehabilitation*, *4*(1), 1–6.

Russo, K. D., Peach, R, K., & Shapiro, L. P. (1998). Verb preference effects in the sentence comprehension of fluent aphasic individuals. Aphasiology, *12*(7/8), 537–545.

Saffran, E. M., Schwartz, M. F., & Linebarger, M. C. (1998). Semantic influences on thematic role assignment: Evidence from normals and aphasics. *Brain and Language*, *62*, 255–297.

Schwartz, M. F., Fink, R. B., & Saffran, E. M. (1995). The modular treatment of agrammatism. *Neuropsychological Rehabilitation*, *5*(1/2), 93–127.

Schwartz, M. F., Saffran, E. M., Fink, R. B., Myers, J. L., & Martin N. (1994). Mapping therapy: A treatment programme for agrammatism. *Aphasiology*, *8*(1), 19–54.

Schwartz, M. F., Saffran, E. M., & Marin, O. S. M. (1980). The word order problem in agrammatism: I. comprehension. *Brain and Language*, *10*, 249–262.

NEUROPSYCHOLOGICAL REHABILITATION, 2004, *14* (1/2), 207–239

Analysis of assets for virtual reality applications in neuropsychology

Albert A. Rizzo[1], Maria Schultheis[2], Kimberly A. Kerns[3], and Catherine Mateer[3]

[1] *Integrated Media Systems Center and School of Gerontology, University of Southern California, Los Angeles, California, USA*
[2] *Kessler Medical Rehabilitation Research and Education Corporation, West Orange, NJ, USA*
[3] *Department of Psychology, University of Victoria, Canada*

Virtual reality (VR) technology offers new opportunities for the development of innovative neuropsychological assessment and rehabilitation tools. VR-based testing and training scenarios that would be difficult, if not impossible, to deliver using conventional neuropsychological methods are now being developed that take advantage of the assets available with VR technology. If empirical studies continue to demonstrate effectiveness, virtual environment applications could provide new options for targeting cognitive and functional impairments due to traumatic brain injury, neurological disorders, and learning disabilities. This article focuses on specifying the assets that are available with VR for neuropsychological applications along with discussion of current VR-based research that serves to illustrate each asset. VR allows for the precise presentation and control of dynamic multi-sensory 3D stimulus environments, as well as providing advanced methods for recording behavioural responses. This serves as the basis for a diverse set of VR assets for neuropsychological approaches that are detailed in this article. We take the position that when combining these assets within the context of functionally relevant, ecologically valid virtual environments, fundamental advancements can emerge in how human cognition and functional behaviour is assessed and rehabilitated.

Correspondence should be addressed to Albert Rizzo, Director, Virtual Environments Laboratory, Integrated Media Systems Center, University of Southern California, 3740 McClintock Ave., Suite 131, Los Angeles, CA 90089-2561, USA. Email: arizzo@usc.edu

http://www.tandf.co.uk/journals/pp/09602011.html DOI:10.1080/09602010343000183

INTRODUCTION

The field of neuropsychology has grown exponentially over the last three decades. Neuropsychologists have been leaders in providing an understanding of brain organisation and brain behaviour relationships, giving new insight into the nature and consequences of brain damage, disease and developmental disorders, as well as normal ageing processes. Neuropsychologists have developed a wide range of measures to assess cognitive, sensory, and motor abilities, as well as behavioural and self-regulatory functions. The field has maintained high standards with regard to ensuring that neuropsychological (NP) measures are reliable and have adequate construct validity. However, a continuing and important challenge for neuropsychologists has been to find ways to better measure, understand, and predict everyday functional capacities (Wilson, 1997). Borrowing principals and themes from cognitive neuroscience, there has been a tendency to explain behaviour by attempting to break it down into separate cognitive abilities or component parts. As a result, although perhaps theoretically useful, many NP tasks themselves appear quite dissimilar to the demands of everyday life. Given the potential mismatch between NP test demands and those of everyday functioning, the predictability of many commonly used NP measures for aspects of adaptive functioning and real-life performance has been called into question. Some neuropsychologists have advocated "top down" tasks, which require integration of a number of cognitive abilities and higher levels of self-monitoring (Shallice & Burgess, 1991) to better emulate real-life demands. Although such tasks are a step in the right direction, they fail to assess the impact of precise presentation and timing of subtle changes to stimuli and do not analyse response characteristics in any detail. Control or measurement of these aspects of tasks and task performance may be quite important in the prediction of actual everyday abilities and real-life function.

Another domain in which cognitive and behavioural assessment play a critical role is in rehabilitation. The identification of useful rehabilitation goals and the measurement of meaningful rehabilitation outcomes are critically dependent on an accurate and reliable assessment of real-world adaptive functioning. Whereas NP assessment may be undertaken for multiple purposes, including diagnosis and description, rehabilitation planning and rehabilitation outcome assessment are critically dependent on tools and techniques that closely predict the individual's ability to function within natural contexts, with all their attendant stimuli and multiplicity of demands. Indeed, the most consistent concern with respect to rehabilitation techniques has been limitations in the ecological validity of the actual rehabilitation activities and resultant limitations in generalisation of new abilities, knowledge, and/or skills (Carney et al., 1999; Park & Ingles, 2001; Ylvisaker & Feeney, 1998).

WHY VIRTUAL REALITY?

The development of virtual reality (VR) technology holds the potential to address many of these areas of concern. By its nature, VR is designed to simulate naturalistic environments. Within these environments, researchers and clinicians can present more ecologically relevant stimuli imbedded in a meaningful and familiar context. Rather than try to predict functional implications from a decontextualised measure of attention, for example, one can look at the effects of systematically increasing ecologically relevant attentional demands in a virtual environment (VE), such as a classroom, office, or store. VR technology allows for exquisite timing and control over distractions, stimulus load and complexity, and can alter these variables in a dynamic way contingent on the response characteristics of the client. Response characteristics in terms of accuracy, timing, and consistency can also be collected to allow a finer and detailed analysis of responses.

When discussion of the potential for VR applications in neuropsychology first emerged in the mid-1990s (Pugnetti et al., 1995; Rizzo, 1994; Rose, Attree, & Johnson, 1996), the technology to deliver on the anticipated "visions" was not in place. Consequently, during these early years VR suffered from a somewhat imbalanced "expectation-to-delivery" ratio, as most users trying systems during that time will attest. The "real" thing never quite measured up to expectations generated by some of the initial media hype, as delivered for example in the films *"The Lawnmower Man"* and *"Disclosure"*. Yet the idea of producing simulated virtual environments that allowed for the systematic delivery of ecologically relevant cognitive challenges was compelling and made intuitive sense. As well, a long and rich history of encouraging findings from the aviation simulation literature lent support to the concept that testing and training in highly proceduralised VR simulation environments would be a useful direction for neuropsychology to explore (Johnston, 1995; Rizzo, 1994). Within this context, a small group of researchers began the initial work of exploring the use of VR technology for applications designed to target cognitive/functional performance in populations with CNS dysfunction. While a good deal of this early work employed non-head mounted display flatscreen environments, these less immersive systems produced encouraging results (Cromby, Standen, Newman, & Tasker, 1996; Rose, Attree, & Johnson 2001; Stanton, Foreman, & Wilson, 1998). This work demonstrated the unique value of the technology, served to inform future applications and created a demand for the assets available with more immersive VR approaches.

Over the last few years, revolutionary advances in the underlying VR enabling technologies (i.e., computation speed and power, graphics and image rendering technology, display systems, interface devices, immersive audio, haptics tools, wireless tracking, voice recognition, intelligent agents, and authoring software) have supported development resulting in more powerful, low-cost PC-driven VR systems. Such advances in technological "prowess" and accessibility have provided the hardware platforms needed for the conduct of human research within more usable and useful VR scenarios. From this, current research efforts to develop more accessible VR systems have produced applications that are delivering encouraging results on a wide range of cognitive, physical, emotional, social, vocational and psychological human issues and research questions (Blascovich et al., 2002; Rizzo, Buckwalter, & van der Zaag, 2002a; Weiss & Jessel, 1998; Zimand et al., in press).

ANALYSIS OF VR ASSETS

What makes VR application development in this area so distinctively important is that it represents the potential for more than a simple linear extension of existing computer technology for human use. This was recognised early on in a visionary article ("The experience society") by VR pioneer, Myron Kruegar (1993), in his prophetic statement that, "...Virtual Reality arrives at a moment when computer technology in general is moving from automating the paradigms of the past, to creating new ones for the future". (p. 163). By way of the capacity of VR to place a person within an immersive, interactive computer-generated simulation environment, new possibilities exist that go well beyond simply automating the delivery of existing paper and pencil testing and training tools on a personal computer. However, while encouraging on a theoretical level, the value of this technology for neuropsychology still needs to be substantiated via systematic empirical research with normal and clinical populations that can be replicated by others. To accomplish this first requires specification as to the real assets that VR offers that add value over existing methodologies, as well as further exploration of its current limitations. Non-immersive computerised testing and training tools have been available for some time and a case can be made that they offer some of the same features found with immersive head-mounted display VR. As well, in spite of the many claims that computers would revolutionise cognitive rehabilitation in the late 1980s, the manifested value of these tools have been questioned by some (Robertson, 1990). Therefore it becomes imperative that research be conducted to determine the incremental value of VR-specific assets (i.e., immersive, naturalistic and/or supra-normal human computer interaction) over already existing methods. To address these issues we will discuss the assets that are available with VR along with examples of NP assessment and rehabilitation research and findings from related fields that illustrate the relevance of these assets. Challenges that still need to be addressed will also be discussed.

The capacity to systematically deliver and control dynamic, interactive 3D stimuli within an immersive environment that would be difficult to present using other means

One of the cardinal assets of any advanced form of simulation technology involves the capacity for systematic delivery and control of stimuli. This asset provides significant opportunities for advancing NP methods. In fact, one could conjecture that the basic foundation of all human research methodology requires the systematic delivery and control of an environment and the subsequent capture and analysis of the behaviour that occurs within the environment. In this regard, an ideal match appears to exist between the stimulus delivery assets of VR simulation approaches and the requirements of NP assessment and rehabilitation. Much like an aircraft simulator serves to test and train piloting ability, VEs can be developed to present simulations that assess and rehabilitate human cognitive and functional processes under a range of stimulus conditions that are not easily controllable in the real world. This "Ultimate Skinner Box" asset can be seen to provide value across the spectrum of NP approaches, from analysis at a molecular level targeting component cognitive processes (e.g., selective attention performance contingent on varying levels of stimulus intensity exposure), to the complex targeting of more molar functional behaviours (e.g., planning and initiating the steps required to prepare a meal in a chaotic setting).

This asset can be seen to allow for the hierarchical delivery of stimulus challenges across a range of difficulty levels. For example, an individual's rehabilitation could be customised to begin at a stimulus challenge level most attainable and comfortable for them, with gradual progression of difficulty level based on that individuals' performance. The rehabilitation of driving skills following traumatic brain injury is one example where individuals may begin at a simplistic level (i.e., straight, non-populated roads) and gradually move along to more challenging situations (i.e., crowded, highway roads) (Schultheis & Mourant, 2001). This asset would also provide the opportunity to identify, implement and modify individual compensatory strategies that can be tested at various hierarchical levels of challenge within a VE modelled after a targeted real-world environment. Repeated practice could result in "successful learning" and produce positive reinforcement of compensatory strategy use that could potentially enhance the generalisation of these strategies to everyday activities. As well, the successful execution of many everyday activities often requires the integration of a variety of cognitive functions, and subsequent component evaluation of these complex behaviours is often challenging to clinicians and researchers. By providing options for stimulus control within a VE, the impact of specific component cognitive assets and limitations may be better isolated, assessed and rehabilitated.

Enhanced stimulus control also can result in better consistency of stimulus presentations. Naturally occurring changes in "everyday" real-world settings typically make the exact repetition of assessment unfeasible and this inconsistency can negatively impact on the standardisation of defining and measuring specific behaviours. For example, current assessment and rehabilitation approaches of everyday functional skills, such as ambulation in the community, are currently limited by the inability to control and repeat exact stimuli in relevant settings (i.e., in the street, within office buildings). Subsequently, assessment and rehabilitation is typically conducted within a more controlled environment (e.g., gymnasium), which may not reflect the actual demands of ambulation in the "real world". The application of VR to this approach would address this limitation by allowing assessment and rehabilitation in more functionally relevant VEs (e.g., city streets) while still allowing clinicians and researchers full control over stimulus presentations. This level of control could serve to improve consistency across assessments and interventions and allow for increased standardisation and validation of methods for assessing complex behaviours. Examples of such VR applications include the development of "virtual cities" and other complex environments for assessing and rehabilitating wayfinding (Brown, Kerr, & Bayon, 1998), the use of public transportation (Mowafty & Pollack, 1995), and a wide range of other instrumental activities of daily living (see review in Rizzo et al., 2002a).

The capacity to create more *ecologically* valid assessment and rehabilitation scenarios

Traditional NP assessment and rehabilitation has been criticised as limited in the area of *ecological* validity, that is, the degree of relevance or similarity that a test or training system has relative to the "real" world (Neisser, 1978). While existing NP tests obviously measure behaviours mediated by the brain, controversy exists as to how performance on analogue tasks relates to complex performance in an "everyday" functional environment. By designing virtual environments that not only "look like" the real world, but actually incorporate challenges that require 'real-world' functional behaviours, the ecological validity of cognitive/functional performance assessment and rehabilitation could be enhanced. As well, the complexity of stimulus challenges found in naturalistic settings could be presented while still maintaining the experimental control required for rigorous scientific analysis and replication. Thus, VR-derived assessment results could have greater predictive validity/clinical relevance and a more direct linkage to both restorative and functional NP rehabilitation approaches.

A number of examples illustrate efforts to enhance the ecological validity of assessment and rehabilitation by designing VEs that are "replicas" of relevant archetypic functional environments. This has included the creation of virtual cities (Brown et al., 1998; Costas, Carvalho, & de Aragon, 2000), supermarkets (Cromby et al., 1996); homes (Rose, Attree, Brooks, & Andrews, 2001); kitchens (Christiansen et al., 1998; Davies et al., 1998), school environments (Stanton et al., 1998; Rizzo et al., 2000), workspaces/offices (McGeorge et al., 2001; Schultheis & Rizzo, 2002); rehabilitation wards (Brooks et al., 1999) and even a virtual beach (Elkind et al., 2001). While these environments vary in their level of pictorial or graphic realism, this factor may be secondary in importance, relative to the actual activities that are carried out in the environment for determining their value from an ecological validity standpoint. Interestingly, when in a virtual environment, humans often display a high capacity to "suspend disbelief" and respond *as if* the scenario was real. It could be conjectured that the "ecological value" of a VR task that needs to be performed may be well supported in spite of limited graphic realism and less immersion (such as in flatscreen systems). In essence, as long as the VR scenario "resembles" the real world, possesses design elements that replicate key real-life challenges and the system responds well to user interaction, then ecological validity is enhanced beyond existing analogue approaches. Evidence to support this view can be drawn from clinical VR applications that address anxiety disorders. While a number of the successful VR scenarios designed for exposure-based therapy of specific phobias would never be mistaken for the real world, clients within these VEs still manifest physiological responses and report subjective units of discomfort levels that suggest they are responding "as if" they are in the presence of the feared stimuli (Wiederhold & Wiederhold, 1998).

This point is also illustrated in a number of examples where VR has been applied to target executive functioning and wayfinding. In the mid-1990s, using graphic imagery that would be considered primitive by today's standards, Pugnetti et al. (1995; 1998) developed a head-mounted display delivered VR scenario that embodied the cognitive challenges that characterise the Wisconsin Card Sorting Test (WCST). The scenario consisted of a virtual building within which users were required to use environmental clues to aid in the correct selection of appropriate doorways needed to pass from room to room through the structure. The doorway choices varied according to the categories of shape, colour and number of portholes. Similar to the WCST, the correct choice criteria were changed after a fixed number of successful trials, and the user was then required to shift cognitive set, look for clues and devise a new choice strategy in order to successfully pass into the next room. In one study, Pugnetti et al. (1998) compared a mixed group of neurological patients (multiple sclerosis, stroke, and traumatic brain injury) with normals' performance on both the WCST and on this head-mounted display executive function system. Results indicated that the VR results mirrored previous anecdotal observations by family members of everyday performance deficits in the patient populations. Although the psychometric properties of the VE task were comparable to the WCST in terms of gross differentiation of patients and controls, weak correlations between the two methods suggested that the methods measured different aspects of these functions. A detailed analysis of the VR task data indicated that specific preservative errors appeared earlier in the test sequence compared to the WCST. The authors suggested that "...this finding depends on the more complex (and complete) cognitive demands of the VE setting at the beginning of the test when perceptuomotor, visuospatial (orientation), memory, and conceptual aspects of the task need to be fully integrated into an efficient routine" (p. 160). The detection of these early "integrative" difficulties for this complex cognitive function may be particularly relevant for the task of predicting real-world capabilities from test results.

This was further evidenced in a detailed single subject case study of a stroke patient using this system. In this report (Mendozzi et al., 1998), results indicated that the VR system was more accurate in identifying executive function deficits in a highly educated patient two years post-stroke, who had a normal WCST performance. The VR system, although using graphic imagery that would never be mistaken for the real world, was successful in detecting deficits that had been reported to be limiting the patient's everyday performance, yet were missed using existing NP tests. These results are in line with the observation that patients with executive disorders often perform relatively well on traditional NP tests of "frontal lobe function", yet show marked impairment in controlling and monitoring behaviour in real-life situations (Shallice & Burgess, 1991).

Similar findings were recently reported by McGeorge et al. (2001) in a study comparing real world and virtual world "errand running" performance in five traumatic brain injury patients and five matched normal controls. The selection of the patient sample for this study was based on staff ratings that indicated poor planning skills. However, the patient and control groups did not differ significantly from normative values on the Behavioural Assessment of the Dysexecutive Syndrome (BADS) battery (Wilson et al., 1996). Videotaped performance of subjects was coded and compared while performing a series of errands in the University of Aberdeen psychology department (real world) and within a flatscreen VR scenario modelled after this environment. Performance in both the real and virtual environment, as defined as the number of errands completed in a 20-minute period, was highly correlated ($r = .79$; $p < .01$). Interestingly, while the groups did not differ on age-corrected standardised scores on the BADS, significant differences *were* found between the groups in both the real world and virtual testing. This finding suggests several things. First, performance in the real and virtual world was functionally similar, second, patient and control groups could be discriminated equally using real and virtual tests while this discrimination was not picked up by standardised testing with the BADS, and third, that both measures of real and virtual world performance showed concordance with staff observations of planning skills. That these results support the view that VR testing may possess higher ecological value is in line with the observation by Shallice and Burgess (1991) that traditional NP tests do not demand the planning of behaviour over more than a few minutes, or the prioritisation of competing subtasks and may result in less effective prediction of real world performance.

In the area of rehabilitation, a number of studies have supported the ecological value of VR training for wayfinding in both developmentally disabled teenagers navigating a supermarket (Cromby et al., 1996) and for school navigation in children in wheelchairs with limited experience in independent wayfinding (Stanton et al., 1998). Further initial support for the ecological value of VR wayfinding training can be found in a case study by Brooks et al. (1999). In this report, a female stroke patient with severe amnesia showed significant improvements in her ability to find her way around a rehabilitation unit following training within a VE modelled after the unit. This was most notable given that prior to training, the patient had lived on the unit for two months and was still unable to find her way around, even to places she had visited regularly. In the first part of the training, improvements on two routes were seen after a three-week period of VE route practice lasting only 15 minutes per weekday and retention of this learning was maintained throughout the patient's stay on the unit. In the second part of the study, the patient was trained on two more routes, one utilising the VE, and the other actually practising on the "real" unit. Within two weeks the patient learned the route practised in the VE, but not the route trained on the real unit, and this learning was maintained throughout the course of the study (Brooks et al., 1999). The authors account for this success as being due in part to the opportunity in the VE for quicker traversing of the environment than in the real world, which allowed for more efficient use of training time. Another factor in this success may be that the VE training did not contain the typical distractions normally present when real-world training is conducted that might have impeded route learning. It might be found that the gradual fading in of distractions would be useful for inoculating the patient to the potentially deleterious impact of their inevitable presence in the real world and further enhance the ecological value of this form of rehabilitation.

These findings lend support to the view that due to the similarity of VR testing or training tasks with the demands of the real world, the enhancement in ecological validity promotes the generalisability of such results to functional real-world performance. Thus, VR assessment results could have enhanced clinical relevance and serve as a basis for the development of both restorative and contextual cognitive rehabilitation approaches. However, before this vision can be fully reached, technological advances need to occur in the area of human–computer interaction interfacing devices. Current technology is still limited in the degree to which a user can naturalistically interact with the challenges presented in a VE. From a human–computer interaction perspective, a primary concern involves how to design more naturalistic and intuitive tools for human interfacing with such complex systems. In order for persons with cognitive impairments to be in a position to benefit from VR applications, they must be able to learn how to navigate and interact within the environment. Many modes of VR interaction (i.e., data-gloves, joy sticks, 3D mice, etc.), while easily mastered by unimpaired users, could present problems for those with cognitive difficulties. Even if patients are capable of using a VR system at a basic level, the extra non-automatic cognitive effort required to interact/navigate could serve as a distraction and limit assessment and rehabilitation processes. In this regard, Psotka (1995) hypothesises that facilitation of a "single egocentre" found in highly immersive interfaces serves to reduce "cognitive overhead" and thereby enhance information access and learning. This is an area that needs the most attention in the current state of affairs for VR applications designed for populations with CNS dysfunction, and an excellent review of these tools and issues can be found in Bowman, Kruijff, LaViola, and Poupyrev (2001).

The delivery of immediate performance feedback in a variety of forms and sensory modalities

The capacity for systematic delivery and control of stimuli presented to users in a VE can serve as a significant asset for the development of NP assessment and rehabilitation scenarios. This asset can also be harnessed to provide immediate performance feedback to users contingent on the status of their efforts. Such automated delivery of feedback stimuli can appear in graded (degree) or absolute (correct/incorrect) forms and can be presented via any or multiple sensory modalities (although mainly audio, visual, or tactile is used) depending on the goals of the application and the needs of the user. This is an intuitively essential component for rehabilitation efforts as performance feedback is generally accepted to be necessary for most forms of learning or skill acquisition (Sohlberg & Mateer, 1989; 2001).

While VR-based feedback can be presented to signal performance status in a form that would not naturally occur in the real world (e.g., a soft tone occurring after a correct response), more relevant or naturalistic sounds can also be creatively applied to enhance both ecological validity and the believability of the scenario. For example, in an Internet delivered VR application designed to help children with learning disabilities practise escape from a house fire (Strickland, 2001), the sound of a smoke detector alarm raises in volume as the child gets near to the fire's location. As the child successfully navigates to safety, the alarm fades contingent on the child choosing the correct escape route. An efficacy study of this application is currently in progress (Dorothy Strickland, personal communication, 21 August, 2002).

The potential value of virtual performance feedback for NP rehabilitation applications can also be conjectured from applications designed to support physical therapy in adults following a stroke (Jack et al., 2001; Deutsch, Latonio, Burdea, & Boian, 2001). These applications use various glove and ankle VR interface devices that translate the user's movements into a visible and somewhat relevant activity that is presented graphically on a flatscreen display. For example, in one application, as the user performs a prescribed hand exercise designed to enhance fractionation (independence of finger motion), the image of a hand appears on the display, playing a piano keyboard, reflecting the actual hand movements of the client. In a similar application, the appropriate hand movement moves a "wiper" that serves to reveal an interesting picture along with display of a graphic rendering of a performance meter representing range of movement. These features not only serve as a mechanism for providing feedback regarding the ongoing status of targeted movement, but could be potentially used as a motivator. Results from this laboratory with stroke patients, presented in a series of seven case studies, reported positive results for rehabilitating hand performance across range, speed, fractionation and strength measures (Jack et al., 2001). In one noteworthy case, functional improvement was reported in a patient who was able to button his shirt independently for the first time post-stroke following two weeks of training with the VR hand interface. As well, by making the repetitive and sometimes boring work of physical therapy exercise more interesting and compelling, patients reported enhanced enjoyment leading to increased motivation.

For assessment purposes, although performance feedback is not typically a component of traditional testing, there may be a well-matched place for it in the emerging area of "dynamic" testing (Sternberg, 1997). In a critique of traditional cognitive and ability performance testing, Sternberg posits that dynamic interactive testing provides a new option that could supplement traditional "static" tests. The dynamic assessment approach requires the provision of guided performance feedback as a component in tests that measure learning. This method appears well suited to the assets available with VR technology. In fact, VEs might be the most efficient vehicle for conducting dynamic testing in an ecologically valid manner while still maintaining an acceptable level of experimental control.

The provision of "cueing" stimuli or visualisation tactics designed to help guide successful performance to support an error-free learning approach

The capacity for dynamic stimulus delivery and control within a VE also allows for the presentation of cueing stimuli that could be used for "error-free" learning approaches in cognitive rehabilitation scenarios. This asset underscores the idea that in some cases it may *not* be desirable for VR to simply mimic reality with all its incumbent limitations. Instead, stimulus features that are not easily deliverable in the real world can be presented in a VE to help guide and train successful performance. In this special case of stimulus delivery, cues are given to the patient *prior* to a response in order to help guide successful error-free performance. Error-free training in contrast to trial and error learning has been shown to be successful in a number of investigations with such diverse subjects as pigeons to persons with developmental disabilities, schizophrenia, as well as a variety of CNS disorders (see Wilson & Evans, 1996 for review).

The basis for these findings regarding error-free learning may lie in reports that indicate that in persons with neurologically based memory impairment, certain memory/learning processes often remain relatively intact. *Procedural,* or skill memory, is one such cognitive operation (Cohen & Squire, 1980; Charness, Milberg, & Alexander, 1988). This type of memory ability concerns the capacity to learn rule-based or automatic procedures including motor tasks, certain kinds of rule-based puzzles, and sequences for running or operating equipment, tools, computers, etc. (Sohlberg & Mateer, 1989). Procedural memory can be viewed in contrast to *declarative,* or fact-based memory, which is usually more impaired following central nervous system (CNS) insult and less amenable to rehabilitative improvement. Additionally, patients often demonstrate an ability to perform procedural tasks without *any* recollection of the actual training. This is commonly referred to as *implicit* memory (Graf & Schacter, 1985) and its presence is indicative of a preserved ability to process and retain new material without the person's conscious awareness of when or where the learning occurred.

VR, by way of its interactive and immersive features, could provide training environments that foster cognitive/functional improvement by exploiting a person's preserved *procedural* abilities. Hence, cognitive processes could be *restored* via procedures practised successfully and repetitively within a VE that contains *functional* real-world demands. Whether the person actually had any declarative recall of the actual training episodes is irrelevant, as long as the learned process or skill is shown to generalise to functional situations. Error-free learning strategies could be well integrated into a VE by way of thoughtful presentation of cueing stimuli within dynamic stimulus presentations. The real challenge would then be to somehow translate difficult declarative (and semantic) tasks into procedural learning activities, with the goal being the restoration of the more complex higher reasoning abilities.

Very few studies have examined the direct or specific effects of providing such cueing stimuli (compared to trial and error training) within a VE. In the only VR-based head-to-head comparison of this type, Connor et al. (2002), has reported a series of case studies on the use of a haptic joystick mediated "Trails B" type training task. In the error-free condition, the haptic joystick restricted movement on a flatscreen trails-type task such that the patient was not allowed to make navigation errors. Mixed findings were reported, but error-free training resulted in significant response speed improvements compared to errorful training in some cases. Other studies have reported on the inclusion of an error-free component embedded within an overall VR training approach with more encouraging findings. For example, in the Brooks et al. (1999) case study previously cited, error-free training for wayfinding in a rehabilitation ward was one component in a VR training system that produced positive transfer to the real ward. Harrison, Derwent, Enticknap, Rose, and Attree (2002) also reported the use of cueing stimuli in a VR system designed to train manoeuvrability and route-finding in novice motorised wheelchair users. This scenario provided a series of arrows that were presented with the caption "Go this way" to guide successful route navigation whenever the user would stray into areas where invisible "collision boxes" were programmed in the environment. Two patients with severe memory impairments took part in route finding training over the course of seven days. Post-testing on the real routes produced mixed results with the patients successfully learning two subsections of the test routes but failing to eradicate errors on two further subsections of the routes. The investigators felt that further collision detection refinement of the system will be required to support accurate prompt delivery to patients before a more systematic group test will be possible.

Cueing stimuli have also been incorporated into a VE designed for executive function assessment and training in the context of a series of food preparation tasks within a virtual kitchen scenario (Christiansen et al., 1998). This scenario consists of a head-mounted display VE of a kitchen in which patients have been assessed in terms of their ability to perform 30 discrete steps required to prepare a can of soup and make a sandwich. Various auditory and visual cues can be presented to help prompt successful performance. However the specific effect of this cueing has not been isolated, nor was a system in place to prevent errors from actually occurring (although successful usability findings—30 patients with minimal side-effects—has been reported along with acceptable test/retest reliability coefficients for use of this system, Christiansen et al., 1998). These researchers report ongoing enhancements to the system regarding the delivery of more complex challenges and increased flexibility in the presentation of cueing stimuli.

Generally, it appears that the provision of cueing stimuli to support error-free rehabilitation in a VE is promising in concept and supported by findings using traditional methods. However, empirical support in the form of systematic group VR data is still lacking. Part of the difficulty up to now has been due to programming challenges for tracking the user's position in the VE as was reported in Harrison et al. (2002), and for accurately providing prompts and restricting errors in an automatic fashion. This has become less of a problem with recent advances in collision detection and "physics" software, but still may be difficult as programming is typically not the clinician's primary skill. However, as better "end-user" programming technologies come along, this may become less of an issue.

Technology challenges aside, VR-based research that could adequately explore the error-free "cueing" issue would require at least an errorless condition that could be compared with trial and error methods as seen in Connor et al. (2002). As well, the sensory mode of cue presentation should be explored to determine whether auditory cueing could be a useful option relative to the types of visual cues typically seen in the form of word captions and arrow pointers. If auditory cueing was found to be of equal effectiveness, it would reduce graphic requirements in system programming. Importantly, auditory prompting may also better resemble and "provoke" self-talk instruction methods that might support generalisation to the real world of self-generated subvocal prompting on the part of the patient. If key prompting statements could be specified in advance, it would be possible to pre-record the patient speaking supportive cues in their own voice. When these cues are played back at strategic choice points within the VE, the patient could be directed more naturalistically by this form of "inner-voice" guidance. Also, since the early reports in this area have thus far mainly focused on spatial navigation and object localisation, cues have been limited to the visual mode for pointing direction and labelling objects. Perhaps more complex tasks could be trained with inclusion of auditory cueing in this manner that could support error free training for the type of integrative problem solving required for effective executive functioning.

Finally, if the user-interfacing tools could be effectively designed, it would be possible to incorporate the use of various electronic compensatory devices into the VR interaction strategy as a method to deliver prompts in a fashion similar to how the patient is being encouraged to use these devices in the real world. This could take the form of assessing what level of "augmentive" information could actually be used by patients to assist in compensatory strategies aimed at improving day-to-day functional behaviour and for training patient's effective use of these devices under a variety of environmental challenges.

The capacity for complete performance capture and the availability of a more naturalistic/intuitive performance record for review and analysis

The review of a client's performance in any assessment and training activity typically involves examination of numeric data and subsequent translation of that information into graphic representations in the form of tables and graphs. Sometimes videotaping of the actual event is used for a more naturalistic review and for behaviour rating purposes. These methods, while of some value, are typically quite labour intensive to produce and sometimes deliver a less than intuitive method for visualizing and understanding a complex performance record. These challenges are compounded when the goal of the review is to provide feedback and insight to clients whose cognitive impairments may preclude a useful understanding of traditional forms of data presentation. VR offers the capability to capture and review a complete digital record of performance in a virtual environment from many perspectives. For example, performance in a VE can be later observed from the perspective of the user, from the view of a third party or position within the VE and from what is sometimes termed, a "God's eye view", from above the scene with options to adjust the position and scale of the view. This can allow a client to observe their performance from multiple perspectives and repeatedly review their performance. Options for this review also include the modulation of presentation as in allowing the client to slow down rate of activity and observe each behavioural step in the sequence in "slow motion".

Advanced programmes to do this have already been developed by the military to conduct what is termed "after action reviews" (Morrison & Meliza, 1999). In military VR applications that often include multiple participants in a shared virtual space, a computerised after action review tool can allow the behaviour of any participant to be reviewed from multiple vantage points at any temporal point in the digital training exercise. This is now standard procedure for military simulation training, but has had limited application in traditional NP approaches. With the exception of less naturalistic review of paper and pencil results and the occasionally review of a client's videotaped performance from a single fixed position, the capacity to provide more intuitive "first-person" perspective views to clients has not been feasible with existing technology.

Thus far, this VR asset has begun to appear as a feature for reviewing navigational performance in a number of wayfinding and place learning applications (Astur, Oriz, & Sutherland, 1998; Jacobs, Laurance, & Thomas, 1997; Skelton et al., 2000). This has mainly been used in applications where a tracked movement record is vital for measuring the dependent variable of exploratory behaviour. Systematic studies of the clinical use of this form of performance record review have yet to appear in the literature, although the capacity to present this information exists with most applications, but requires additional programming to extract and display it. In this regard, the first author's laboratory has developed a visual record review method for replaying children's head movements while they are tracking stimuli within a virtual classroom. This application (Rizzo et al., 2000; 2002b) takes data from a magnetic field tracking device positioned on top of the head-mounted display and represents the captured movement via a virtual representation of a person's head. The head faces outward on the screen and "straight forward" head position represents the attentive gaze at the virtual blackboard where target hit stimuli are displayed to the child. During playback, it is possible to observe the child's head movements during discrete periods when distracting stimuli are presented around the classroom. Head movements away from the centre of the screen represent the child's actual movements to follow the distracting stimuli on each side of the classroom instead of the face forward position required to view the target stimuli. This presentation format delivers an extremely intuitive understanding of the distractibility of children diagnosed with attention deficit hyperactivity disorder (ADHD) during VR classroom performance testing. In the initial prototype of this system, we can deliver side-by-side concurrent performance of both a non-diagnosed and ADHD child and observe the stark contrast in their head turning away from the target stimuli during distraction periods. Thus far in selected case comparisons, the non-diagnosed children are noticed to turn in the direction of the distraction very briefly, but nearly immediately return to the on-task position. By contrast, the children with ADHD are often observed to look away and then continue off task for varying extended periods of time resulting in subsequent omission performance errors. The "head to head" playback of these head movements serves to underscore, in an intuitive manner, the significant findings of off task head position that were revealed from the complex statistical analyses of these movement data. Integration of this form of intuitive performance record review could serve to provide insight for understanding the behaviour of ADHD children to professionals, parents and perhaps even the tested child, in a manner not possible with graphs and data tables. This is an asset in which VR may add value across all areas of performance testing and training that is not readily available with existing traditional tools.

The capacity to pause assessment, treatment and training for discussion and/or integration of other methods

In the assessment and rehabilitation of complex behaviour and/or functional activities, feedback is often an integral component. Similar to the previous asset regarding the availability of a naturalistic performance record, VR allows for a cumulative record to be reviewed at *any* point in the testing and training sequence. Specifically, immediate external therapist response to client performance is one form of feedback that is commonly seen in the rehabilitation of clinical populations. This may be of particular value for clinical populations who have memory difficulties that require more frequent review and feedback during a training session. While this may be possible through "traditional" approaches (i.e., one can always pause analogue NP testing and training), VR's unique assets offer the opportunity to pause or "freeze time" in the middle of a functional "real-world" simulated task. This can result in additive learning benefits, whereby you can "stop and evaluate" not only individual performance, but also by examining what environmental elements may be affecting performance. For example, during activities in a VR kitchen for the completion of a simple task (i.e., heating soup from a can), performance may be paused for the correction of errors (missed procedure steps), evaluation of safety elements of the task (where are the sharp objects?) or discussion of perceptual difficulties (inappropriate visual scanning).

Thus, the ability to pause performance "mid-digitalstream" may also foster better processing and discussion of decision making elements of performance. This may be useful for individuals with frontal lobe damage who have compromised executive skills and subsequently may benefit from an on the spot review of their step-by-step decision making process. In addition, VR may allow for the clinician to monitor performance and provide problem solving guidance to test out potential alternative solutions, that when integrated into the rehabilitation intervention, may help increase client self-awareness of assets and limitations. For some tasks, the opportunity of combining immediate feedback and processing/discussion, obtainable through VR, may offer safety options not possible in the real world. For example, in driver re-training for individuals with cognitive compromise, the ability to pause performance mid-task and provide guidance may support an increased level of "awareness", which may serve to enhance learning and recall. Participants experiencing an "accident" in a driving VE, can be immediately "pulled over" and assisted in identifying errors that lead to the accident. This may result in fostering a heightened client awareness of the rehabilitation experience due to the immediacy and better specificity of performance feedback.

The design of safe testing and training environments that minimise the risks due to errors

As alluded to in the VR driving example above, when developing certain functionally based assessment and rehabilitation approaches, one must consider the possibility of safety risks that may occur during activities designed to test and train abilities in the real world. Driving would probably represent one of the more risk-laden activities that a client with CNS dysfunction would undertake in order to achieve functional independence. However, even simple functional activities can lead to potential injury when working with persons having CNS-based impairments. Such potential risks can be seen in the relatively "safe" environment of a kitchen (i.e., burns, falls, getting cut with a knife) as well as in more naturally dangerous situations such as street crossing, the operation of mechanical/industrial equipment and driving a motor vehicle. Additionally, the risk for client/therapist injury and subsequent liability concerns, may actually limit the functional targets that are addressed in the rehabilitation process. These "overlooked" targets may actually put the client at risk later on as they make their initial independent efforts in the real world without having such targets addressed thoroughly in rehabilitation.

This is an area where VR provides an obvious asset by creating options for clients to be tested and trained in the safety of a simulated digital environment. The value of this has already been amply demonstrated in the predecessor field of aviation simulator research where actual flying accidents dropped precipitously following the early introduction of even very crude aircraft simulation training (Johnston, 1995). Thus far, this asset has served as a driving force for VR system design and research with clinical and "at-risk" normal populations. Such applications include: street crossing with unimpaired children (McComas, MacKay, & Pivak, 2002), populations with learning and developmental disabilities (Strickland, 2001; Brown et al., 1998), and adult traumatic brain injury groups with neglect (Naveh, Katz, & Weiss, 2000); kitchen safety (Rose, Brooks, & Attree, 2000); escape from a burning house with autistic children (Strickland, 2001); preventing falls with at-risk elderly people (Jaffe, 1998); use of public transportation (Mowafty, & Pollock, 1995) and driving with a range of clinical populations (Liu, Miyazaki, & Watson, 1999; Rizzo, Reinach, McGehee, & Dawson, 1997; Schultheis, & Mourant, 2001). In addition to the goal of promoting safe performance in the real world, some researchers have reported positive results for building a more rational awareness of limitations using a VR approach. For example, Davis and Wachtel (2000), have reported a number of instances where older adults, post-stroke, had decided *not* to continue making a return to driving a primary immediate goal after they had spent time in a challenging VR driving system. It is expected that the VR driving literature will grow as more attention is focused on preventing risk in both novice and aged populations.

Finally, one concern that may exist with this asset involves the potential that practice of activities that are dangerous in real life, within the safety of a VE, might create a false sense of security or omnipotence that would put the client at risk upon subsequent action in the real world. In essence, can *safe* transfer of training occur in the real world when the consequences of errors are prevented from occurring in the VE? This is a very challenging concern that will need to be considered carefully. Perhaps one option would be to provide a noxious sound cue, contingent on the occurrence of dangerous errors in the VE, as a means to condition a proper attitude of caution in clients. This concern further underscores the need for a professional to closely monitor client activity in order to recognise possible patterns of risk-taking behaviour that could emerge when using such VEs.

The capacity to improve availability of assessment and rehabilitation by persons with sensorimotor impairments via the use of adapted interface devices and tailored sensory modality presentations built into VE scenario design

One of the current challenges in neuropsychology concerns the adaptation of NP assessment and rehabilitation methods for use by clients with significant sensory and motor impairments. And when such adaptations are attempted, the question often arises as to how much does a client's performance reflect centrally based cognitive dysfunction vs. artefacts due to more peripheral sensorimotor impairments. VR offers two ways in which this challenge may be addressed in the testing and training of cognitive and everyday functional abilities in persons with sensorimotor impairments.

One approach places emphasis on the design of adapted human–computer interface devices in a VE to promote usability and access. The thoughtful integration of adapted interface devices between the person and VR system could assist those with motor impairments to navigate and interact in functional testing and training VR applications (beyond what might be possible in the real world). Such interface adaptations may support actuation by way of alternative or augmented movement, speech, expired air, tracked eye movement and by way of neurofeedback-trained biosignal activity. While an extensive literature exists in the area of interface design for persons with disabilities and on concerns about an emerging "digital divide" (LaPlant, 2001), those domains are beyond the scope of this article. However, two examples should serve to illustrate this potential in the VR area. One basic example involves the use of a gaming joystick to navigate in a VE that was found effective for teaching wayfinding within a VE modelled after an amnesic client's rehabilitation unit (Brooks et al., 1999). These authors partially attributed the observed positive training effects to the client's capability for quicker traversing of the VE using a joystick compared to what her ambulatory impairments would allow in the real environment. This strategy supported efficient use of training time. A more technically complex approach uses "biosignals", as seen in the use of the "Cyberlink" system (Doherty, Bloor, & Cockton, 1999). Initial results using this system suggested that persons with extreme motor and language impairments following stroke and traumatic brain injury were able to communicate using an EEG/EOG/EMG-driven cursor on a flatscreen computer. With continued advances in adapted interface technology, these approaches could support VE navigation and interaction in persons with motor impairments and serve to promote better access to cognitive and functionally based assessment and rehabilitation. As well, by minimising the impact of peripheral impairments on performance, centrally based performance components may be more efficiently tested and trained.

A second approach to this challenge has been to tailor the sensory modality components of the VE around the needs of persons with visual impairments. The few efforts in this area have mainly attempted to build simulated structures around the use of enhanced 3D sound (Lumberas & Sanchez, 2000) and tactile stimuli (Connor, 2002: see Asset 4). For example, Lumbreras et al. (2000), aiming to design computer games for blind children, created a 3D audio VR system referred to as "AudioDOOM". In this application, blind children use a joystick to navigate the mazelike game environment exclusively on the basis of 3D audio cues (i.e., footstep sounds, doors that "creak" open, echoes, etc.) while chasing "monsters" around the environment. Following varied periods of time in the VE, the children are then given Lego to construct their impression of the structure of the layout. The resulting Lego constructions are often noteworthy in their striking resemblance to the actual structure of the audio-based layout of the maze. Children using this system (who never actually have "seen" the physical visual world) often appear to be able use the 3D sound cues to create a spatial-cognitive map of the space and then accurately represent this space with physical objects (i.e., Lego, clay, sand). Examples of some of these constructions are available on the Internet (http://www.dcc.uchile.cl/~mlumbrer/audiodoom/audiodoom.html). While still in the "proof of concept" stage, it would be possible to conceive of such 3D audio-based environments as providing platforms for testing and training of persons with visual impairments at any age.

Finally, the use of haptic simulation tools has been investigated as a method to create VE applications for persons with visual impairments (Jansson, 2000). However, the technology to deliver convincing touch-based simulations is still in the very early stages of development and readers interested in further details are referred to McLaughlin, Hespanha, & Sukhatme (2002).

The introduction of "gaming" features into VR rehabilitation scenarios as a way to enhance motivation

Plato was reputed to have said, "You can discover more about a person in an hour of play than in a year of conversation." (cited in Moncur & Moncur, 2002). This ancient quote may have particular relevance for future applications of VR in neuropsychology. Observing and/or quantifying a person's approach or strategy when participating in a gaming activity may provide insight into cognitive functioning similar to the types of challenges found in traditional performance assessments. However, a more compelling clinical direction may involve leveraging gaming features and incentives for the challenging task of enhancing motivation levels in clients participating in rehabilitation. In fact, one possible factor in the mixed outcomes found in cognitive rehabilitation research may be in part due to the inability to maintain a client's motivation and engagement when confronting them with a repetitive series of retraining challenges, whether using word list exercises or real-life functional activities. In this regard, an understanding of gaming features and their integration into VR-based rehabilitation systems to enhance client motivation may be a useful direction to explore for a number of reasons.

There is general agreement that the peak ages for traumatic brain injury are in the 15–24 year age range (Lezak, 1995). This same age group also makes up the largest percentage of users of commercial interactive computer gaming applications and this popularity is also extending to other age groups at a rapid pace (Lowenstein, 2002). In fact, the computer gaming industry has now surpassed the "Hollywood" film industry in total entertainment market share, and in the USA sales of computer games now outnumber the sale of books (Digiplay Initiative, 2002). As such, it appears that gaming applications have become a standard part of the "digital homestead" as delivered on PCs and specific gaming boxes (i.e., Playstation, X-Box, etc.). From this, interactive gaming has become well integrated into the lifestyles of many people who at some point may require rehabilitative services. For this segment of the population, familiarity with and preference for interactive gaming could become useful assets for enhancing client motivation and engagement when designing VR-based rehabilitation tasks.

Thus far, the integration of gaming features into a VE has been reported to enhance motivation in adult client's undergoing physical therapy following a stroke (Jack et al., 2001). As well, Strickland (2001) reports that children with autism were observed to become very engaged in the VR safety training applications that she has developed which incorporate gaming features. Further anecdotal observations suggest that children diagnosed with ADHD often have a fascination for the type of stimulus environments that occur with computer/video games (Greenhill, 1998). Parents are often puzzled when they observe their children focusing on video games intently, while teacher reports indicate inattention in the classroom. Additionally, in the first author's clinical experience, it was observed that some of the young adult traumatic brain injury clients, who had difficulty maintaining concentration on traditional cognitive rehabilitation tasks, would easily spend hours at a time playing the computer game "Sim City". These observations suggest that designers of rehabilitation tasks might benefit from examining the formulas that commercial game developers use in the creation of interactive computer games. These formulas govern the flow and variation in stimulus pacing that provide linkage to a progressive reward and goal structure. When delivered within a highly interactive graphics-rich environment, users are observed to become extremely engaged in this sort of gameplay. Neuroscience research in the area of rapid serial visual presentation (RSVP) may provide some scientific insight into the human attraction to these fast-paced stimulus environments. In this regard, Biederman (2002) suggests that a gradient of opiate-like receptors in the portions of the cortex involved in visual, auditory, and somatosensory perception and recognition drives humans to prefer experiences that are novel, fast, immersive, and readily interpreted. This may partly underlie the enhanced motivation that is observed for the types of activities that are presented in interactive gaming environments. While many reasons may contribute to the allure of current interactive computer gaming, a proper discussion of these issues is beyond the scope of this article. However, the potential value of gaming applications in general education and training is increasingly being recognised and an excellent presentation of these topics can be found in Prensky (2001) along with an extensive gaming bibliography that is available at the Digiplay Initiative (2002). As VR systems in neuropsychology begin to enter the mainstream, investigation on how to integrate gaming features within rehabilitation applications is likely to become an area of intense interest in the future.

The integration of virtual human representations (avatars) for systematic applications addressing social interaction

Over the last few years, continuing advances in the underlying VR enabling technologies has allowed for the creation of more realistic and compelling virtual environment *structures*. One needs only to look at the recent offerings from the interactive computer gaming industry to appreciate the enhanced level of realism that is afforded by the current state of computer graphics technology. This graphics revolution has also driven the creation of ever more realistic virtual human representations, commonly referred to as "avatars". A compelling case can be made for "populating" VEs with avatars for clinical purposes. More believable virtual humans inhabiting VEs would open up possibilities for assessment and rehabilitation scenarios that target social interaction, naturalistic communication and awareness of social cues. As well, avatars could perhaps serve as "personal" guides that provide instruction or feedback to users operating in a VE. The existence of avatars in VEs could also serve to enhance the realism of VR scenarios that may in turn promote the experience of presence. Such enhanced presence or suspension of disbelief while in a VE might serve to increase psychological engagement in a training scenario, and hence, could foster better generalisation to the real world.

However, while advances in avatar design can be readily appreciated in the highly processed fixed forms typically found in computer gaming and in the film, *Final Fantasy*, the creation of believable characters that can support real time interaction within a VE is still a non-trivial endeavour. Indeed, Alessi and Huang (2000) have pointed out that until recently, "virtual humans" have mainly appeared in mental health scenarios to "... serve the role of props, rather than humans" (p. 321). This has been mainly due to challenges for both the creation of avatars that can dynamically communicate non-verbal implicit signals via facial and body gestures and in the capacity to *drive* such avatar expression/interaction with some form of artificial intelligence. Research on these issues is actually quite active from a basic science perspective (Rickel, Marsala, Gratch, Hill, Traum, & Swartout, 2002; Rizzo et al., 2001a), but high development costs and technical challenges have thus far limited progress for all but the most basic direct *clinical* applications.

In the clinical area, VEs populated with avatars have mainly been designed for use in exposure therapy for specific anxiety disorders. For example, early research in this area is investigating the use of video and computer graphics methods to render virtual humans for treatment of public speaking and social phobias (Anderson, Rothbaum, & Hodges, in press; North, North, & Coble, 2002; Pertaub, Slater, & Barker, 2002; Rizzo, Neumann, Pintaric, & Norden, 2001b). These are application areas that require the presence of human representations to effectively target the specific fear structure in treatment. Some of these applications have used two-dimensional photographic paste-ups of human forms (Moore, Wiederhold, Wiederhold, & Riva, 2002; Riva et al., 1999). Such applications allow the clinician to select the number of avatars that appear in the scenario (i.e., supermarkets, parties, auditoriums, subways, etc.) in order to hierarchically target anxiety as part of an exposure-based treatment approach. At a somewhat higher level of complexity, graphics-based avatars capable of dynamic expressions have been used by Pertaub et al. (2002) to target public speaking anxiety. In this study, subjects gave an oral presentation in a VR conference room with avatars in the audience whose eyes were programmed to follow the speaker's movement. The avatars were also programmed to dynamically display facial and body cues that represented states of appreciation/interest, boredom/hostility and neutral cues. Random autonomous behaviours (i.e., twitches, blinks, nods, etc.) were also programmed into these continuously animated avatars. Results with non-phobics revealed significantly lower self-reported speech confidence when in the presence of the negative audience and higher negative ratings by females when using a head-mounted display compared to flatscreen delivery. A second study reported in this article indicated that high speech anxiety subjects had more discomfort (as measured by heart rate and self-reported anxiety) simply when speaking in the presence of avatars compared to a no avatar condition. For our purposes, these results indicate that subjects were reacting to avatars "as if" they were real members of an audience. Along these lines another research group has used avatars in a group of scenarios as part of a research programme that is replicating traditional social psychology studies on social distance, behavioural facilitation/inhibition and conformity. This work has also revealed the occurrence of a similar suspension of disbelief, with subjects responding to graphics-based virtual humans in a manner similar to previous experiments using real people (Blascovich et al., 2002).

Other groups have begun experimenting with the incorporation and VR delivery of dynamic video clips of humans for public speaking anxiety (Anderson et al., 2000) and for social phobia and anger management (Rizzo et al., 2001b). Early case study results on the head-mounted display speech anxiety applications that use "pasted-in" videos of audiences that vary in size and demeanour have been positive (Anderson et al., 2000). Our social phobia and anger management scenarios using 360-degree panoramic video (Rizzo et al., 2001b) has produced 15 test scenarios (party and work scenarios) that are currently being evaluated. The incorporation of 2D video in a VE may provide more realistic rendering of actual scenes, but also has some limitations, among them restrictions in the user's capacity to explore and navigate "within" the environment as is possible in 3D graphics. Also, once video is captured, it becomes a "fixed" medium that can limit the flexible control of events that is needed for some types of training applications.

The integration of avatars is a potential asset for VEs designed to target NP issues, although this "asset" has rarely been implemented in any systematic fashion for applications with persons with CNS dysfunction. This may primarily be due to an early emphasis on testing and training performance on "tasks" in VEs that mainly involve navigation and perception/interaction with objects. For example, Rizzo et al. (2000, 2002b) has incorporated a virtual teacher within a VR classroom designed to assess attention processes, but this avatar is only capable of delivering instructions and providing verbal commands for various cognitive challenges using fixed audio file inputs. Other avatars appear in the VR classroom to serve as "distracters" during testing, by way of their position in adjacent seats and via their entrance in and departure from the classroom scenario. In an environment similar in concept to the VR classroom, this same approach is being developed in a VR office scenario designed to assess a wider range of cognitive processes (Schultheis & Rizzo, 2002). In this application, avatars that represent co-workers and supervisors exist in the office as distracters and to deliver verbal commands to look out for and report the occurrence of various target stimuli at a later time as part of a prospective memory assessment. Avatars that represent animals that have anthropomorphic features have also been used in VEs as guides to assist children with learning disabilities on street crossing, yard safety and escape from a burning house (Strickland, 2001).

These sorts of applications illustrate the types of first steps that have been taken for VR avatar integration in NP applications. However, with technological advances, it is likely that avatars could play a more dynamic role in VR assessment and rehabilitation applications. Already, advanced research is demonstrating the feasibility of developing avatars that are "fuelled" with artificial intelligence, aimed at fostering more "authentic" real-time interaction between "real" humans and virtual characters for training purposes. For example, Rickel and Johnson (1999) have reported success in the implementation of an avatar with artificial intelligence named "Steve" who serves the role as "instructor" for a virtual training environment targeting the operation and maintenance of equipment on a battleship. As well, similar avatar applications for testing and actual training of tactical decision making performance for crisis responses in US Army peace-keeping operations are under development (Rickel et al., 2002). These applications could be said to emulate the type of interactions that occur with holographic characters as has been portrayed on the "holodeck" in various versions of the science "fiction" TV series "*Star Trek*". With these research efforts in mind, it is reasonable to consider that future avatar-based VEs could be designed to address self-awareness, social interaction, emotional and vocational targets in persons with CNS dysfunction. This would allow for VE application development that is in line with a "holistic" conceptualisation of NP rehabilitation (Prigatano, 1997), while at the same time serving to better integrate cognitive and learning theory-based approaches (Wilson, 1997) within a unified assessment and rehabilitation platform.

The potential availability of low-cost libraries of VEs that could be easily accessed by professionals

The future evolution of VR as a useful and usable tool in neuropsychology will be driven by three key elements. First, continuing advances in the underlying enabling technologies necessary for VR delivery, along with concomitant hardware cost reductions, will allow VR to become more available and usable by independent clinicians and researchers. Second, this potential for increased access and the impact of market forces will result in further development of new VR applications that target a broader range of clinical and research targets. And finally, continued research aimed at determining reliability, validity and utility will help establish certain VR applications as mainstream NP tools. Contingent upon the occurrence of these events, it will be possible that in the future, neuropsychologists will be able to purchase a VR system that provides them with a suite of environments (i.e., home, classroom, office, community, etc.) within which, a variety of testing and training tasks will be available. This has already occurred in the area of VR anxiety disorder applications with no less than three companies marketing systems in this manner. Internet access to libraries of downloadable VR scenarios will become a likely form of distribution. Data mining, scoring and report writing features will also become available similar to what currently exists with certain standardised tests. As well, highly flexible "front end" interface programs will allow clinicians and researchers to modify stimulus delivery/

response capture parameters within some VEs and tailor system characteristics to more specifically meet their targeted purposes. This level of availability could provide professionals with unparalleled options for using and evolving standard VR applications in the service of their clients and for scientific aims.

In anticipation of these possibilities, a parallel objective within ongoing VR research is to determine the most efficient and ethical mechanisms for creation and distribution of VEs. Although promising in concept, the evolution of VR as a clinical tool raises numerous questions regarding the application of technology with clinical populations. One concern is the potential impact on the patient–therapist relationship. Earlier applications of computers in cognitive remediation were met with criticism from professionals who argued that the introduction of computers was equivalent to the removal of the therapist. As well, will greater access to VR applications via the Internet encourage individuals to undertake self-treatment without feeling the need for professional guidance? Will slick marketing of costly VR rehabilitation programs that lack evidence for effectiveness entice naïve clients and deliver no tangible benefit? For a review of some of the ethical issues relevant to the use of VR in clinical practice and overall societal impact, the reader is referred to Rizzo, Schultheis, and Rothbaum, (2002c).

Such concerns underscore the need for the careful definition of VR as a clinical *tool*, not unlike the various instruments currently used by therapists for assessment and rehabilitation (e.g., psychometric tests, biofeedback procedures). Ultimately, the goal of providing "low cost libraries" of VR applications will be driven by both scientific evidence and market forces. While this will provide options for professionals, the clinical judgement as to what VR applications are appropriate should remain an individualised decision between an informed patient and clinician, as is the case with currently available NP methods.

The option for self-guided independent testing and training by clients when deemed appropriate

Independent self-assessment and "home-based" skills practice by clients are common components of most forms of rehabilitation. Generally, it is accepted that by having clients do "homework", that this will promote generalisation of skills learned in treatment proper, to everyday behaviour. The widespread increase in access to personal computing over the last decade has also encouraged the autonomous use of computerised cognitive self-help software by clients (for better or worse). As such, it is likely that the independent use of VR will also become more common as access to systems and software expands in the future. Notwithstanding the potential for shoddy VR applications to reach the marketplace with little evidence to support their efficacy or value, the option for independent VR use (when "guided" by an appropriate professional) could be viewed as an asset for a number of reasons. When compared with existing computerised testing and training formats, VR is distinguished by its capacity to provide higher levels of both immersion and interactivity between the user and the VE. These unique features are seen to enhance the suspension of disbelief required to generate a sense of presence within the VE. When this psychological state of presence occurs, it is conjectured to create a user experience that may influence task performance (Sadowski & Stanney, 2002). This user experience may produce behaviours that are different from what typically occurs in persons undergoing traditional testing and training due to the user's attention being more occupied "within" the VE. As well, the user experience may be less "self-conscious" due to the perceived removal of the test administrator from the immediate personal and attentional space. This experience could provide a unique qualitative window into how people perform tasks when operating in a more independent and autonomous fashion. For example, if clients were allowed to interact freely within a functional VE (i.e., office, shopping mall, home, etc.) that contained very subtle test challenges, the recording and later observation of more naturalistic client behaviours would be possible. This could include observing how individualised compensatory or problem-solving strategies are spontaneously employed when challenged with a complex situation. As well, this may also be of value for monitoring decision-making in the assessment of potentially hazardous real-world skills in a VE, such as driving an automobile.

Another approach might involve the development of a scenario that allows for repeated visits in which the user must monitor and make adjustments in controllable events occurring in the VE over longer periods of time (with progress "saved" at the end of each visit and carried over to the next). This would be akin to what occurs in the game Sim City and might provide insight into the factors that influence client performance extended over long periods of time. Similarly, for the retraining of specific skills, a client's autonomous interaction with the dynamic features of a VE could help capitalise on the established benefits of active learning over more passive approaches. In this area, differential learning effects have been reported in VR training, with active interaction better supporting route learning (Rose et al., 2001) and mental rotation training (Rizzo et al., 2001c) compared to passive observation training. Such studies lend support for a rehabilitation perspective that underscores the significance of empowering individuals by providing active opportunities for error and experience. While traditional NP rehabilitation may value the opportunities for self-guided evaluations and practice, often feasibility is limited for a variety of reasons (i.e., limited therapy time, safety concerns). In this regard, the use of VEs may provide a mechanism for allowing safe, repeatable, self-guided, independent testing and training.

While this asset may offer a useful option for clinical assessment and retraining, it is not without the potential for risk. That is, while immersion and interactivity may enhance the "realism" of a VE, these same features may also create difficulties for certain individuals with psychiatric conditions or cognitive impairments that produce distorted reality testing. Specifically, such conditions could result in increased vulnerability for negative emotional responses during or following VR exposure. Although such incidents have yet to be reported in the VR literature, insurances for monitoring behaviour and responses during VR exposure become an ethical responsibility for the professional. While current therapeutic uses of VR still require a clinician to be present, future applications may not have this requirement and this potential "opportunity" again underscores the need for advance consideration of the ethical issues pertinent to the use of VR as a clinical tool.

CONCLUSIONS

It is our view that the use of computer-based VR simulation technology will play an increasing role in how NP assessment and rehabilitation is done in the future. Advances in the underlying enabling technologies and continuing cost reductions in system hardware are expected to make it possible for VR shortly to become a mainstream tool in this area. With this view in mind, this article has aimed to provide a detailed specification of the assets that are available when using VR for NP approaches. VR is not a panacea for all challenges in neuropsychology. It may also be unlikely that any one application would make use of all of the assets specified in this article. However, it is hoped that neuropsychologists with an interest in developing and/or applying VR applications will find this detailed asset specification useful for targeting areas that could maximise value in their area of expertise. Although some overlap between certain assets may seem to appear at first glance, each asset is seen to represent a unique facet that could be harnessed to address specific challenges in neuropsychology. Also, by integrating examples of current NP rationales and applications with specific reference to component VR assets, it is hoped that clinicians and researchers may use this information to communicate more effectively with computer science-based VR system developers. The task of building really *good* VR/NP systems that are both usable and useful is a challenging endeavour that requires a multidisciplinary mix of domain-specific knowledge. This can be best accomplished by combining an informed view of what is possible with the technology with what makes the most sense from a clinical perspective. With proper attention to these issues, it is hoped that effective VR system development will bring the benefits of the information age to those with impairments due to CNS dysfunction.

REFERENCES

Alessi, N. E., & Huang, M. P. (2000). Evolution of the virtual human: From term to potential application in psychiatry. *CyberPsychology and Behavior, 3*, 321–326.

Anderson, P., Rothbaum, B. O., & Hodges, L. F. (in press). Virtual reality in the treatment of social anxiety: Two case reports. *Cognitive and Behavioral Practice.*

Astur, R. S., Oriz, M. L., & Sutherland, R. J., (1998). The characterization of performance by men and women in a virtual Morris water task: A large and reliable sex difference. *Behavioral Brain Research, 93*, 185–190.

Biederman, I. (2002). *A neurocomputational hypothesis of perceptual and cognitive pleasure.* Invited paper presented at the 9th Joint Symposium on Neural Computation. California Institute of Technology, Pasadena, May, 2002. (Available at: http://www.its.caltech.edu/~jsnc/program.html).

Blascovich, J., Loomis, J., Beall, A. C., Swinth, K. R., Hoyt, C. L., & Bailenson, J. N. (2002). Immersive virtual environment technology as a methodological tool for social psychology. *Psychological Inquiry, 13*, 103–124.

Bowman, D., Kruijff, E., LaViola, J. J., & Poupyrev, I. (2001). An introduction to 3-D user interface design. *Presence: Teleoperators and Virtual Environments, 10*, 96–108.

Brooks, B. M., McNeil, J. E., Rose, F. D., Greenwood, R. J., Attree, E. A., & Leadbetter, A. G. (1999). Route learning in a case of amnesia: A preliminary investigation into the efficacy of training in a virtual environment. *Neuropsychological Rehabilitation, 9*, 63–76.

Brown, D. J., Kerr, S. J., & Bayon, V. (1998). The development of the Virtual City: A user centred approach. In P. Sharkey, D. Rose, & J. Lindstrom (Eds.), *Proceedings of the 2nd European Conference on Disability, Virtual Reality and Associated Techniques* (pp. 11–16). Reading, UK: University of Reading.

Carney, N., Chesnut, R. M., Maynard H., Mann, N. C., Patterson, P., & Helfand, M. (1999). Effect of cognitive rehabilitation on outcomes for persons with traumatic brain injury: A systematic review. *Journal of Head Trauma Rehabilitation, 14*, 277–307.

Charness, N., Milberg, W., & Alexander, M. P. (1988). Teaching an amnesic a complex cognitive skill. *Brain Cognition, 8*, 253–272.

Christiansen, C., Abreu, B., Ottenbacher, K., Huffman, K., Massel, B., & Culpepper, R. (1998) Task performance in virtual environments used for cognitive rehabilitation after traumatic brain injury. *Archives of Physical Medicine and Rehabilitation, 79*, 888–892.

Cohen, N. J., & Squire, L. R. (1980). Preserved learning and retention of pattern-analyzing skill in amnesia: Dissociation of "knowing how" and "knowing that." *Science, 210*, 207–209.

Connor, B., Wing, A. M., Humphreys, G. W., Bracewell, R. M., & Harvey, D. A. (2002). Errorless learning using haptic guidance: Research in cognitive rehabilitation following stroke. In P. Sharkey, C. S. Lanyi, & P. Standen (Eds.), *Proceedings of the 4th International Conference on Disability, Virtual Reality, and Associated Technology* (pp. 77–86). Reading, UK: University of Reading.

Costas, R., Carvalho, L., & de Aragon, D. (2000). Virtual city for cognitive rehabilitation. In P. Sharkey, A. Cesarani, L. Pugnetti, & A. Rizzo (Eds.), *Proceedings of the 3rd International Conference on Disability, Virtual Reality, and Associated Technology* (pp. 305–313). Reading, UK: University of Reading.

Cromby, J., Standen, P., Newman, J., & Tasker, H. (1996). Successful transfer to the real world of skills practiced in a virtual environment by student with severe learning disabilities. In: P. M. Sharkey (Ed.), *Proceedings of the 1st European Conference on Disability, Virtual Reality and Associated Technologies* (pp. 305–313). Reading, UK: University of Reading.

Davies, R. C., Johansson, G., Boschian, K, Lindén, A., Minör, U., & Sonesson, B. (1998). A practical example using virtual reality in the assessment of brain injury. In P. Sharkey, D. Rose, & J. Lindstrom (Eds.), *Proceedings of the 2nd European Conference on*

Disability, Virtual Reality and Associated Techniques (pp. 61–68). Reading, UK: University of Reading.

Davis, E. S., & Wachtel, J, (2000). *Interactive driving simulation as a tool for insight development and motivation in a rehabilitation setting.* Paper presented at the 8th Annual Medicine Meets Virtual Reality Conference, Newport Beach, CA. January 22, 2000.

Deutsch, J. E., Latonio, J., Burdea, G., & Boian, R. (2001) Post-stroke rehabilitation with the Rutgers Ankle System: A case study. *Presence: Teleoperators and Virtual Environments, 10,* 416–430.

Digiplay Initiative (2002). http://www.digiplay.org.uk/index2.php

Doherty, E., Bloor, C., & Cockton, G. (1999). The "Cyberlink" brain–body interface as an assistive technology for persons with traumatic brain injury: Longitudinal results from a group of case studies. *CyberPsychology and Behavior, 3,* 249–260.

Elkind, J. S., Rubin, E., Rosenthal, S., Skoff, B., & Prather, P. (2001). A simulated reality scenario compared with the computerized Wisconsin Card Sorting test: An analysis of preliminary results. *Cyberpsychology and Behavior, 4,* 489–496.

Graf, P., & Schacter, D. L. (1985). Implicit and explicit memory for new associations in normal and amnesic patients. *Journal of Experimental Psychology: Learning, Memory, & Cognition, 11,* 501–518.

Greenhill, L. L. (1998). Diagnosing attention-deficit/hyperactivity disorder in children. *Journal of Clinical Psychiatry 59* (Suppl. 7), 31–41.

Harrison, A., Derwent, G., Enticknap, A., Rose, F. D., & Attree, E. A. (2002). The role of virtual reality technology in the assessment and training of inexperienced powered wheelchair users. *Disability and Rehabilitation, 24,* 599–606.

Jack, D., Boian, R., Merians, A., Tremaine, M., Burdea, G., Adamovich, S., Recce, M., & Poizner, H. (2001). Virtual reality-enhanced stroke rehabilitation. *IEEE Transactions on Neurological Systems and Rehabilitation Engineering, 9,* 308–318.

Jacobs, W. J., Laurance, H. E., & Thomas, K. (1997). Place learning in virtual space I: Acquisition, overshadowing and transfer. *Learning and Motivation, 28,* 521–541.

Jaffe, D. L. (1998). *Use of virtual reality techniques to train elderly people to step over obstacles.* Paper presented at the Technology and Persons with Disabilities Conference, Los Angeles, CA.

Jansson, G. (2000). Basic issues concerning visually impaired people's use of haptic displays. In P. Sharkey, A. Cesarani, L. Pugnetti, & A. Rizzo (Eds.), *Proceedings of the 3rd International Conference on Disability, Virtual Reality, and Associated Technology* (pp. 33–38). Reading, UK: University of Reading.

Johnston, R. (1995). Is it live or is it memorized? *Virtual Reality Special Report, 2,* 53–56.

Krueger, M. W. (1993). The experience society. *Presence: Teleoperators and Virtual Environments, 2,* 162–168.

LaPlante, W. P. (2001). *A proposal for a research agenda in computer human interaction.* Paper presented at the ACM SIGCHI 2001 State of the Science Exchange. Available at: http://www.icdri.org/technology/indexbp.htm

Lezak, M. D. (1995). *Neuropsychological assessment.* New York: Oxford University Press.

Liu, L., Miyazaki, M., & Watson, B. (1999). Norms and validity of the DriVR: A virtual reality driving assessment for persons with head injuries. *Cyberpsychology & Behavior, 2,* 53–67.

Lowenstein, D. (2002). Essential facts about the video and computer game industry. http://www.idsa.com/pressroom.html

Lumbreras, M., & Sanchez, J. (2000). Usability and cognitive impact of the interaction with 3D virtual interactive acoustic environments by blind children. In P. Sharkey, A. Cesarani, L. Pugnetti, & A. Rizzo (Eds.), *Proceedings of the 3rd International Conference on Disability, Virtual Reality, and Associated Technology,* (pp. 129–136). Reading, UK: University of Reading.

McComas, J., MacKay, M., & Pivak, J. (2002). Effectiveness of virtual reality for teaching pedestrian safety. *CyberPsychology and Behavior, 5*, 185–190.

McGeorge, P., Phillips, L. H., Crawford, J. R., Garden, S. E., Della Sala, S., Milne, A. B., Hamilton, S., & Callander, J. (2001). Using virtual environments in the assessment of executive dysfunction. *Presence-Teleoperators and Virtual Environments, 10*, 375–383.

McLaughlin, M. L., Hespanha, J. P., & Sukhatme, G. (2002). *Touch in virtual environments.* Upper Saddle River, NJ: Prentice-Hall/IMSC Press.

Mendozzi, L., Motta, A., Barbieri, E., Alpini, D., & Pugnetti, L. (1998). The application of virtual reality to document coping deficits after a stroke: Report of a case. *Cyberpsychology & Behavior, 1*, 79–91.

Moore, K., Wiederhold, B. K., Wiederhold, M. D., & Riva, G. (2002). Panic and agoraphobia in a virtual world. *Cyberpsychology And Behavior, 5*, 197–203.

Moncur, M., & Moncur, L. (2002). QuotationsPage.com. At: http://www.quotationspage.com/quotes/Plato/

Morrison, J. E., & Meliza, L. L. (1999). Foundations of the after action review process. *US Army Research Institute for the Behavioral and Social Sciences* Special Report No. 42.

Mowafty L., & Pollack, J. (1995). Train to travel. *Ability, 15*, 18–20.

Naveh, Y., Katz, N., & Weiss, P. (2000). The effect of interactive virtual environment training on independent safe street crossing of right CVA patients with unilateral spatial neglect. In P. Sharkey, A. Cesarani, L. Pugnetti, & A. Rizzo (Eds.), *Proceedings of the 3rd International Conference on Disability, Virtual Reality, and Associated Technology* (pp. 243–248). Reading, UK: University of Reading.

Neisser, U. (1978). Memory: What are the important questions? In M. M. Gruneberg, P. E. Morris, & R. N. Sykes (Eds.), *Practical aspects of memory* (pp. 3–24). London: Academic Press.

North, M., North, S., & Coble, J. (2002). Virtual reality therapy: An effective treatment for psychological disorders. In K. Stanney (Ed.), *Handbook of virtual environments* (pp. 1065–1079). New York: Lawrence Erlbaum.

Park, N. W., & Ingles, J. L. (2001). Effectiveness of attention rehabilitation after an acquired brain injury: A meta-analysis. *Neuropsychology, 15*, 199–210.

Pertaub, D., Slater, M., & Barker, C. (2002). An experiment on public speaking anxiety in response to three different types of virtual audience. *Presence-Teleoperators and Virtual Environments, 11*, 68–71.

Prensky, M. (2001). *Digital game-based learning.* New York: McGraw-Hill.

Prigatano, G. P. (1997). Learning from our successes and failures: Reflections and comments on "Cognitive rehabilitation: How it is and how it might be". *Journal of the International Neuropsychological Society, 3*, 497–499.

Psotka, J. (1995). Immersive training systems: Virtual reality and education and training. *Instructional Science, 23*, 405–431.

Pugnetti, L., Mendozzi, L., Motta, A., Cattaneo, A., Barbieri, E., & Brancotti, S. (1995). Evaluation and retraining of adults' cognitive impairments: Which role for virtual reality technology? *Computers in Biology and Medicine, 25*, 213–227.

Pugnetti, L., Mendozzi, L., Attree, E., Barbieri, E., Brooks, B. M., Cazzullo, C. L., Motta, A., & Rose, F. D. (1998). Probing memory and executive functions with virtual reality: Past and present studies. *CyberPsychology and Behavior, 1*, 151–162.

Rickel, J., & Johnson, W. L. (1999). Animated agents for procedural training in virtual reality: Perception, cognition, and motor control. *Applied Artificial Intelligence, 13*, 343–382.

Rickel, J., Marsala, S., Gratch, J., Hill, R., Traum, R., & Swartout, W. (2002). Toward a new generation of virtual humans for interactive experiences. *IEEE Intelligent Systems, 17*, 32–38.

Riva, G., Bacchetta, M. Baruffi, M., Rinaldi, S., & Molinari, E. (1999). Virtual reality based experiential cognitive treatment of anorexia nervosa. *Journal of Behavior Therapy and Experimental Psychiatry, 30*, 221–230.

Rizzo, A. A. (1994). Virtual reality applications for the cognitive rehabilitation of persons with traumatic head injuries. In H. J. Murphy (Ed.), *Proceedings of the 2nd International Conference on Virtual Reality And Persons With Disabilities*. Northridge, CA: California State University. (http://www.csun.edu/cod/conf/1994/proceedings/Table94.htm)

Rizzo, A. A., Bowerly, T., Buckwalter, J. G., Schultheis, M. T., Matheis, R., Shahabi, C., Neumann, U., Kim, L., & Sharifzadeh, M. (2002b). Virtual environments for the assessment of attention and memory processes: The virtual classroom and office. In P. Sharkey, C. S. Lanyi, & P. Standen (Eds.), *Proceedings of the 4th International Conference on Disability, Virtual Reality, and Associated Technology* (pp. 3–12). Reading, UK: University of Reading.

Rizzo, A. A., Buckwalter, J. G., Bowerly, T., McGee, J., van Rooyen, A., van der Zaag, C., Neumann, U., Thiebaux, M., Kim, L., Pair, J., & Chua, C. (2001c). Virtual environments for assessing and rehabilitating cognitive/functional performance: A review of projects at the USC Integrated Media Systems Center. *Presence: Teleoperators and Virtual Environments, 10*, 359–374.

Rizzo, A. A., Buckwalter, J. G., Humphrey, L., van der Zaag, C., Bowerly, T., Chua, C., Neumann, U., Kyriakakis, C., van Rooyen, A., & Sisemore, D. (2000). The virtual classroom: A virtual environment for the assessment and rehabilitation of attention deficits. *CyberPsychology and Behavior, 3*, 483–499.

Rizzo, A. A., Buckwalter, J. G., & van der Zaag, C. (2002a). Virtual environment applications for neuropsychological assessment and rehabilitation. In K. Stanney (Ed.), *Handbook of virtual environments* (pp. 1027–1064). New York: Lawrence Erlbaum Associates, Inc.

Rizzo, A. A., Neumann, U., Pintaric, T., & Norden, M. (2001b). Issues for application development using immersive HMD 360 degree panoramic video environments. In M. J. Smith, G. Salvendy, D. Harris & R. J. Koubek (Eds.), *Usability evaluation and interface design* (pp. 792–796). New York: Lawrence Erlbaum Associates, Inc.

Rizzo, A. A., Neumann, U., Enciso, R., Fidaleo, D., & Noh, J. Y. (2001a). Performance driven facial animation: Basic research on human judgments of emotional state in facial avatars. *CyberPsychology and Behavior, 4*, 471–487.

Rizzo, M., Reinach, S., McGehee, D., & Dawson, J. (1997). Simulated car crashes and crash predictors in drivers with Alzheimer's disease. *Archives of Neurology, 54*, 545–551.

Rizzo, A. A., Schultheis, M. T., & Rothbaum, B. (2002c). Ethical issues for the use of virtual reality in the psychological sciences. In S. Bush & M. Drexler (Eds.), *Ethical issues in clinical neuropsychology* (pp. 243–280). Lisse, The Netherlands: Swets & Zeitlinger Publishers.

Robertson, I. (1990). Does computerized cognitive rehabilitation work? A review. *Aphasiology, 4*, 381–405.

Rose, F. D., Attree. E. A., Brooks, B. M., & Andrews, T. K. (2001). Learning and memory in virtual environments: A role in neurorehabilitation? Questions (and occasional answers) from UEL. *Presence-Teleoperators and Virtual Environments, 10*, 345–358.

Rose, F. D., Attree, E. A., & Johnson, D. A. (1996). Virtual reality: An assistive technology in neurological rehabilitation. *Current Opinions in Neurology, 9*, 461–467.

Rose, D., Brooks, B. M., & Attree, E. A. (2000). Virtual reality in vocational training of people with learning disabilities. In P. Sharkey, A. Cesarani, L. Pugnetti, & A. Rizzo (Eds.), *Proceedings of the 3rd International Conference on Disability, Virtual Reality, and Associated Technology* (pp. 129–136). Reading, UK: University of Reading.

Sadowski, W., & Stanney, K. (2002). Presence in virtual environments. In K. Stanney (Ed.), *Handbook of Virtual Environments* (pp. 791–806). New York: Lawrence Erlbaum Associates, Inc.

Schultheis M. T., & Mourant, R. R. (2001). Virtual reality and driving: The road to better assessment of cognitively impaired populations. *Presence: Teleoperators and Virtual Environments, 10*, 436–444.

Schultheis, M. T., & Rizzo, A. A. (2002). *The virtual office: Assessing and re-training vocationally relevant cognitive skills.* Paper presented at the 10th Annual Medicine Meets Virtual Reality Conference, Newport Beach, CA. 26 January, 2002.

Shallice T., & Burgess P. (1991). Higher order cognitive impairments and frontal lobe lesions in man. In: H. S. Levin, H. M. Eisenberg, & A. L. Benton (Eds.), *Frontal lobe function and dysfunction* (pp. 125–138). Oxford: Oxford University Press.

Skelton, R. W., Bukach, C. M., Laurance, H. E., Thomas, K.G., & Jacobs, J. (2000). Humans with traumatic brain injuries show place learning deficits in computer generated virtual space. *Journal of Clinical Experiments in Neuropsychology, 22*, 157–175.

Sohlberg, M. M., & Mateer, C. A. (1989). *Introduction to cognitive rehabilitation.* New York: Guilford Press.

Sohlberg, M. M., & Mateer, C. A. (2001). *Cognitive rehabilitation: An integrative neuropsychological approach.* New York: Guilford Press.

Stanton, D., Foreman, N., & Wilson, P. (1998). Uses of virtual reality in clinical training: Developing the spatial skills of children with mobility impairments. In G. Riva, B. Wiederhold, & E. Molinari (Eds.), *Virtual reality in clinical psychology and neuroscience* (pp. 219–232). Amsterdam: IOS Press.

Sternberg, R. J. (1997). Intelligence and lifelong learning: What's new and how can we use it? *American Psychologist, 52*, 1134–1139.

Strickland, D. (2001). *Virtual reality and multimedia applications for mental health assessment and treatment.* Paper presented at the ACM SIGGRAPH 2001 Conference. 16 August, 2001.

Wiederhold, B. K., & Wiederhold, M. D. (1998). A review of virtual reality as a psychotherapeutic tool. *CyberPsychology and Behavior, 1*, 45–52.

Weiss, P., & Jessel, A. S. (1998). Virtual reality applications to work. *Work, 11*, 277–293.

Wilson, B. A. (1997). Cognitive rehabilitation: How it is and how it might be. *Journal of the International Neuropsychological Society, 3*, 487–496.

Wilson, B. A., Alderman, N., Burgess, P. W., Emslie, H., & Evans, J. J. (1996). *BADS: Behavioural Assessment of the Dysexecutive Syndrome.* Bury St Edmunds, UK: Thames Valley Test Company.

Wilson, B. A., & Evans, J. J. (1996). Error-free learning in the rehabilitation of people with memory impairments. *Journal of Head Trauma Rehabilitation, 11*, 54–64.

Ylvisaker, M., & Feeney, T. (1998). Everyday people as supports: Developing competencies through collaboration. In. M. Ylvisaker (Ed.), *Traumatic brain injury: Children and adolescents.* Newton, MA: Butterwort-Heinemann.

Zimand, E., Anderson, P., Gershon, G., Graap, K., Hodges, L., & Rothbaum, B. (in press). Virtual reality therapy: Innovative treatment for anxiety disorders. *Primary Psychiatry.*

NEUROPSYCHOLOGICAL REHABILITATION, 2004, *14* (1/2), 241–249

Evaluating digital "on-line" background noise suppression: Clarifying television dialogue for older, hard-of-hearing viewers

A. R. Carmichael

Age and Cognitive Performance Research Centre, University of Manchester, UK

It is known that older people have disproportionately greater difficulties perceiving speech embedded in noise or otherwise degraded than do younger people. The Independent Television Commission (ITC) receives a number of complaints about programmes having excessive background "noise". The Broadcasting Act 1990 gives the ITC responsibility for addressing the needs of elderly and disabled viewers of all independent television in the UK, and thus established a research consortium with the aim of reducing the impact of background noise.

The findings presented in this paper are drawn from DICTION, a multidisciplinary project partially funded by the DTI-LINK initiative, which has developed digital signal processing technology that identifies and suppresses the background noise of television programmes in real-time. A sample of elderly volunteers (63–84 years) underwent pure tone audiometry and provided data based on objective tests of intelligibility per se, and on their subjective impressions of the auditory material (e.g., clarity of dialogue, intrusiveness of background noise, etc.). The findings illustrate the effects of age and hearing loss and the dissociation of objective and subjective measures. They also show that under certain noise conditions clear-cut improvements in intelligibility are beyond current signal processing techniques although apparent improvements in clarity (etc.) are not.

INTRODUCTION

It has been well documented that older people tend to have disproportionately greater difficulty perceiving speech than do their younger counterparts

Correspondence should be addressed to Dr. A. R. Carmichael, ITC Research Fellow, Division of Applied Computing, University of Dundee, Dundee, DD1 4HN. Tel: +44 1382 345054, E-mail: acarmichael@computing.dundee.ac.uk

http://www.tandf.co.uk/journals/pp/09602011.html DOI:10.1080/09602010343000192

(Bergman, 1971). Similarly, factors found to have a negative impact on speech intelligibility for listeners with "normal" hearing tend to have a greater impact for those with age-related hearing problems (Helfer & Wilber, 1988). Such negative factors can be categorised into two closely related but fundamentally distinct types. That is to say, there are external factors that degrade the speech signal itself (e.g., "peak clipping", frequency band limitation, etc.) and there are ones that interfere with the speech signal (e.g., background noise) without necessarily damaging it per se (Luce, 1993). Further, the main source of the difficulties older listeners have with speech tend to mirror these external factors with internal ones, such that age-related damage to peripheral sections of the hearing system will represent the incoming signal less accurately so that the speech (and other incoming sound) becomes degraded (Fozard, 1990). Also, age-related decrements in the nerve pathways through to the cognitive system introduce further "noise" to the already degraded signal (Cervellera & Quaranta, 1982). This puts a significant extra burden on the relevant cognitive systems which are themselves slower and less efficient due to age-related changes (Stine, Wingfield, & Poon, 1986; Rabbitt, 1990). Given the above and the ephemeral and "informationally dense" nature of speech it is perhaps not surprising that older listeners will have intelligibility problems in anything other than optimal listening conditions.

It is likely that the age-related changes in hearing outlined above are the main bases for the relatively high number of complaints received by the ITC from older viewers about excessive background noise making programmes difficult to follow. Many of these complaints are couched in terms of "intelligibility" which raises an accessibility issue in regard to the Broadcasting Act 1990. Attempts to solve this problem at the production end of the broadcast chain have been unsuccessful for a variety of reasons beyond the scope of the present article. However, as digital signal processing technology for noise reduction has developed significantly during recent years it seemed a potentially useful approach to improving clarity at the reception end. That is to say, a suitably adapted processing unit could feasibly be incorporated into a set-top box or digital TV at little (if any) extra cost as one element of the government's drive to ease the change-over from analogue to digital TV broadcasting. This led to the research and design project from which the present human factors data have been drawn (DICTION Digitally Improving the Clarity of Television Narrative for hard-of-hearing viewers, a DTI-LINK project[1]).

---

[1] The DICTION project was partially funded by the DTI Link Broadcast Research Initiative. The Project was managed by the Independent Television Commission. Partners were the University of Surrey's Centre for Communication Systems Research; the University of Manchester's Age and Cognitive Performance Research Centre; Premier Electonics (GB) Ltd; Skinka Electronics; and Broadcast Project Research Ltd.

Given the above, an obvious focus for the human factors involved in such a project is a measurable improvement in intelligibility. In addition it is always important also to probe people's subjective impressions about any proposed solution. That is, a proposed solution proven to enhance intelligibility may still fail as an actual solution if it is then found to be unacceptable on more aesthetic grounds (e.g., too "tinny"). Further, earlier human factors research by the present author (see Rabbitt & Carmichael, 1994) has shown the possibility for totally unexpected mismatches between such objective and subjective measures (also in the domain of digitally processed speech). This project developed technology for "low bit-rate" digital coding of speech for the transmission of Audio Description for Television. Anecdotally the impression of the development team (all with relatively "young ears") was that the proposed options all seemed equally intelligible, but that the cheaper options sounded more "warbly". In contrast to this, subsequent research with older listeners found that the cheaper options produced significantly (and markedly) poorer intelligibility, whereas there appeared to be nothing that subjectively distinguished them for the older volunteer sample (i.e., they were all felt to be equally—and positively—clear, pleasant, etc.).

Digital signal processing for background noise reduction relies in a simple sense on two main parameters for separating the speech signal from unwanted noise (Chabries et al., 1987). One of these is the known acoustic properties of speech (and to some extent those of likely types of noise) and the other is the tendency for the speech to be "louder" than the noise. Thus with regard to something like background traffic noise it is relatively straightforward to separate the speech from the noise and suppress (or remove) the latter. "Noise" such as music is somewhat more problematic as it shares more in common (frequencies, etc.) with speech, but as music has certain relatively predictable regularities (that differ from speech) these can be utilised to some effect. Perhaps most problematic is background speech such as in a "cocktail party" scenario (Moore, 1997). Here the only distinction is the signal-to-noise ratio (and to some extent the generally predictable regularities of speech, which are much less evident in the "babble" produced by several speakers). On this basis it was agreed that this "worst case scenario" would be a suitable "acid test" for the candidate processes. Thus, the Revised Speech In Noise Test (SPIN(R); Bilger, 1984; Bilger, Nuetzel, Rabinowitz, & Rzeczkowski, 1984) was chosen as a suitable standardised test. Other benefits of this test are that it minimises the role of deafness per se, as the test material is presented to each volunteer at a volume level determined by their individual pure-tone audiometric profile. Also, the speech and (12-talker "babble") noise are presented in "mono" so that no spatial cues can help distinguish speech and noise, as will be the case in some television broadcasts. Finally the developers of the SPIN(R) Test recommend (for older listeners) a signal-to-noise ratio of 8 dB and it would seem that general "good practice" in audio engineering means that this is rarely violated in TV programme soundtracks.

The data presented here are from a series of iterative experiments which examined the impact, both objectively and subjectively, of a developing sequence of signal-processing techniques. Comparisons are made with a "baseline" of the original test recordings and an established "audio engineering" approach of two-band compression. This applies differential compression to lower and higher frequencies in the speech wave so that, in general, it presents a better "fit" to the profile of hearing loss experienced by many older people (i.e., disproportionately greater loss at higher frequencies). Although this approach does not address background noise per se, it does tend to improve intelligibility in such sub-optimum conditions. The digital signal processor used consists, in simple terms, of three modules. The first of these is concerned with speech/non-speech detection, which separates the overall sound wave into that which is considered (foreground) speech, and that which is effectively (background) "noise". The next module aims at identifying the type of "noise" thus detected, in order that it can be most accurately reduced. The final module is the Adaptive Pass-band Estimator and is involved with, on the one hand, effecting the required "noise" reduction, and on the other, with enhancing the speech component (using an approach loosely analogous with two-band compression). A more complete and detailed account of this processor is given by Stefanovic and Kondoz (2000). It will be argued below that while such digital processes are effective for many people and with many types of noise, the special requirements of older listeners and speech-like noise (particularly in a "real-time" context) seems to highlight some potentially important limitations.

METHOD

The data presented here were drawn from a series of experimental sessions carried out over a period of approximately one year. Generally, the sample sizes for each session were in the region of 40 to 50 volunteers. However, the analyses reported below only include data from those volunteers who attended all the relevant sessions (thus allowing for within-subjects analyses). Therefore the results presented are based on the contributions of 20 volunteers.

Volunteer sample

The volunteers taking part in these experimental sessions ranged in age from 64 to 83 years, giving a mean age of 73.4 years. As would be expected, this group presented a broad range of hearing ability (pure-tone audiometry) although none wore a hearing aid. The original analyses showed that both age and hearing ability had marked effects on performance. However, partly due to the relatively small sample size and for ease of explication, these are not reported here.

Materials

The audio material, on which the data presented here are based, was all drawn from various of the parallel forms of the SPIN(R) Tests (Bilger, 1984). High quality digital recordings were made of each test list. These recordings then underwent (audio or digital) processing to produce the test material. The baseline lists used in each session were also "recorded" for a second time so that all material (regardless of processing condition) represented second generation copies of the originals. Answer sheets were provided for each set of test material. For the SPIN(R) Test a page of suitably numbered boxes allowed insertion of the target words. For the subjective responses a page of rating scales similar to that below were used.

Very unclear Quite unclear Neutral Quite clear Very clear

|——————|——————|——————|——————|

Volunteers were asked to put a mark on the line where it fitted best with regard to the categories provided. The position of these marks was measured from the extreme left of the line to give a percentage score.

Procedure

All volunteers attended an initial session which included a pure tone audiometry test, completion of a questionnaire about their views on their own hearing ability and a "test run" to familiarise them with the SPIN(R) Test. In addition to familiarisation per se, the test run was also used to explain to volunteers that following each test list they completed they would also be asked to give subjective ratings on various aspects of the audio they had just heard. These ratings included the clarity and pleasantness of the speech, the intrusiveness of the babble noise, and others. Only data from the clarity ratings are presented here. Testing took place in a sound deadened test cubicle (2 m × 3 m approx.). Volunteers sat in a chair with their answer sheets on a small table at a suitable height for writing. The audio material was played from CD on a Pentium II PC with a SoundBlaster AWE64 Gold sound card connected to KLH 610A speakers. The speakers were positioned 2 m in front of the volunteer with each one 0.75 m either side of centre (i.e., 1.5 m apart).

RESULTS AND DISCUSSION

The results are illustrated in Figure 1. It can be seen that the relationship between baseline and 2-band compression is similar on both measures. Such that 2-band compression produced significantly better intelligibility, $F(1, 19) = 6.15$, $p < .05$, and better clarity ratings, $F(1, 19) = 4.72$, $p < .05$, than did baseline. Similarly, among the four digital noise suppression algorithms a significant trend of improvement emerges across the time span of the project for both intelligibility, $F(3, 57) = 7.71$, $p < .001$, and clarity ratings, $F(3, 57) = 3.26$, $p < .01$. Beyond this, the main difference between the upper and lower panels is the relationship between the digital processes and the baseline and compressed material. That is to say, there is a relatively greater disparity between objective clarity (intelligibility) and subjectively perceived clarity for all the digitally processed material than for the other two conditions. The initial digital algorithm (which has previously been successfully implemented in the context of commercial mobile telephony) produced significantly lower intelligibility than baseline, $F(1, 19) = 11.65$, $p < .001$, while several iterations later, the "final" digital algorithm improved intelligibility to a level not significantly different, $F(1, 19) = 2.64$, $p > .05$, although this was still significantly lower than 2-band compression, $F(1, 19) = 5.37$, $p < .05$. In comparison to this, the initial algorithm produced perceived clarity comparable to baseline, $F(1, 19) = 2.23$, $p > .05$, whereas the "final" one improved this to a level significantly better than both baseline, $F(1, 19) = 5.53$, $p < .05$, and 2-band compression, $F(1, 19) = 4.62$, $p < .05$.

It is worth pointing out that the improvements over baseline produced by 2-band compression occurred without any differential treatment of the signal and the noise. That is to say, the improvements were due solely to the compression of higher frequencies (in both the speech *and* the noise) so as to achieve a better "fit" for most older people's hearing abilities, and thereby improve their ability to cognitively "suppress" the unwanted noise. Digital processing for noise suppression was (and will continue to be) developed on the grounds that it has greater *potential* to improve the listening environment for a much wider range of hearing impaired listeners, particularly as digital sound transmission becomes more ubiquitous.

Although it is apparent that the experiments and data described fall somewhat short of rigorously supporting the claims to be made below, the present author feels they adequately justify raising a potentially important, albeit speculative issue (particularly in light of the previous findings outlined in the introduction). That is to say, the notable drop in intelligibility between baseline and the initial digital process is likely to be due to the algorithm erroneously identifying certain elements of the speech signal as "noise" and thus suppressing them (further, there does not appear to be any evidence in the literature to eliminate the possibility that, at an even more basic level, the

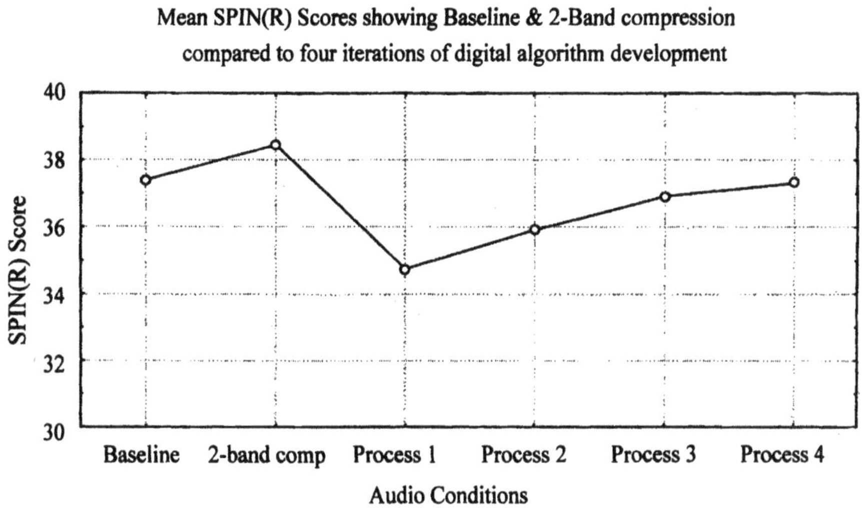

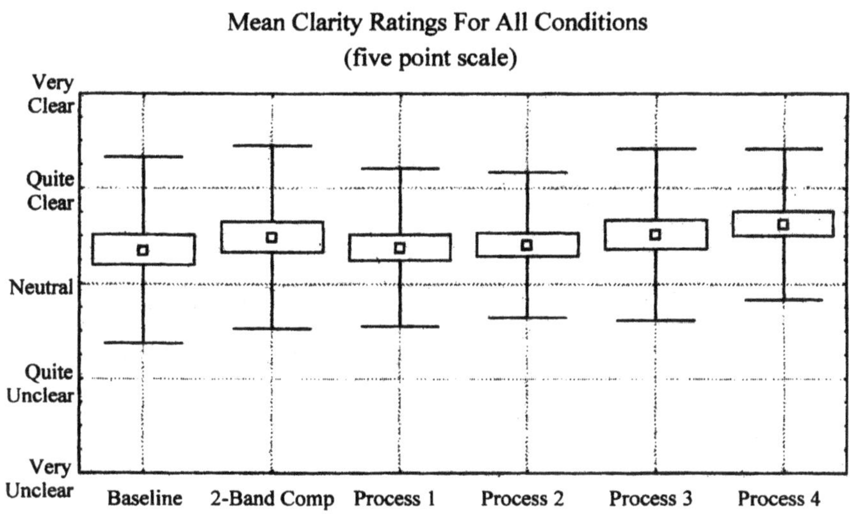

Figure 1. Performance on the SPIN(R) intelligibility test (upper panel) and the associated subjective judgements of clarity (lower panel). Note that the Y axis has been expanded in both cases in order to emphasise the relatively small differences between conditions.

problem is caused by the digitisation process itself). To listeners with "normal" hearing this damage to the speech wave goes unnoticed because their relatively efficient hearing system can still capitalise on the remaining redundancy. Whereas for older listeners, the age-related decrements (both sensory and cognitive) in their hearing ability means they require relatively more redundancy to achieve adequate intelligibility and that in this case (and that of the "low bit-rate" speech mentioned above) not enough remains to adequately achieve this.

Therefore, the suggestion here is that the relative decrement in intelligibility is due to degraded speech rather than to the effectiveness (or not) of noise suppression per se. The subjective ratings and other, purely technical measures of improvement in the signal-to-noise ratio (in terms of dB) suggest that "noise suppression" was effective. However, it seems reasonable to accept that something about the digital processing involved is having an effect on sound quality which is not being captured by accepted acoustic and audiological measures. This indicates a need for further research to help define more suitably the redundancy of speech (and its adequacy for various hearing abilities and listening environments) in terms of the digitisation process itself and in terms of the various forms of digital processing commonly applied to recorded speech, such as noise suppression (as touched on here), and also the wide variety of approaches to compression and transmission. There would also likely be benefits in similarly addressing computer-generated synthetic speech which seems to be finding favour as an economical method for transmitting linguistic information. Beyond simply "further research" there would also seem to be a need for a substantial increase in "cross-fertilisation" of expertise between the various disciplines connected to this issue. It would seem especially fruitful if such "cross-fertilisation' could be fostered separately from (but perhaps parallel to) any such "further (multi-disciplinary) research" as may be supported in the future.

REFERENCES

Bergman, M. (1971). Hearing and aging. *Audiology, 10*, 164–171.

Bilger, R. (1984). Speech recognition test development. *ASHA Reports Series American Speech Language Hearing Association, 14*, 2–15.

Bilger, R. C., Nuetzel, J. M., Rabinowitz, W. M., & Rzeczkowski, C. (1984). Standardization of a test of speech perception in noise. *Journal of Speech and Hearing Research, 27*, 32–48.

Cervellera, G., & Quaranta, A. (1982). Audiologic findings in presbycusis. *Journal of Auditory Research, 22*(3), 161–171.

Chabries, D., Christiansen, R., Brey, R., Robinette, M., & Harris, R. (1987). Application of adaptive digital signal-processing to speech enhancement for the hearing-impaired. *Journal of Rehabilitation Research Development, 24*(4), 65–74.

Fozard, J. L. (1990). Vision and hearing in aging. In J. E. Birren & K. W. Schaie (Eds.), *Handbook of the psychology of aging* (3rd ed., pp. 150–170). London: Academic Press.

Helfer, K. S., & Wilber, L. A. (1988). Speech understanding and aging. *Journal of the Acoustical Society of America, 83*, 859–893.

Luce, R. D. (1993). *Sound and hearing: A conceptual introduction.* Hillsdale, NJ: Lawrence Erlbaum Associates, Inc.

Moore, B. C. J. (1997). *An introduction to the psychology of hearing.* (4th ed.). London: Academic Press.

Rabbitt, P. (1990). Mild hearing loss can cause apparent memory failures which increase with age and reduce with IQ. *Acta Otolaryngolgica, supplementary*, 1–10.

Rabbitt, P. M. A., & Carmichael, A. R. (1994). Designing communications and information-handling systems for disabled and elderly users. In J. Snel & R. Cremer (Eds.), *Work and aging: A European perspective*, (pp. 173–195). London: Taylor and Francis.

Stefanovic, M., & Kondoz, A. (2000). An overview of general noise pre-processing and speech enhancement algorithm for television audio. *Deliverable 3.4 of the DTI-ESRC/LINK funded, DICTION (Digitally Improving the Clarity of Television Narrative for hard-of-hearing viewers) Project.*

Stine, E. L., Wingfield, A., & Poon, L. W. (1986). How much and how fast: Rapid processing of spoken language in later adulthood. *Psychology and Aging, 1*(4), 303–311.

Subject index

For Product Safety Concerns and Information please contact our EU
representative GPSR@taylorandfrancis.com
Taylor & Francis Verlag GmbH, Kaufingerstraße 24, 80331 München, Germany

www.ingramcontent.com/pod-product-compliance
Ingram Content Group UK Ltd.
Pitfield, Milton Keynes, MK11 3LW, UK
UKHW020011200926
475702UK00014B/1817

* 9 7 8 1 1 3 8 8 7 7 9 7 9 *